P9-CKX-175

WITHDRAWN

JUN ~ ~ ~4

DAVID O. McKAY LIBRARY
BYU-IDAHO

9-10-90 KF

DATE DUE

APR 1 6 1998			
OCT 3 1 2000			
JUN 2 2001			
APR 2 6 2002			
NOV 1 7 2004			

Demco

RICKS COLLEGE
DAVID O. McKAY LIBRARY
REXBURG, IDAHO 83440

Modern Language Association of America

Approaches to Teaching World Literature

Joseph Gibaldi, Series Editor

25. Barry N. Olshen and Yael S. Feldman, eds. *Approaches to Teaching the Hebrew Bible as Literature in Translation.* 1989.
26. Robin Riley Fast and Christine Mack Gordon, eds. *Approaches to Teaching Dickinson's Poetry.* 1989.
27. Spencer Hall, ed. *Approaches to Teaching Shelley's Poetry.* 1990.
28. Sidney Gottlieb, ed. *Approaches to Teaching the Metaphysical Poets.* 1990.

Approaches to Teaching the Metaphysical Poets

Edited by

Sidney Gottlieb

The Modern Language Association of America
New York   1990

Copyright © 1990 by The Modern Language Association of America

Library of Congress Cataloging-in-Publication Data

Approaches to teaching the metaphysical poets / edited by Sidney
  Gottlieb.
        p.   cm. — (Approaches to teaching world literature ; 28)
    Includes bibliographical references.
    ISBN 0-87352-529-9   ISBN 0-87352-530-2 (pbk.)
    1. English poetry—Early modern, 1500-1700—History and criticism.
  2. English poetry—Early modern, 1500-1700—Study and teaching.
  3. Metaphysics in literature—Study and teaching.   4. Metaphysics in
  literature I. Gottlieb, Sidney.   II. Series.
  PR545.M4A68   1990
  821'.309—dc20   89-13650

Cover illustration of the paperback edition: Gianlorenzo Bernini, *Apollo and
Daphne*, marble, Galleria Borghese, Rome, 1622–25. Photograph: Alinari/Art
Resource.

Published by the Modern Language Association of America
10 Astor Place, New York, New York 10003-6981

In loving memory of Ned Gottlieb
23 March 1916–24 September 1989

CONTENTS

PREFACE TO THE SERIES

In *The Art of Teaching* Gilbert Highet wrote, "Bad teaching wastes a great deal of effort, and spoils many lives which might have been full of energy and happiness." All too many teachers have failed in their work, Highet argued, simply "because they have not thought about it." We hope that the Approaches to Teaching World Literature series, sponsored by the Modern Language Association's Publications Committee, will not only improve the craft—as well as the art—of teaching but also encourage serious and continuing discussion of the aims and methods of teaching literature.

The principal objective of the series is to collect within each volume different points of view on teaching a specific literary work, a literary tradition, or a writer widely taught at the undergraduate level. The preparation of each volume begins with a wide-ranging survey of instructors, thus enabling us to include in the volume the philosophies and approaches, thoughts and methods of scores of experienced teachers. The result is a sourcebook of material, information, and ideas on teaching the subject of the volume to undergraduates.

The series is intended to serve nonspecialists as well as specialists, inexperienced as well as experienced teachers, graduate students who wish to learn effective ways of teaching as well as senior professors who wish to compare their own approaches with the approaches of colleagues in other schools. Of course, no volume in the series can ever substitute for erudition, intelligence, creativity, and sensitivity in teaching. We hope merely that each book will point readers in useful directions; at most each will offer only a first step in the long journey to successful teaching.

Joseph Gibaldi
Series Editor

PREFACE TO THE VOLUME

Unlike all previous volumes in the Modern Language Association series *Approaches to Teaching World Literature,* this one focuses on a group of writers, not a single author or work. Perhaps a strong argument could be made for devoting a volume to Donne alone or even to Herbert. But it seems more important and useful to teachers to broaden the focus and consider Donne, Herbert, Vaughan, Crashaw, and Marvell as they are most often examined in the classroom: as a group.

We should not underestimate the differences that separate and distinguish those writers. Nor should we be totally happy with that troublesome designation *metaphysical.* One of the first completed questionnaires I received at the beginning of my work on this project queried, "Do we still use that obsolete term?" It seems to me that we do, and perhaps we should, but we should use it as a term to be debated or dissected, rather than as a critical straitjacket. The intention of this book is not to perpetuate a lazy, uncritical use of the term *metaphysical poets;* rather, it aims to aid in the classroom process of discriminating among the varieties of poetry, metaphysical and otherwise, practiced by five important seventeenth-century poets.

The first section of the volume, "Materials," is a descriptive (rather than consciously evaluative) review of sources relevant to teaching the poets: editions, anthologies, reference and critical works, and audiovisual aids. I have tried to be as thorough as space allows, but part of the purpose of the review section is to be focused and selective in order to give instructors a manageable overview of textbook options and preferred critical works. Whenever possible, I include references to comprehensive bibliographies to facilitate further research.

The heart of the volume is "Approaches," eighteen essays on a variety of topics. Like Herbert's poems in *The Temple,* stars that set up constellations as they shine and reflect on one another, the essays fall into shimmering patterns as they take up common themes, often from divergent perspectives. Annabel Patterson's essay, which serves as an introduction, proposes that we teach *against* the traditional Dryden-Johnson-Eliot approach to the metaphysical poets. In one way or another, nearly every essay that follows comments on that issue. It is impossible to cover all the important backgrounds necessary for a full understanding of Donne, Herbert, Vaughan, Crashaw, and Marvell, but the essays in the next section, "General Discussions and Backgrounds," focus on such important topics as seventeenth-century love poetry, religion, iconography, and representations of and addresses to women in metaphysical poetry. The attention throughout the essays to detailed scholarship, concrete pedagogical methods, and class assignments makes the section particularly useful to instructors who worry about what is often a great gap between research and undergraduate teaching. Next, five essays explore various course contexts in which the metaphysical poets appear, including not only the ubiquitous survey course but also a humanities-based composition course. Finally, in "Approaches to Specific Poets" each of the five poets is discussed in a separate essay. That there is not room for several essays on each is partially compensated for by the suggestions and the techniques for teaching each of the poets that are included in nearly all the preceding essays.

The list of participants in the survey of instructors inadequately acknowledges my gratitude to those who not only filled out questionnaires but also sent in syllabi, course materials, bibliographies, examinations, and generous letters describing classroom experiences and techniques. I especially thank the teacher-scholars who contributed essays to this volume for their patience, goodwill, and wisdom as we advised and instructed each other through the long process of composing and revising this book.

The Sacred Heart University Research and Creativity Council generously supported this project by granting funds for release-time and research-related expenses. On a personal level, I have benefited a great deal from constant discussions about undergraduate education with my friends and colleagues Ralph Corrigan and David Curtis, English department chairperson *extraordinaire*.

Finally, I am fortunate to come from a family of teachers—not academics but wise teachers nonetheless—and it is to my mother, father, sister, and brother that I owe much of my continuing interest in the process of seeking and sharing knowledge. And I am also joyfully indebted to Becky Abbott, whose knowledge of things physical and metaphysical is perpetually wonderful.

SG

Part One

MATERIALS

Sidney Gottlieb

Editions

Many teachers find the choice of books for a course covering John Donne, George Herbert, Henry Vaughan, Richard Crashaw, and Andrew Marvell an agonizing decision, in part because of the inevitable compromises required. Teachers generally agree that the reading material in such a course should be comprehensive (either complete or including a substantial and representative selection of poems); well edited, with reliable texts, useful notes, and supplementary matter; and modernized (if at all) according to principles that are defensible and consistent and that do not disregard the shape, the arrangement, and the visual disposition or structure of the poems. That those high ideals are frequently met in individual volumes on each of the metaphysical poets is the cause for some celebration, but instructors cannot ask undergraduates to buy a full set of those increasingly expensive texts, especially for a course in which other books may be required. Anthologies provide a way out of the problem, but they raise as many problems as they resolve. Criticisms of anthologies in general as badly edited, cheaply printed, and idiosyncratically annotated have not disappeared completely, and those criticisms have been compounded by a new sensitivity to the role anthologies play in canon formation and canon restriction.

What follows is not an attempt to settle the implicit argument between those who (in the words of one colleague) "most certainly do not believe in using an anthology of seventeenth-century poetry" and those who, for one reason or another, choose to use an anthology. Nor is what follows a comprehensive list of all available editions and anthologies or a fully developed critical review of them. It is, rather, a brief description of those texts mentioned by respondents, including enough information to help instructors decide which texts suit their particular needs. (The focus is on paperback books, although some of the anthologies are hardbound.) The comments offered by the respondents are sometimes blunt, and I include them not to endorse or to damn a text but to give samples of the range of opinions.

For consistency and ease of reference, I modernize titles of works by the metaphysical poets—though this should not necessarily be taken as indicating that I prefer to teach from modernized texts. The spelling varies, however, in the individual essays in this volume; some contributors modernize spelling, others do not, according to the editions they prefer to use for teaching.

Individual Authors

Instructors are fortunate to have a variety of Donne texts to choose from, a variety that diminishes considerably when we come to the other poets. Each of the Donne editions has a particular attraction. Of the full collections, John T. Shawcross's *Complete Poetry of John Donne* is recommended by several respondents, especially because of its affordability and good notes. Some explanatory notes are inconveniently gathered at the end of the volume, but the notes beneath the poems are useful and occasionally provocative; the textual notes are particularly extensive and scrupulous. In *John Donne: The Complete English Poems* A. J. Smith uses modernized spelling, takes some liberties with the arrangement of the poems—the *Songs and Sonnets*, for example, are placed in alphabetical order—and is bolder than most other editors in making determinations about poems dubiously attributed to Donne. His main concern, Smith says, "is to make an old and difficult author as intelligible as is now possible to readers today" (15). He does so largely through a commentary covering more than three hundred pages.

The notes in C. A. Patrides's *Complete Poems of John Donne* are not as extensive, though they are certainly illuminating, but Patrides's edition contains features that may be especially useful for undergraduate readers. For example, Patrides includes a long critical introduction, touching briefly on Donne's metrics, conceits, dramatic devices, and lifelong concern for themes of love and death. Like Shawcross, Patrides includes a few elegies and commendatory poems on Donne but also reprints Alexander Pope's versions of "Satire 3" and "Satire 4." And the forty-six page bibliography near the end is of interest not only to students but also to their teachers. The editions by Shawcross, Smith, and Patrides have collectively superseded Herbert J. C. Grierson's Oxford Standard Authors edition of *Donne: Poetical Works*, an offshoot of Grierson's pathbreaking textual work on Donne but lacking in critical annotations, which are essential in a modern student's text.

Of the editions of selected poetry by Donne, A. L. Clements's Norton Critical Edition, *John Donne's Poetry*, was the most popular with the respondents. Clements updates the punctuation, the spelling, and the capitalization, but, where an interpretive point is in question, he usually refers to the original in his textual notes. At first glance there seems to be an imbalance, as the poems take up only 100 pages of a 273-page book, but the selection is serviceable, including all the *Songs and Sonnets* and *Holy Sonnets*, seven elegies, "Satire 3," *The First Anniversary*, *La Corona*, three religious hymns, several verse letters, and one epithalamium. The bulk of the volume is taken up with a valuable, though now somewhat dated, collection of critical essays: "Donne and Metaphysical Poetry," "Donne's Love Poetry," and "Donne's Divine Poems and the Anniversaries." Clements includes the classic statements on those subjects by Dryden, Johnson, Coleridge, Grierson, and Eliot and modern commentaries by such critics as Cleanth Brooks, Joseph A. Mazzeo, Louis L. Martz, and Helen Gardner.

Marius Bewley's modernized edition *The Selected Poetry of Donne* does not have that critical apparatus, but it does contain a full introduction, helpful notes, and a substantially broader selection than Clements's book, including all that the Clements volume contains and all the satires and elegies, *The Second Anniversary, The Progress of the Soul*, and other divine poems. Some respondents praised Frank J. Warnke's *John Donne: Poetry and Prose*, particularly because it is a reasonably priced paperback that contains both the poetry and a decent selection of prose, including the "Meditations" from *Devotions upon Emergent Occasions* and *Death's Duel* and two other sermons. That description also fits *John Donne: Selected Poetry and Prose*, edited by T. W. Craik and R. J. Craik, a modernized text that includes a generous variety of the secular and sacred poetry and six *Devotions* and extracts from ten sermons. The introduction, the commentary, and the notes are extensive and helpful.

Joseph H. Summers's *Selected Poetry of George Herbert* is long out of print but has been ably replaced by C. A. Patrides's edition, *The English Poems of George Herbert*, which was highly recommended by many respondents as a good teaching text with useful notes. Patrides reprints *The Temple* in full and the six poems that appear only in the Williams manuscript and the two sonnets to Herbert's mother printed in Izaak Walton's *Life of Herbert*. The introductory essay (focusing on the artful complexity just beneath Herbert's much-commented-on simplicity), short note on typology, the appendixes, and the full bibliography help make it a useful and attractive volume.

Gareth Reeves's *Selected Poems of George Herbert* suffers somewhat by comparison because it does not include *The Temple* in full: "The Church-Porch" and "The Church Militant" are excluded completely; since less than half of "The Church" is printed, the sequences and the patterns are inevitably disturbed. Reeves's introduction and commentary are extensive, though, and he also includes brief extracts from Herbert's prose work *The Country Parson*. The importance of that prose work and its relevance to *The Temple* is underscored by John N. Wall, Jr., as he includes both in their entirety (with modernized spelling and punctuation) in *George Herbert:* The Country Parson, The Temple. The second edition corrects the many errors of the imperfectly printed first edition but still makes no attempt to retain the original shape and line spacing of the poems, often a crucial aspect of Herbert's artistry. Wall's detailed introduction focuses on "the extent to which Herbert's didactic understanding of the priestly life underlies the contents" of his prose and poetry (27–28). Louis L. Martz's *George Herbert and Henry Vaughan* in the Oxford Authors series includes modernized texts of *The Temple*, supplementary poems, and *The Country Parson*. The convenience of having so much of Herbert and Vaughan (discussed below) in one volume, along with Martz's authoritative and detailed commentary, makes the edition extremely valuable.

Instructors have a few options in choosing an individual volume of Vaughan's poems. French Fogle's *Complete Poetry of Henry Vaughan* is lightly annotated but carefully edited and printed to preserve the shape of the poems and the use of italics, often highly significant in Vaughan. Fogle includes translations of all the Latin poems (as well as the originals) and prints the full biblical text (in a footnote) on the many occasions when Vaughan gives a particular citation at the beginning or the end of a poem. Much more fully annotated is Alan Rudrum's *Henry Vaughan: The Complete Poems* which concludes with more than 260 pages of carefully documented, informative notes, backing up the prefatory claim that the book is "by far the most comprehensively annotated edition of Vaughan's poems yet to appear" (18). Rudrum modernizes the spelling but not the punctuation or the use of italics, and the edition is handsomely laid out and easy to read. Louis L. Martz's *George Herbert and Henry Vaughan* does not include all Vaughan's poetry, but it does contain a generous selection; there is nothing from *Olor Iscanus* and *Thalia Rediviva*, but both parts of *Silex Scintillans* (1650, 1655) are reprinted in their entirety, along with everything in Vaughan's earlier collection *Poems* (1646) except his translation of Juvenal's tenth satire. As in the Herbert section, the annotations on Vaughan are extensive, and Martz pays careful attention to alchemical imagery and allusions to both Herbert and the Bible.

At present, George Walton Williams's *Complete Poetry of Richard Crashaw* is the only comprehensive volume of Crashaw's poems readily available to students. The poems are lightly annotated but glossed by numerous informative headnotes and illustrations. Williams arranges the poems in two main sections, sacred and secular, and part of the reason the volume is so bulky (more than seven hundred pages long) is that he includes all Crashaw's poems and translations (alternative versions as well), the texts Crashaw translated, and prose translations of his poetic works in Latin and Greek.

The volume of Marvell's poems most frequently recommended by the respondents was Elizabeth Story Donno's *Andrew Marvell: The Complete English Poems*. Donno modernizes the spelling, while retaining the original punctuation, and arranges the poems in chronological order. English translations of the Latin and Greek poems are reprinted from the authoritative edition of William A. McQueen and Kiffin A. Rockwell. Donno's notes on the poems, gathered at the end of the volume, are extensive and helpful. George deF. Lord's *Andrew Marvell: Complete Poetry* arranges the poems in the following sections: "Lyric Poems," "The Cromwell Era," "The Era of Charles II," "Poets and Heroes," "Poems in Latin and Greek" (with a translation following each poem), and "Poems of Doubtful Authorship." Lord gives few notes for the lyrics, but he annotates the overtly political and satiric poems much more fully to clarify for modern readers the seventeenth-century events and characters Marvell anatomizes. Lord's introduction is a substantive summary of Marvell's characteristic themes and techniques, but his one-page bibliography basically lists only other editions and fails to steer the reader to any helpful critical works. Robert Wilcher's *Andrew Marvell: Selected Poetry and Prose* includes a substantive introduction, a selected bibliography, a critical commentary, and notes. Modernized texts of the poems are supplemented by a thirty-six-page sampling of Marvell's prose, including a few letters.

Anthologies

Anthologies are an area of great concern, even a sore spot. Some respondents were adamant; one insisted, "I *never* use anthologies, especially about the metaphysical poets," and some complained that anthology selections are often skimpy, stale, or otherwise hard to work with. Other respondents were simply frustrated, asserting that no completely satisfactory anthology of metaphysical poetry is in print. But many respondents were more pleased with current anthologies, valuing them for their convenience, availability, and reasonable cost. Anthologies can carve up authors, leaving behind apparently permanent monuments of their greatest hits; but, some argue, anthologies can also help contextualize literary works (as opposed to single-author volumes, which may emphasize individuality) and effectively fulfill their purpose as *introductions* to a variety of authors.

The debate has by no means been resolved, but the survey of instructors showed that anthologies covering the metaphysical poets are used frequently. The most popular anthology among the respondents is volume 1 of *The Norton Anthology of English Literature* (gen. ed. Abrams). Some respondents said that they use it only because of departmental mandate and despite its poor notes and conservative canon, but it also received much praise as the best textbook available for such courses. The section "The Early Seventeenth Century (1603–1660)," edited by Robert M. Adams and George M. Logan, opens with an essay largely on the historical context and literary crosscurrents, and each author's section is introduced by a brief biographical headnote. Donne's *Songs and Sonnets* are fairly well represented by twenty poems, and the selection also includes two elegies, "Satire 3," "The Storm," *The First Anniversary* in full, nine poems from *Holy Sonnets*, "Good Friday, 1613," three hymns, three prose meditations, and one sermon. (Other sections of the volume contain brief extracts from Izaak Walton's *Life of Donne* and Johnson's "Life of Cowley.") The selections from Herbert have increased from previous editions and now total twenty-three poems, all from "The Church." Vaughan is represented by "A Rhapsody" and eight poems from *Silex Scintillans*. Crashaw is represented by seven poems, including "In the Holy Nativity of Our Lord God," "To . . . the Countesse of Denbigh," "The Flaming Heart," and four brief sacred epigrams. The metaphysical side of Marvell is captured in the thirteen poems selected from his works, but only "An Horatian Ode" stands in for the political verse that occupied much of his time. All the texts are modernized, and the annotations and appended brief bibliographies are helpful. Although readers will always complain about the light, somewhat transparent paper it is printed on, the *Norton Anthology* fulfills its aim of introducing students "to the excellence and variety of English literature" by presenting "accurate and readable texts" (xxix).

Nearly as popular with the respondents is *Seventeenth-Century Prose and Poetry*, edited by Alexander M. Witherspoon and Frank K. Warnke. This classic text (the first version dates back to 1929) provoked some serious criticism, including complaints that "the notes are inadequate, the modernizations are dubious, and the selections are dated" and that the book is "bad, bowdlerized, unperceptive." But praise for the anthology outweighed those comments, and it was described as "the best available," "convenient, cheap, comprehensive," and the "standard" text for the period. Its double-column format is growing increasingly unpopular, but only that layout and the decision to keep the notes at a minimum allowed a great deal of material to fit one volume. The selections from Donne include thirty-three poems from *Songs and Sonnets*, six elegies, "Satire 3," one verse letter, ten poems from *Holy Sonnets*, "Good Friday, 1613," and three hymns. In the prose section, Witherspoon and Warnke also print thirteen meditations, three complete sermons, extracts from twenty-two other sermons, and Walton's *Life of Donne*. The selections from Herbert include thirty-eight poems from "The Church," sections from "The Church-Porch," two sonnets to his mother, and brief extracts from *The Country Parson*, along with a substantial part of Walton's *Life of Herbert*. Vaughan is represented by twenty-six poems (all but one from *Silex Scintillans*), Crashaw by nine, and Marvell by sixteen, including an extract from "Upon Appleton House." The editors have modernized the texts, included brief headnotes and bibliographies, and compiled a useful "Critical Miscellany" as an appendix, gathering brief but important essays and comments by such critics as Samuel Johnson, T. S. Eliot, Morris Croll, Austin Warren, Louis L. Martz, Joseph A. Mazzeo, and Frank J. Warnke.

The respondents found much to praise in the Renaissance section of *The Oxford Anthology of English Literature*, edited by Frank Kermode and John Hollander. More than the Norton anthology and the Witherspoon and Warnke edition, the Oxford text (modernized throughout) offers extensive annotations, a detailed glossary, and a particularly attractive series of illustrations, including paintings, emblems, and engravings. Respondents noted that the "visuals are useful in teaching," the "notes are excellent," and the selections are "comprehensive," offering "ample enough materials for the student to browse in." The Donne section contains one of his paradoxes (from *Juvenilia*), two elegies, twenty poems from *Songs and Sonnets*, "Satire 3," part of *The Second Anniversary* (lines 254–300), six poems from *Holy Sonnets*, "Good Friday, 1613," two hymns, two meditations, and one sermon; the section on prose contains part of Walton's *Life of Donne*. Nineteen poems by Herbert (rearranged freely), seven by Vaughan, six by Crashaw (including parts of "The Flaming Heart"), and twelve by Marvell (including a long section from "Upon Appleton House," 369–568) also appear in the Oxford anthology.

Mario A. Di Cesare's Norton Critical Edition *George Herbert and the Seventeenth-Century Religious Poets* does not attempt to be as comprehensive as the previously mentioned anthologies: it does not include Donne (although it has a section on Thomas Traherne), and, while it contains some secular poems by Crashaw and Marvell, the focus is on religious verse. Respondents were particularly pleased by the carefully edited and modernized texts, "sensible and restrained footnotes," and "good critical section." Furthermore, Di Cesare's suggestion that within seventeenth-century poetry there is a "school of Herbert" to be reckoned with neatly complements much current critical work. The anthology contains a large selection of poems by Herbert—eighty from "The Church" (although nothing from "The Church-Porch" or "The Church Militant") and the two sonnets from Walton's *Lives*—along with forty-five poems from Vaughan's *Silex Scintillans*, sixteen poems by Crashaw, and eighteen by Marvell (including "Upon Appleton House" in full). Unlike many other Norton Critical Editions, the commentary section here focuses almost exclusively on modern criticism, and Di Cesare has compiled a useful collection of essays, including at least three on every poet in the anthology and an introductory overview by Anthony Low, "Metaphysical Poets and Devotional Poets."

Among other texts mentioned less frequently in the responses to the survey, Louis L. Martz's *English Seventeenth-Century Verse* (vol. 1) was the first choice of several instructors, but that excellent collection is now out of print. Of the hardcover comprehensive texts, *Seventeenth-Century Verse and Prose* (vol. 1)—edited by Helen C. White, Ruth C. Wallerstein, Ricardo Quintana, and A. B. Chambers—was adopted by a number of teachers, as were two paperback collections: Hugh Kenner's *Seventeenth-Century Poetry: The Schools of Donne and Jonson*, recommended because it covers both groups of poems, and Helen Gardner's *The Metaphysical Poets*, because it is inexpensive and has an adequate selection of the religious poetry of Donne, Herbert, Crashaw, Vaughan, and Marvell and samples from other seventeenth-century poets.

Required and Recommended Readings for Students

Many of the instructors surveyed do not regularly assign supplementary readings; one observed, "Even in my upper level courses I am somewhat dubious of secondary reading." Because of time constraints within a semester and perhaps a lingering New Criticism orientation, some respondents said that they urged students to concentrate on the primary texts. But others offered detailed bibliographies to their students, sometimes assigning, sometimes simply recommending a core of readings that are accessible (although not always easy) and important introductions to Donne, Herbert, Vaughan, Crashaw, and Marvell. The majority of the works mentioned below contain discussions of or are otherwise relevant to all those poets, but I conclude with a few titles that focus specifically on them individually. For ease of reference I occasionally use a book's short title, but the complete title is given in "Works Cited" at the end of this volume.

For supplementary readings, instructors often turn first to classical or contemporary primary sources. Not many were as ambitious as one respondent, who required two book reports from each student on such topics as the *Canzoniere*, Martial, Juvenal, Horace, Persius, Sidney's poems, More's epigrams, Heywood's epigrams, Augustine on altars, Thomas Vaughan's works, recusant prose, classical eclogues, and various church fathers. But most respondents agreed that students should be acquainted with the Authorized Version of the Bible (especially the Book of Psalms), the Book of Common Prayer, samples of Petrarchan poems, and perhaps Continental models of metaphysical poetry (easily available in Frank J. Warnke's anthology *European Metaphysical Poetry*). Regarding secondary sources, many instructors wanted their students to read the two classic statements on metaphysical poetry, Samuel Johnson's comments in his "Life of Cowley" and T. S. Eliot's in his essay "The Metaphysical Poets." The one indispensable reference work is the *Oxford English Dictionary*, often used as the basis of an assignment (see Steven Marx's essay in this volume) or in tandem with demonstrations of the complexity of metaphysical and other forms of wit found in such studies as William Empson's *Seven Types of Ambiguity* and Cleanth Brooks's *Well-Wrought Urn*.

For general historical background, students may consult the following: Christopher Hill's *Century of Revolution, 1603–1714*, Godfrey Davies's *Early Stuarts, 1603–1660*, and G. P. V. Akrigg's *Jacobean Pageant*. Studies that consider early seventeenth-century poetry in the light of contemporary events and conditions include Cecily Veronica Wedgwood's *Poetry and Politics under the Stuarts*, Julia Briggs's *This Stage-Play World: English Literature and Its Background, 1580–1625*, and Graham Parry's

Seventeenth-Century Poetry: The Social Context. Three books in particular were recommended as introductions to the basic intellectual framework of the seventeenth century: E. M. W. Tillyard's *Elizabethan World Picture*, Basil Willey's *Seventeenth-Century Background*, and Louis I. Bredvold's *Intellectual Milieu of John Dryden*. But some instructors found those texts (particularly Tillyard) too dated, conservative, and misleading, and they recommended that their students become acquainted with the way the seventeenth-century world picture is repainted in such books as Stephen Greenblatt's *Renaissance Self-Fashioning* and Jonathan Dollimore's *Radical Tragedy*. Less contentious is Isabel Rivers's *Classical and Christian Ideas in English Renaissance Poetry*, which defines and explores key topics (such as cosmology, Protestantism, humanism, and allegory) in readable analytic essays, well-chosen extracts from primary sources, and a briefly annotated bibliography. The eleven essays in *The Age of Milton*, edited by C. A. Patrides and Raymond B. Waddington, can be consulted individually or collectively for information about such topics as seventeenth-century theology, science, fine arts, education, and politics.

Several literary histories were recommended as especially useful for students: Douglas Bush's *English Literature in the Earlier Seventeenth Century, 1600–1660* is magisterial; George Parfitt's *English Poetry of the Seventeenth Century* contains many fine insights but may be somewhat difficult for a student to consult for information on a particular poet because it is arranged by genre; and *From Donne to Marvell*, volume 3 of The New Pelican Guide to English Literature, edited by Boris Ford, is handy, wide-ranging, and inexpensive, though occasionally in need of updating. The two critical studies most highly recommended as essential were Louis L. Martz's *Poetry of Meditation* and Barbara Kiefer Lewalski's *Protestant Poetics and the Seventeenth-Century Religious Lyric*. Some instructors even suggested that the contrast between Martz's focus on the legacy of Catholic meditational techniques and Lewalski's emphasis on distinctively Protestant texts and techniques can be the basis of student essays or class discussions. Other critical studies recommended as helpful for students include Joan Bennett's *Five Metaphysical Poets*, A. Alvarez's *School of Donne*, Anthony Low's book *Love's Architecture*, and Earl Miner's *Metaphysical Mode from Donne to Cowley*. As indicated above, instructors who use Witherspoon and Warnke or one of the Norton Critical Editions frequently assign critical essays contained therein; William R. Keast's collection of modern essays in criticism, *Seventeenth-Century English Poetry*, was also praised as comprehensive and convenient.

The following studies, each focusing on an individual poet, were recommended as useful for students. The respondents noted that Walton's *Life of Donne* provides an important introduction, which some felt may be supplemented by John Carey's controversial *John Donne: Life, Mind, and Art*. Frank J. Warnke's Twayne volume on Donne provides an uncontroversial brief introduction to the life and works. James Winny's *Preface to Donne* is lively and well-illustrated. Two fine anthologies of criticism on Donne are out of print but usually available in libraries: *John Donne*, edited by Helen Gardner, in the Twentieth-Century Views series and *Discussions of John Donne*, edited by Frank Kermode.

For Herbert, the respondents overwhelmingly named Joseph H. Summers's *George Herbert: His Religion and Art* as the best place to begin a study of his life and works. Stanley Stewart's *George Herbert* in the Twayne series avoids, rather than emulates, the bland objectivity that surfaces in many of the other volumes in that series and presents an interesting argument for a less "Protestant" Herbert than many modern critics envision. Several respondents also admitted rather mischievously that they like to liven up class discussions by assigning readings from Stanley E. Fish's section on Herbert in *Self-Consuming Artifacts* or Barbara Leah Harman's *Costly Monuments: Representations of the Self in George Herbert's Poetry*. There is the Twayne series volume *Henry Vaughan* by Kenneth Friedenreich, but Jonathan F. S. Post's *Henry Vaughan: The Unfolding Vision* is equally accessible and more authoritative. Readers studying Crashaw are steered toward Austin Warren's *Richard Crashaw*, a fine biographical and critical study. Finally, George deF. Lord's Twentieth-Century Views series volume *Andrew Marvell* (out of print but widely available in libraries) contains highly recommended essays by T. S. Eliot and Joseph H. Summers among various other selections and provides a useful starting point for the study of that elusive poet. (The section "The Instructor's Library" lists many other general and specialized studies that a student can consult when doing more extensive work in the area.)

Aids to Teaching

Many instructors were enthusiastic about the results of integrating audio-visual materials into their courses: as one respondent explained, "Students are so visual these days that it really helps to work through a visual medium, especially for undergraduates." In addition, critics have repeatedly stressed the importance of audiovisual dimensions in the metaphysical poets. Much attention, for example, has been paid to Donne's meditative composition of place, Herbert's interest in music and emblematic devices, Vaughan's visual descriptions of moments of illumination, Crashaw's debt to baroque art, and Marvell's emblems and complex use of voices in poetic dialogues and debates. The instructors sometimes exposed students to those contexts by requiring or recommending secondary sources, such as the following: Wylie Sypher's *Four Stages of Renaissance Style* and Arnold Hauser's *Mannerism: The Crisis of the Renaissance and the Origin of Modern Art* on contemporary painting, John Hollander's *Untuning of the Sky: Ideas of Music in English Poetry, 1500–1700*, Ernest B. Gilman's *Curious Perspective: Literary and Pictorial Wit in the Seventeenth Century*, Louis L. Martz's *Poetry of Meditation*, Barbara Kiefer Lewalski's well-illustrated discussion of Protestant emblematics in *Protestant Poetics and the Seventeenth-Century Religious Lyric*, Rosemond Tuve's iconographic *Reading of George Herbert*, and Marc F. Bertonasco's *Crashaw and the Baroque*.

More frequently, though, instructors work in class with primary sources. The respondents mentioned many visual aids, including some easily overlooked, such as the blackboard; one instructor wrote, "As simple as this seems, I have found that attempting to draw metaphysical conceits in front of the class is most effective." In addition, slides, prints of sixteenth- and seventeenth-century paintings, photographs of sculpture and architecture, and facsimiles of emblem books are helpful in suggesting backgrounds for or analogues of figurative expressions by the poets. One instructor used "slides of anamorphic paintings to get students to think about illusion in metaphysical poetry" and noted that "slides of baroque architecture, juxtaposed with slides of classical buildings, have worked well in encouraging students to think about metaphysical conceits." Teaching Crashaw in particular almost necessitates the use of visual aids, and various respondents noted that they used illustrations of Bernini's sculptures to help communicate to students some concept of the emotional force, deliberate asymmetry, and heavy reliance on illusion that characterize Crashaw's baroque artistry. Other instructors used portraits and photographs of estates and houses to give students a view of seventeenth-century men, women, and places. And a short animated film, *Damon the Mower*—made by George Dunning, the cartoon artist more widely known for his pop-art film *The Yellow Submarine*—is based on a Marvell poem.

Many metaphysical poems are meant to be scripts for astonishing rhetorical, dramatic, or musical performances, and instructors frequently read poems out loud in class, ask their students to read aloud, or play selections from the records and cassettes currently available. Perhaps the best known and most highly recommended record is Richard Burton's reading of poems by Donne, but also useful are the Caedmon recordings *Sermons and Meditations of John Donne* by Herbert Marshall and *Metaphysical Poetry* by Cedric Hardwicke and Robert Newton, which excludes Donne but includes (among others) eight poems by Herbert, three by Vaughan, and two each by Crashaw and Marvell. One instructor emphasized music, even inviting "a musicologist to give a lecture on the development of music during this period." Others examined musical settings for lyrical poems and played samples of contemporary music, such as Dowland lute songs. Instructors looking for information on music and metaphysical poetry may consult recent scholarly works by Louise Schleiner and Paul L. Gaston, which contain much information on seventeenth- and twentieth-century settings of poems by Herbert and Donne in particular.

Other audiovisual teaching aids vary in usefulness. Such television series as Jacob Bronowski's *Ascent of Man* and Kenneth Clark's *Civilisation*, available in many university and public libraries, contain sections that may help acquaint students with the intellectual and aesthetic concerns of the Renaissance and the seventeenth century. The Films for the Humanities videocassette *Milton and Seventeenth-Century Poetry* (virtually identical to their filmstrip of the same title) concentrates on the metaphysical poets, Milton, and the epic, but it is somewhat sketchy. Far more useful and informative are the Audio Learning cassettes containing discussions of metaphysical poetry (by Paulina Palmer and Paul Merchant), Herbert and Marvell (Palmer and Merchant), Donne's poetry (Barbara Hardy and A. J. Smith) and seventeenth-century literature, including a general overview of metaphysical poetry and a particular analysis of Donne and Marvell (Frank Kermode and A. J. Smith). Students are often willing to supplement class discussions and reading assignments with those interesting tapes.

The above paragraphs provide just a brief summary of the many teaching aids that may prove helpful in a course including Donne, Herbert, Vaughan, Crashaw, and Marvell. Further information can be found not only in the detailed list of books in the following section, "The Instructor's Library," but also in several essays in the section "Approaches." The importance of imaginative immersion into seventeenth-century life is discussed by both P. G. Stanwood and E. R. Gregory, and the essays by Albert C. Labriola, Huston Diehl, Faye Pauli Whitaker, Nicholas Jones, and John R. Roberts emphasize the centrality of visual- and aural-performance contexts for a full understanding of the metaphysical poets.

The Instructor's Library

What follows is not a comprehensive bibliography or an evaluatively annotated list of essential secondary sources—a judgment that varies a great deal
from one instructor to another. Instead, I am simply providing an overview
of some of the material available on the metaphysical poets, both collectively
and individually, that may be particularly useful to teachers and serious
students. The focus is on book-length works recommended by the respondents to the questionnaire, but I have not hesitated to supplement the titles
in a few places, especially to broaden the list in categories not covered
specifically by the questionnaire. For ease of reference, each of the sections
below first discusses general studies and then goes on to discuss works on the
individual poets.

Reference Works

The dramatic increase in scholarly and critical studies of the metaphysical
poets since the 1920s is well documented in a number of specialized bibliographies, including Theodore Spencer and Mark Van Doren's *Studies in
Metaphysical Poetry: Two Essays and a Bibliography* (covering up to 1939),
Lloyd E. Berry's continuation, *A Bibliography of Studies in Metaphysical
Poetry, 1939–1960*, and Arthur E. Barker's Goldentree Bibliography *The
Seventeenth Century: Bacon through Marvell*, which is particularly useful
because it lists many background studies, as well as works on individual
authors. Also helpful are Douglas Bush's bibliographical listings in his *English Literature in the Earlier Seventeenth Century* and the relevant sections
of A. E. Dyson's *English Poetry: Select Bibliographical Guides*. Much
briefer but handy, especially because of its brevity, is John T. Shawcross's
summary "Research and the State of Studies in Seventeenth-Century British
Literature (1600–1660)."

In addition to consulting those comprehensive surveys, readers may want
to turn to more detailed bibliographies for each individual poet. John R.
Roberts's *John Donne: An Annotated Bibliography of Modern Criticism,
1912–1967* and *John Donne: An Annotated Bibliography of Modern Criticism, 1968–1978* are carefully researched and easy to use. Equally authoritative is Roberts's revised and expanded *George Herbert: An Annotated
Bibliography of Modern Criticism, 1905–1984*. Readers looking for a less
extensive survey will find a valuable resource in Jerry Leath Mills's "Recent
Studies in Herbert," which was updated in a separate essay in the same
series by Robert H. Ray. A full bibliography for Vaughan is available in E. L.
Marilla's *Comprehensive Bibliography of Henry Vaughan* and E. L. Marilla

and James D. Simmonds's *Henry Vaughan: A Bibliographical Supplement, 1946–1960*. "Recent Studies in Henry Vaughan" by Robert E. Bourdette, Jr., provides a helpful brief overview. Crashaw is well served by John R. Roberts's *Richard Crashaw: An Annotated Bibliography of Criticism, 1632–1980* and Albert R. Cirillo's "Recent Studies in Crashaw." Dan S. Collins's *Andrew Marvell: A Reference Guide* is fully annotated and comprehensive, but Gillian Szanto's "Recent Studies in Marvell" is still a welcome guide.

For up-to-date references, readers should consult annual bibliographies, such as the *MLA International Bibliography, Year's Work in English Studies*, and the Modern Humanities Research Association's *Annual Bibliography of English Language and Literature*. Many scholarly journals regularly publish essays on the metaphysical poets, but a few specialize in the area: each Winter issue of *Studies in English Literature* contains essays on Renaissance and seventeenth-century authors and a lengthy review essay surveying the previous year's books in the field; *English Literary Renaissance* contains essays, texts, and bibliographical articles in a series titled "Recent Studies in the English Renaissance"; *Seventeenth-Century News* prints book reviews, notes, and abstracts of articles; *The Seventeenth Century* covers literature, history, theology, and philosophy, among many other subjects; and both the *John Donne Journal* and the *George Herbert Journal* include essays, notes, and reviews on a broader range of seventeenth-century topics than their titles indicate.

The one indisputably essential reference work for linguistic studies of the metaphysical poets is the *Oxford English Dictionary*. More detailed analyses are facilitated by concordances available for each poet: by Homer C. Combs and Zay R. Sullens for Donne, Mario A. Di Cesare and Rigo Mignani for Herbert, Imilda Tuttle for Vaughan's *Silex Scintillans*, Robert M. Cooper for Crashaw, and George R. Guffey for Marvell.

Background Studies and Critical Works

Some modern critics suggest that the notion of a background is more problematic than was previously believed. Indeed, it is often difficult to determine what constitutes a legitimate background and to analyze a fluid and complicated relation between text and context. In addition, researchers in metaphysical poetry should also bear in mind a somewhat more mundane reminder: the metaphysical age spans a long time, from Donne's birth in 1572 to Vaughan's death in 1695. The general studies listed below, therefore, apply unequally to the individual poets.

It would take a lifetime to master the historical works on the period, but a variety of useful and comprehensive introductions are available. Godfrey

Davies's *Early Stuarts, 1603–1660* and George N. Clark's *Later Stuarts, 1660–1714*, both part of the Oxford History of England series, are thorough and contain detailed bibliographies. Christopher Hill, in some respects the controversial dean of historians of seventeenth-century England, emphasizes economic developments and corresponding shifts in social relations in *The Century of Revolution, 1603–1714* and in the many important specialized studies collected in *Puritanism and Revolution* and *Society and Puritanism in Pre-Revolutionary England*. Conrad Russell's *Crisis of Parliaments: English History 1509–1660* surveys the growing and ultimately mismanaged tensions culminating in the Civil War, and David Ogg covers the post-Restoration period in overwhelming detail in *England in the Reign of Charles II* and *England in the Reign of James II and William III*. A general reader may not want to get mired in the often bitter controversies among historians over various seventeenth-century topics (the nature of parliament, the rise of the gentry, the causes of the Civil War, and so on), but it is helpful to know something about the current debate over revisionist interpretations of the period, summarized concisely (but with full references) by Christopher Hill in "Parliament and People in Seventeenth-Century England" (*Collected Essays* 3: 21–67). Each of the above historical works rewrites but does not replace several classics of seventeenth-century history still worth consulting: Samuel R. Gardiner's *History of England from the Accession of James I to the Outbreak of the Civil War* and G. M. Trevelyan's *England under the Stuarts*.

Studies of the social history of the period focused for a long time on the court and the nobility, and such works as G. P. V. Akrigg's *Jacobean Pageant: Or, The Court of King James I* and Lawrence Stone's *Crisis of the Aristocracy, 1558–1641* continue to be important. But the tremendous increase in attention to local history and the conditions and the culture of lower- and middle-class men and women has substantially broadened our view of seventeenth-century life. Louis B. Wright's literature-based *Middle-Class Culture in Elizabethan England* is a pioneering work in the field, and both Lawrence Stone's *Family, Sex and Marriage in England 1500–1800* and Richard L. Greaves's *Society and Religion in Elizabethan England* provide an extraordinary amount of material on the manners, habits, customs, and beliefs of the time. The title of Keith Thomas's great work *Religion and the Decline of Magic* does not capture the extent to which it is an encyclopedic work of social history.

Studies of intellectual history are particularly important for poets known to have ransacked many realms of human knowledge for words, images, and themes, some of which may be foreign to the modern mind. A number of works focus on the medieval heritage of the Renaissance mind; they include E. M. W. Tillyard's *Elizabethan World Picture*, A. O. Lovejoy's *Great*

Chain of Being, and C. S. Lewis's *Discarded Image*. C. A. Patrides gives a handy introduction to a dozen recurrent topics (such as the cessation of oracles, numerology, and the order of angels) in *Premises and Motifs in Renaissance Thought and Literature*. Renaissance psychology and the place of human beings in the created world are surveyed in J. B. Bamborough's *Little World of Man* and Theodore Spencer's *Shakespeare and the Nature of Man*. Perry Miller's *New England Mind* presents information about the old England mind as well, John R. Mulder's *Temple of the Mind* contains a brief introduction to the rhetorical and logical habits reinforced by seventeenth-century education, and Rosalie Colie focuses on contradiction and contrariety in *Paradoxia Epidemica: The Renaissance Tradition of Paradox*. The pivotal place of the seventeenth century in the transition from an aural-oral culture to a print culture is examined in Elizabeth L. Eisenstein's *Printing Press as an Agent of Change* and Walter J. Ong's *Presence of the Word* and *Interfaces of the Word*. Among the volumes that survey a variety of backgrounds, the following are especially useful: Isabel Rivers's *Classical and Christian Ideas in English Renaissance Poetry*, Joseph A. Mazzeo's *Renaissance and Revolution: Backgrounds to Seventeenth-Century Literature*, Basil Willey's *Seventeenth-Century Background*, Louis I. Bredvold's *Intellectual Milieu of John Dryden*, and *The Age of Milton*, edited by C. A. Patrides and Raymond B. Waddington.

Within the history of ideas relevant to the metaphysical poets, studies of science are particularly important. The effects of the new science on a firmament of Christian humanism and optimism are examined in Herschel Baker's *Dignity of Man* and *The Wars of Truth*, Victor Harris's *All Coherence Gone*, R. F. Jones's *Ancients and Moderns*, and Marjorie Hope Nicolson's *Breaking of the Circle*. Although they do not discuss literature and science, the following books present information about seventeenth-century scientific developments: Thomas S. Kuhn's *Copernican Revolution*, Alexander Koyré's *From the Closed World to the Infinite Cosmos*, and A. A. Wolf's *History of Science, Technology, and Philosophy in the Sixteenth and Seventeenth Centuries*. Christopher Hill focuses on science and social transformations in *Intellectual Origins of the English Revolution*, as does Charles Webster in *The Great Instauration: Science, Medicine, and Reform, 1626–1660*.

The above general studies of the historical and intellectual contexts of the seventeenth century continue to be influential, but they are in the process of being reevaluated and, more than occasionally, attacked by some modern scholars and critics who focus on new sources of information (history from below, rather than from above, for example), challenge the notion of a basic unity and coherence in any seventeenth-century system of ideas, and analyze how poems often subtly undermine the ideology and the social relations they seem to celebrate. Cecily Veronica Wedgwood's *Poetry and*

Politics under the Stuarts and Jonathan Goldberg's *James I and the Politics of Literature* adopt radically different critical methods—Wedgwood is in most respects a traditional historian, and Goldberg writes under the spell of postmodern theories of textual indeterminacy—but both provide compelling evidence that even the court culture commissioned by or aimed at the king was shot through with subversion and discontent. Goldberg's *Voice Terminal Echo* is less directly concerned with historical matters but contains essays on Herbert and Marvell, among others, written from a poststructuralist perspective that he acknowledges is combative and controversial, as well as vital. Annabel M. Patterson's *Censorship and Interpretation* stresses that the pressures of censorship (surely very strong in the seventeenth century) greatly influenced not only what writers did not write about but also the peculiar language and the structures of what they did write about. Her notion that allegory and obscurity are political, as well as stylistic, strategies offers a new way of studying metaphysical wit. Christopher Hill also examines the political restrictions on writers caused by ecclesiastical and governmental censorship in volume 1 of his *Collected Essays*, which contains studies of Vaughan, Marvell, and many other seventeenth-century authors.

Other valuable books include Raymond Williams's *Country and the City*, David Norbrook's *Poetry and Politics in the English Renaissance*, Guy Fitch Lytle and Stephen Orgel's collection of essays *Patronage in the Renaissance*, and Leah Sinanoglou Marcus's *Politics of Mirth*. Arguably the two most provocative and influential recent studies in the field do not discuss metaphysical poetry directly but are being used as models for new studies of Donne, Herbert, and Marvell in particular: Stephen Greenblatt's *Renaissance Self-Fashioning* brilliantly examines the many countervailing forces that lie behind the difficult task of creating a poetic and public career; and Jonathan Dollimore's *Radical Tragedy*, though it focuses primarily on drama, contains an extensive critique of such "essentialist" works as Tillyard's *Elizabethan World Picture* and suggests that the great writers of the time questioned or subverted the ideology Tillyard champions. The variety of historical approaches to late sixteenth- and seventeenth-century literature and culture is displayed in four collections of essays: *The Historical Renaissance: New Essays on Tudor and Stuart Literature and Culture*, edited by Heather Dubrow and Richard Strier; *Renaissance Historicism: Selections from* English Literary Renaissance, edited by Arthur F. Kinney and Dan S. Collins; *"The Muses Common-Weale": Poetry and Politics in the Seventeenth Century*, edited by Claude J. Summers and Ted-Larry Pebworth; and *Politics of Discourse: The Literature and History of Seventeenth-Century England*, edited by Kevin Sharpe and Steven N. Zwicker. Taken together, those volumes confirm that the "old" historicism is not dead but is capable of remarkable flexibility and revision and that the "new" historicism is alive and well and is anything but monolithic or dogmatic.

As several essays later in this volume note, the relation between metaphysical poetry and the various fine arts is important. The influence of emblem books is discussed in Rosemary Freeman's *English Emblem Books* and Rosalie Colie's *Resources of Kind*. Mario Praz's *Studies in Seventeenth-Century Imagery* is essential for any serious study of emblems, and Jerome S. Dees's "Recent Studies in the English Emblems" lists many other works. Clark Hulse's "Recent Studies of Literature and Painting in the English Renaissance" is a handy checklist, and important works in the field include Wylie Sypher's *Four Stages of Renaissance Style*, Jean Seznec's *Survival of the Pagan Gods*, Ernest B. Gilman's *Curious Perspective: Literary and Pictorial Wit in the Seventeenth Century*, and Louis L. Martz's "English Religious Poetry, from Renaissance to Baroque." The term *baroque* remains slippery, but it is examined with reference to various arts, as well as literature, in Carl Friedrich's *Age of the Baroque* and H. James Jensen's *The Muses' Concord: Literature, Music, and the Visual Arts in the Baroque Age*. Finally, John Hollander's *Untuning of the Sky: Ideas of Music in English Poetry, 1500–1700* is a comprehensive introduction and may be supplemented by works listed in Louise Schleiner's "Recent Studies in Poetry and Music of the English Renaissance."

The precise theological context of metaphysical poetry continues to be a topic of much controversy. Horton Davies provides a comprehensive overview in *Worship and Theology in England*, volumes 1, *From Cranmer to Hooker, 1534–1603*, and 2, *From Andrewes to Baxter and Fox, 1603–1690*. In *The Protestant Mind of the English Reformation, 1570–1640*, Charles H. George and Katherine G. George emphasize the broad spectrum of agreement on basic theological matters that they think characterized the early seventeenth century. That position is reinforced by Patrick Collinson's *Religion of Protestants: The Church in English Society 1559–1625*, in which he warns that we must be careful not to read the later sects and divisions into the early prerevolutionary period. Nicholas Tyacke's book on the rise of Arminianism expands on the main thesis of his influential article "Puritanism, Arminianism, and Counter-Revolution": that the rise of a powerful Arminian party in the 1620s, headed by William Laud, precipitated the breakup of what had been a flexible consensus. J. Sears McGee's *Godly Man in Stuart England* is a study of some key differences between Puritanism and Anglicanism, and William Haller's *Rise of Puritanism* is still useful. Before engaging in a serious study of those hotly debated issues, scholars should look over Richard L. Greaves's long review essay "The Puritan-Nonconformist Tradition in England, 1560–1700: Historiographical Reflections," an extensive critical review of scholarship in the area.

Works on seventeenth-century religious issues that may be of particular interest to literary scholars include C. A. Patrides's *Grand Design of God: The Literary Form of the Christian View of History*, Helen C. White's

English Devotional Literature, 1600–1640, and Malcolm M. Ross's *Poetry and Dogma: The Transfiguration of Eucharistic Symbols in Seventeenth Century English Poetry*. The reference points for an ongoing critical debate are Louis L. Martz's *Poetry of Meditation*, which emphasizes the centrality of Roman Catholic devotional techniques to seventeenth-century poets, and Barbara Kiefer Lewalski's analysis of an alternative tradition in *Protestant Poetics and the Seventeenth-Century Religious Lyric*.

Several modes of thought and expression are vital to an understanding of the metaphysical poets. For a full introduction to typology, one can consult Jean C. Daniélou's *From Shadows to Reality: Studies in the Typology of the Fathers* and William G. Madsen's *From Shadowy Types to Truth*. Other useful studies are Paul J. Korshin's *Typologies in England 1650–1820*; a collection of essays edited by Earl Miner, *Literary Uses of Typology*; and Ira Clark's *Christ Revealed: The History of the Neotypological Lyric in the English Renaissance*. The standard works on allegory are Rosemond Tuve's *Allegorical Imagery: Some Medieval Books and Their Posterity* and Angus Fletcher's *Allegory: The Theory of a Symbolic Mode*. Itrat Husain examines the mystical in great detail in *The Mystical Element in the Metaphysical Poets of the Seventeenth Century*. Wit is one of the characteristic marks of metaphysical poetry, and there are important explanations of the backgrounds of wit (see especially T. S. Eliot's essay "The Metaphysical Poets," S. L. Bethell's "Nature of Metaphysical Wit," Earl Miner's *Metaphysical Mode from Donne to Cowley*, and Joseph A. Mazzeo's "Critique of Some Modern Theories of Metaphysical Poetry") and stunning demonstrations of how wit functions in a poem (see especially William Empson's *Seven Types of Ambiguity* and Cleanth Brooks's influential reading of Donne's "Canonization" in *The Well-Wrought Urn*).

The growth in critical studies of the metaphysical poets has been astonishing (analyzed in a monograph, *The Revival of Metaphysical Poetry*, by Joseph E. Duncan). Works that provide substantial general introductions to Donne, Herbert, Vaughan, Crashaw, and Marvell include: A. Alvarez's *School of Donne*, Joan Bennett's *Five Metaphysical Poets*, J. B. Leishman's *Metaphysical Poets*, Helen C. White's *Metaphysical Poets*, George Williamson's *Donne Tradition* and *Six Metaphysical Poets: A Reader's Guide*, Joseph H. Summers's *Heirs of Donne and Jonson*, and Anthony Low's study *Love's Architecture*. Several useful anthologies of criticism are those edited by Frank Kermode, *The Metaphysical Poets*; William R. Keast, *Seventeenth-Century English Poetry: Modern Essays in Criticism*; Malcolm Bradbury and David Palmer, *Metaphysical Poetry*; Harold Bloom, *John Donne and the Seventeenth-Century Metaphysical Poets*; and Claude J. Summers and Ted-Larry Pebworth, *"Bright Shooters of Everlastingnesse": The Seventeenth-Century Religious Lyric*.

A number of critical studies emphasize a particular theme or approach while discussing the entire group of metaphysical poets. Seventeenth-century poetic theory and styles are the focal points in Rosemond Tuve's *Elizabethan and Metaphysical Imagery*, Ruth Wallerstein's *Studies in Seventeenth-Century Poetic*, Earl Miner's volumes *The Metaphysical Mode from Donne to Cowley* and *Seventeenth-Century Imagery: Essays on Uses of Figurative Language from Donne to Farquhar*. M. M. Mahood examines the legacy of Renaissance humanism in *Poetry and Humanism*, Stanley Stewart traces a recurrent image and theme in *The Enclosed Garden: Tradition and Image in Seventeenth-Century Poetry*, and Harold Toliver discusses the importance of place in general in *Lyric Provinces in the English Renaissance*. Camille Wells Slights discusses *The Casuistical Tradition in Shakespeare, Donne, Herbert, and Milton*, and Patrick Grant examines the metaphysical poets' responses to Augustinianism in *The Transformation of Sin: Studies in Donne, Herbert, Vaughan, and Traherne*. Michael McCanles's *Dialectical Criticism and Renaissance Literature* establishes a dialectical model to resolve the apparent split between formalist and historicist approaches to literary analysis; more influential is Stanley E. Fish's *Self-Consuming Artifacts: The Experience of Seventeenth-Century Literature*, which has persuaded a whole generation of critics to look for ways in which metaphysical poetry teases and tricks its readers and sets up structures only to tear them down. Louis L. Martz analyzes variations on the theme of human and divine love in *The Wit of Love: Donne, Carew, Crashaw, Marvell*, and Leah Sinanoglou Marcus's *Childhood and Cultural Despair: A Theme and Variations in Seventeenth-Century Literature* contains many observations on the poetic, psychological, and political significance of images of childhood in seventeenth-century poetry. The essays in *Poems in Their Place: The Intertextuality and Order of Poetic Collections*, edited by Neil Fraistat, range from classical to modern, but several authors examine the idea of the book in seventeenth-century poetry and the interpretive importance of a poem's location within a larger collection. William Halewood's *Poetry of Grace: Reformation Themes and Structures in English Seventeenth-Century Poetry* (written before Lewalski's *Protestant Poetics*) emphasizes the Protestant backgrounds of the major metaphysical poets, while Anthony Raspa's *Emotive Image* argues, not entirely successfully, for the importance of a Jesuit poetics in early seventeenth-century poetry in England.

Studies of Individual Poets

The following sections discuss works that focus on individual poets and that supplement the brief review of such critical studies at the end of "Required and Recommended Readings for Students." Many of the books listed in

"Reference Works" contain chapters on or discussions of the individual poets; I have generally not repeated citations to those books. Occasionally, I mention individual articles, but the emphasis is on book-length critical works, although some of the most valuable work on the poets comes out in articles not always expanded into books. (The prose works of Donne, Herbert, and Vaughan in particular are essential to a full understanding of those writers but lie outside the scope of this volume.) Since the respondents repeatedly emphasized the authoritative modern editions and biographies of each poet, I begin each section with a quick survey of those works.

Donne. For vital information about the texts of Donne's poems and much learned and provocative commentary, teachers may consult the following editions: Helen Gardner, *The Divine Poems* and *The Elegies and the Songs and Sonnets*; Wesley Milgate, *The Epithalamions, Anniversaries and Epicedes* and *The Satires, Epigrams and Verse Letters*; Theodore Redpath, *The Songs and Sonnets of John Donne*; and Frank Manley, *The Anniversaries.* A long-term Donne variorum project is currently under way; it will completely reexamine and reedit the texts and summarize centuries of critical discussion. R. C. Bald's *John Donne: A Life* remains the standard biography, although Edward S. Le Comte's *Grace to a Witty Sinner* and John Carey's controversial *John Donne: Life, Mind, and Art* offer additional lively opinions. Arthur F. Marotti's *John Donne, Coterie Poet* presents persuasive readings of many poems in the light of Donne's biographical background and social-historical position.

The most frequently recommended general introduction to Donne was J. B. Leishman's *Monarch of Wit*, which provides a comprehensive overview of Donne's life and work. Leonard Unger's brief book *Donne's Poetry and Modern Criticism* surveys modern definitions of the term *metaphysical* and examines a variety of poems by Donne to assert that their complexity resists reduction to any one critical term. James Winny's *Preface to Donne* (mentioned above as recommended to students) contains materials on numerous contemporary contexts of Donne's poems, while Wilber Sanders's *John Donne's Poetry* is a much more text-centered study, examining the modulations of voice and wit in the entire range of Donne's poetry. Clay Hunt focuses on a more limited number of poems in *Donne's Poetry: Essays in Literary Analysis* and uses detailed close readings to examine the characteristic and intriguing "strangeness" in seven key texts. Other specialized studies of Donne's style include Pierre Legouis's *Donne the Craftsman*, Arnold Stein's *John Donne's Lyrics: The Eloquence of Action*, and Murray Roston's *Soul of Wit: A Study of John Donne.* Each of those studies emphasizes the seriousness and the integrity of Donne's art; Legouis counters the claims that Donne was an untidy craftsman, Stein dramatizes Donne's rhetorical and logical structures, and Roston notes that we need to pay more attention to Donne's continuity, rather than to the breach between his secular and his sacred poems.

Donne's poems always attract critics seeking to fathom the biographical and psychological complexities that lie behind them; for example, in *The Progress of the Soul* Richard E. Hughes uses the poetry and the prose to study what he calls in his subtitle *The Interior Career of John Donne*; and much of Judith Stampfer's *John Donne and the Metaphysical Gesture* is taken up with analyzing the deeply private and personal components of Donne's verse. Other important critical works, however, focus on the poetic and the intellectual backgrounds vital to an understanding of Donne. For example, Donne's Petrarchan heritage is examined in Donald L. Guss's *John Donne, Petrarchist: Italianate Conceits and Love Theory* and in Silvia Ruffo-Fiore's book *Donne's Petrarchism: A Comparative View*. A similar comparative view is taken in L. Elaine Hoover's study of Donne and a contemporary Spanish poet *John Donne and Francisco de Quevedo: Poets of Love and Death*. N. J. C. Andreason's *John Donne: Conservative Revolutionary* argues that Donne's style was new in many respects but that the *Elegies* and *Songs and Sonnets* still fit neatly into traditional categories of Ovidian, Petrarchan, and Christian Platonic verse.

In the essays collected in *The Disinterred Muse: Donne's Texts and Contexts*, David Novarr argues eloquently for the necessity of responsible scholarly work to understand Donne's poems and to save him from being "kidnapped" by readers with intriguing but faulty, unhistorical approaches. (That whole topic is the subject of much debate these days.) Scholarly studies of the historical and intellectual backgrounds of Donne's poems include Charles M. Coffin's *John Donne and the New Philosophy*, an influential study of Donne's interest in what he termed the "new science"; Dwight Cathcart's *Doubting Conscience: Donne and the Poetry of Moral Argument*, stressing the role of casuistry in Donne's thought; William Zunder's *Poetry of John Donne*, an ambitious though brief reading of Donne's works in the context of "literature and culture in the Elizabethan and Jacobean period"; and Terry G. Sherwood's *Fulfilling the Circle: A Study of John Donne's Thought*, an analysis of Donne's views on epistemology and psychology. Thomas Docherty's *John Donne, Undone* relies heavily on modern poststructural theory and examines Donne in the context of a troublesome historical moment when the major systems of discourse—political, sociocultural, and aesthetic—were unstable.

If book-length studies of Donne focus on any one genre, most—like Patricia Garland Pinka's *This Dialogue of One: The* Songs and Sonnets *of John Donne*—focus on the lyrics. But there are two notable exceptions: M. Thomas Hester's *Kinde Pitty and Brave Scorn: John Donne's* Satyres and

Barbara Kiefer Lewalski's *Donne's "Anniversaries" and the Poetry of Praise: The Creation of a Symbolic Mode.*

Apart from the anthologies of criticism already noted in previous sections, several collections of essays on Donne are particularly important. A. J. Smith's *John Donne: The Critical Heritage* gathers many commentaries up to the twentieth century. Twentieth-century criticism is well represented in John R. Roberts's *Essential Articles for the Study of John Donne's Poetry*, which contains thirty-nine previously published articles on a variety of themes. Other useful volumes are *John Donne: Essays in Celebration*, edited by A. J. Smith, which contains sixteen original essays; *A Garland for John Donne*, edited by Theodore Spencer, eight essays in honor of the tercentenary of Donne's death; *Just So Much Honor*, eleven essays collected by Peter Amadeus Fiore; and *The Eagle and The Dove: Reassessing John Donne*, fifteen essays edited by Claude J. Summers and Ted-Larry Pebworth.

Herbert. The standard edition of Herbert's writings is F. E. Hutchinson's *Works of George Herbert*, which lacks complete textual notes and translations of the Latin and Greek works but contains a full biographical and critical introduction and an extensive commentary. The modern translation *The Latin Poetry of George Herbert* (including the Greek poems) by Mark McCloskey and Paul R. Murphy is handy, as are facsimile editions with full critical introductions of the two important manuscript versions of Herbert's poems, The Williams manuscript (ed. Amy M. Charles) and the Bodleian manuscript (ed. Amy M. Charles and Mario A. Di Cesare). A fully annotated edition of the poems for the Longman series is in preparation. Amy M. Charles's meticulous and carefully documented *A Life of George Herbert* is the definitive biography, but other useful lives of the poet include Marchette Chute's *Two Gentle Men: The Lives of George Herbert and Robert Herrick*, aimed at the common reader; Stanley Stewart's volume *George Herbert* in the Twayne series, and T. S. Eliot's brief but influential and provocative pamphlet *George Herbert* in the Writers and Their Work series.

Among the respondents, by far the most often and most highly recommended study of Herbert was Joseph H. Summers's *George Herbert: His Religion and Art*, which contains extensive chapters on Herbert's life, influence, religious background, poetic form, and metrical inventiveness. Consonant with Louis L. Martz's sections on Herbert in *The Poetry of Meditation*, which emphasize the influence of Catholic meditative texts and structures in *The Temple*, Rosemond Tuve's *Reading of George Herbert* demonstrates that many of Herbert's themes and figures, inexplicable to the modern reader, were clear to the seventeenth-century reader schooled in readily available medieval iconography and Bible commentaries. A number of recent studies directly challenge Martz and Tuve and focus on Herbert's debt to Protestant theology and meditative practices: Herbert is one of Barbara Kiefer Lewalski's central figures in her encyclopedic study *Protestant Poetics and the Seventeenth-Century Religious Lyric*; Richard Strier stresses Herbert's debt to Lutheran theology in *Love Known: Theology and Experience in George Herbert's Poetry* and provides insightful analyses of many key poems; A. D. Nuttall envisions Herbert's confronting a Calvinist God in *Overheard by God: Fiction and Prayer in Herbert, Milton, Dante and St. John*; Gene Edward Veith, Jr., examines the broad background of Protestant theology and its effect on Herbert in *Reformation Spirituality: The Religion of George Herbert*; and Donald R. Dickson explores how a Protestant interpretation of a common typological figure affects the imagery and the arrangement of Herbert's poems in *The Fountain of Living Waters: The Typology of the Waters of Life in Herbert, Vaughan, and Traherne*. Unhappy with the limitations of the Martz versus Lewalski polarity, John N. Wall, Jr., in *Tranformations of the Word: Spenser, Herbert, Vaughan*, focuses on the liturgical background of Herbert's poems and attempts to place Herbert in an Anglican church that is a "distinctive 'third stream' within Western Christendom alongside Roman Catholicism and the reformed church traditions" (2–3).

Other studies recommended by the respondents reflect the wide variety of critical approaches to Herbert. Helen Vendler offers detailed close readings of many lyrics in *The Poetry of George Herbert* and analyzes Herbert's penchant for writing poems of reinvention and self-correction. Stanley E. Fish's *Living Temple: George Herbert and Catechizing* grounds in catechetical practices the recurrent pattern in which Herbert's speakers and poems undo themselves, a theme also discussed in Fish's earlier chapter on Herbert in *Self-Consuming Artifacts: The Experience of Seventeenth-Century Literature*. While differing from Fish in several ways, Barbara Leah Harman similarly emphasizes the ways Herbert's poems collapse and dissolve and the problems his speakers have in telling coherent stories in *Costly Monuments: Representations of the Self in George Herbert's Poetry*. More tradition-minded critics are by no means blind to the problems and difficulties addressed in *The Temple* but approach them from different angles and set them in a framework of poetic order and stability: Margaret Bottrall's *George Herbert* stresses his harmony and joyous devotional spirit, and both Robert B. Shaw's *Call of God: The Theme of Vocation in the Poetry of Donne and Herbert* and Diana Benet's *Secretary of Praise: The Poetic Vocation of George Herbert* examine Herbert's achievements in his dual vocation of priest and poet. Recent critics, though, have begun to emphasize the "world of strife" that Herbert lived in and presented in his writings. Marion White Singleton goes far beyond Shaw and Benet in studying how Herbert transformed, rather than simply abandoned, secular goals and codes of conduct in the strenuous process of fashioning himself in his life and his poems as "God's courtier." Studies of how deeply Herbert's writings are embedded in the social and political circumstances of his times include articles by Sidney Gottlieb, Cristina Malcolmson, and Michael C. Schoenfeldt.

Herbert's style attracts attention, and, apart from Joseph H. Summers's *George Herbert: His Religion and Art,* the two major studies of Herbert's poetic skill are Mary Ellen Rickey's *Utmost Art: Complexity in the Verse of George Herbert*—a wide-ranging analysis of Herbert's classical allusions, puns, purposeful titles, thoughtful revisions, and overall deceptive simplicity—and Arnold Stein's *George Herbert's Lyrics,* which discusses Herbert's prosody, "art of plainness," and creation of a lyric mode that allows for the expression and the mastery of powerful personal feelings. In *Equivocal Predication: George Herbert's Way to God,* Heather A. R. Asals argues, with key references to Augustine, that Herbert's language and poetics are thoroughly Anglican, sacramental, and incarnational; through divine equivocation, the unrelenting dual focus of words, his poems bridge the gap between human beings and God. Other books that explore Augustinian backgrounds include Mark Taylor's *Soul in Paraphrase: George Herbert's Poetics* and Richard Todd's *Opacity of Signs: Acts of Interpretation in George Herbert's* The Temple. Coburn Freer explains some of Herbert's poetic inventiveness in terms of the many psalm translations in *Music for a King: George Herbert's Style and the Metrical Psalms,* and in *Spelling the Word: George Herbert and the Bible* Chana Bloch emphasizes the centrality of the Bible for Herbert as a source of themes, images, and poetic techniques. Bart Westerweel's *Patterns and Patterning: A Study of Four Poems by George Herbert* is an exhaustive illustrated study of sources and visual analogues for two of Herbert's most obviously shaped poems, "The Altar" and "Easter-wings," and two of his less obviously patterned narratives, "The Pilgrimage" and "Love" (3). Robert H. Ray's *Herbert Allusion Book* is an invaluable listing of allusions to Herbert in the seventeenth century and provides important material on Herbert's immediate reputation and influence.

Allusions to and critical comments on Herbert from the early seventeenth century to the first part of the twentieth century are gathered in *George Herbert: The Critical Heritage,* assembled by C. A. Patrides. *Essential Articles for the Study of George Herbert's Poetry,* edited by John R. Roberts, reprints thirty-four modern essays; *"Too Rich to Clothe the Sunne": Essays on George Herbert,* edited by Claude J. Summers and Ted-Larry Pebworth, contains fifteen new essays; *Like Season'd Timber: New Essays on George Herbert,* edited by Edmund Miller and Robert DiYanni, contains twenty-one essays, many of which cover neglected topics, such as Herbert's prose and his influence in the eighteenth century; and *A Fine Tuning: Studies of the Religious Poetry of Herbert and Milton*, edited by Mary Maleski, includes six essays on Herbert. Together, those collections give a panoramic view of much of the work that constitutes the modern critical revival of interest in Herbert.

Vaughan. L. C. Martin's *Works of Henry Vaughan* remains the standard scholarly edition for the study of Vaughan, but it has been supplemented and in some respects corrected and improved by several modern editions that follow up on Martin's pathbreaking work. French Fogle's texts of the English and Latin poems in *The Complete Poetry of Henry Vaughan* are the result of a more extensive collation of early editions than Martin was able to undertake, and E. L. Marilla's *Secular Poetry of Henry Vaughan* and especially Alan Rudrum's *Henry Vaughan: The Complete Poems* take into account the current research on Vaughan in their extensive annotations. Vaughan's life continues to attract attention, and many critical articles focus on his conversion from secular to sacred poetry, his relationship with his brothers, and his experiences during the civil war. The major book-length biography is F. E. Hutchinson's *Henry Vaughan: A Life and Interpretation*. Kenneth Friedenreich's Twayne series volume *Henry Vaughan* similarly blends biography and criticism.

The two critical studies recommended most highly by the respondents to the questionnaire were E. C. Pettet's *Of Paradise and Light: A Study of Silex Scintillans* and Jonathan F. S. Post's *Henry Vaughan: The Unfolding Vision*. Pettet offers insightful analyses of some individual poems but is also attentive to sequences, clusters of images, and large structural patterns that connect parts 1 and 2 of the collection. Post provides a comprehensive, integrating view of Vaughan's body of work and does a better job than most other critics of emphasizing the poet's relationship to Herbert without turning Vaughan into a derivative epigone. James D. Simmonds's *Masques of God: Form and Theme in the Poetry of Henry Vaughan* is also a valuable study of the continuity of Vaughan's secular and sacred poetry.

Many critical works focus on Vaughan's mysticism or his reliance on alchemical imagery. Elizabeth Holmes stresses the influence of hermeticism in general and his brother Thomas in particular in *Henry Vaughan and the Hermetic Philosophy*; those subjects are also pursued in Thomas O. Calhoun's *Henry Vaughan: The Achievement of Silex Scintillans*. R. A. Durr defines Vaughan's central theme as a quest for regeneration in *On the Mystical Poetry of Henry Vaughan*. In *Henry Vaughan: Experience and the Tradition* and *The Unprofitable Servant in Henry Vaughan*, Ross Garner does not deny Vaughan's quest for regeneration or his frequent flights from reason but situates them in orthodox contexts: they are themes sanctioned not only by hermetic philosophers but also by Augustine and key biblical texts. Louis L. Martz's work on Vaughan, in *The Poetry of Meditation* and *The Paradise Within*, also emphasizes the importance of Augustine and later meditative practices. The chapter on Vaughan in Donald R. Dickson's *Fountain of Living Waters* focuses on an important typological figure in Vaughan's poems; and, in a long chapter in *Transformations of the Word*, John N. Wall, Jr., studies how allusions to the Bible, the Book of Common Prayer, and Herbert's *Temple* allowed Vaughan to keep alive the idea of an Anglican church that was physically under siege during the time of Puritan rule.

Frank Kermode's "Private Imagery of Henry Vaughan" is only one brief article in the midst of many long studies arguing for Vaughan's debts to systems of mystical philosophy, but it restores a certain balance by focusing on his lyric and literary powers. Mary Ellen Rickey's "Vaughan, *The Temple*, and Poetic Form" examines Vaughan's impressive debt to Herbert—impressive not only because it is extensive but also because it involves complex imitations and transformations of poetic structures. I note those two essays in particular because they are not included in Alan Rudrum's collection *Essential Articles for the Study of Henry Vaughan*. Also useful is the *George Herbert Journal* special issue on Vaughan, edited by Jonathan F. S. Post, which comprises eight essays on such topics as Vaughan's versification, neglected poems and prose, and sense of self in *Silex Scintillans*.

Crashaw. The standard edition of Crashaw's poems is L. C. Martin's *Poems, English, Latin, and Greek, of Richard Crashaw*. George Walton Williams's *Complete Poetry of Richard Crashaw* is also authoritative and in some respects particularly handy to use because Williams reorders the poems according to two categories—secular and sacred—includes brief but useful explanatory headnotes, and puts English translations of the Latin and Greek poems on facing pages. The best biography is also one of the most highly recommended critical works, Austin Warren's *Richard Crashaw: A Study in Baroque Sensibility*. Paul A. Parrish's Twayne volume *Richard Crashaw* surveys the poet's life and works and, while not discounting Crashaw's baroque sensibility, argues that the concept does not completely explain his talent and interests.

George Walton Williams's *Image and Symbol in the Sacred Poetry of Richard Crashaw* was frequently recommended by the respondents for its examination of recurrent images—water, dust, the colors white and red—that are central to Crashaw's religious poems. Ruth Wallerstein also emphasizes the intense power of images in the poems; her *Richard Crashaw: A Study in Style and Poetic Development* traces Crashaw's special debts to Giambattista Marino, Jesuit epigrams, religious music, and emblems as he composes poems that are provocatively sensuous and emotional. In *Rhyme and Meaning in Richard Crashaw*, Mary Ellen Rickey is aware of possible models and backgrounds for Crashaw's style but focuses primarily on his artistry, especially his use of rhyme to structure poems.

Most of the book-length studies of Crashaw explore his relationship to European movements in art and religious devotion and attempt to define his style as baroque—a term as slippery as it is necessary. The long section on Crashaw in Mario Praz's influential *Flaming Heart* places the poet squarely in the Continental Counter-Reformation tradition and suggests that in his enthusiastic wit, daring conceits, and erotic and devotional enthusiasm he outdoes even Marino, one of his crucial models. (For a more detailed comparison of the two poets, see Claes Schaar, *Marino and Crashaw: Sospetto d'Herode: A Commentary.*) Robert T. Petersson similarly emphasizes the energetic, "ecstatic" qualities of Crashaw's poetry in *The Art of Ecstasy: Teresa, Bernini, and Crashaw*; Petersson uses the autobiography of Saint Teresa of Avila and Bernini's Cornaro Chapel in Rome as key analogues and interpretive contexts for Crashaw's "Hymn to Saint Teresa." A different view is evident in Marc Bertonasco's revisionary *Crashaw and the Baroque*, which emphasizes not turbulent sensuousness but a controlled and thoughtful but still affective devotional style akin to that of Saint Francis de Sales. Other devotional models for Crashaw are also proposed: Patrick Grant offers a comparison in "Richard Crashaw and the Capucins" (*Images* 89-128), and Anthony Raspa argues for the influence of the Ignatian mode of meditation on Crashaw and others in *The Emotive Image: Jesuit Poetics in the English Renaissance*. R. V. Young interprets Crashaw against the background of Spanish culture and poetry in *Richard Crashaw and the Spanish Golden Age*.

Important essays on Crashaw can be located easily by referring to the annotated bibliographies by Cirillo and Roberts. No anthology presents the "essential articles on Crashaw," but the twelve original studies in Robert M. Cooper's *Essays on Richard Crashaw* cover key poems and themes, including the funeral elegies and the musical and emblematic aspects of Crashaw's style.

Marvell. The standard scholarly edition of Marvell's poetry is H. M. Margoliouth's *Poems and Letters of Andrew Marvell*, revised in 1971 by Pierre Legouis and E. E. Duncan-Jones with added textual notes and annotations. Elizabeth Story Donno's commentary in *Andrew Marvell: The Complete English Poems* is detailed and authoritative. William A. McQueen and Kiffin A. Rockwell have edited and translated *The Latin Poetry of Andrew Marvell*. The best place to study Marvell's later satires is in volume 1 of *Poems on Affairs of State: Augustan Satirical Verse, 1660–1714*, edited by George deF. Lord, where the satires not only are heavily glossed but also appear alongside the contemporary poems to which they frequently respond. Pierre Legouis's *Andrew Marvell: Poet, Puritan, Patriot* remains the fullest biographical study; other useful surveys of the life and works include M. C. Bradbrook and M. G. Lloyd-Thomas's *Andrew Marvell*, John Dixon Hunt's *Andrew Marvell: His Life and Writings*, and Michael Craze's *Life and Lyrics of Andrew Marvell*. John Press's pamphlet *Andrew Marvell* in the Writers and Their Work series is a good introduction, as is Lawrence W. Hyman's more detailed treatment in his Twayne series volume *Andrew Marvell*. William Empson's *Using Biography* contains three essays that investigate several biographical cruxes vital to an understanding of the historical context and the transmission of Marvell's poems.

The critical study of Marvell most highly recommended by the respondents was Rosalie Colie's *"My Ecchoing Song": Andrew Marvell's Poetry of Criticism*, which contains extensive analyses of how such key poems as "The Garden" and "Upon Appleton House" absorb but also undermine and transform emblematic and generic conventions. Also highly recommended were J. B. Leishman's *Art of Marvell's Poetry*, which offers close readings of numerous poems in their literary (rather than social-historical) context, and Ann E. Berthoff's *Resolved Soul: A Study of Marvell's Major Poems*, which explores the recurrent theme of the pressures the personae face in a time-bound world. Harold Toliver emphasizes Marvell's habitual attempt to balance, rather than reconcile, opposite viewpoints in *Marvell's Ironic Vision*; and Robert Wilcher uses a variety of critical approaches to synthesize much modern scholarly work in his introductory study *Andrew Marvell*.

Many specialized studies focus on the aesthetic, philosophical, and political contexts of Marvell's poems and either explicitly or implicitly challenge the common New Critical approach that separates the poems from the poet's historical circumstances. The second part of Ruth Wallerstein's *Studies in Seventeenth-Century Poetic* argues for the importance of Neoplatonism and traditional Christian imagery and thought by analytic readings of "An Horatian Ode," "Upon Appleton House," and "The Garden." R. I. V. Hodge focuses not so much on political as on intellectual and scientific revolutions in his study *Foreshortened Time: Andrew Marvell and Seventeenth Century Revolutions*. Marvell's relation to the pastoral tradition is explored in Patrick Cullen's *Spenser, Marvell, and Renaissance Pastoral*, Donald M. Friedman's book *Marvell's Pastoral Art*, and Michael Long's intriguing comparative study *Marvell, Nabokov: Childhood and Arcadia*. The often-neglected religious context of Marvell's poems is discussed in Bruce King's book *Marvell's Allegorical Poetry*, John Klause's *Theodicy and the Moral Imagination of Andrew Marvell*, and Warren L. Chernaik's *Poet's Time: Politics and Religion in the Work of Andrew Marvell* (though that last work is primarily concerned with analyzing Marvell's responses to the revolution and its aftermath). Margarita Stocker interprets the major poems in the light of contemporary ideas on the Second Coming in *Apocalyptic Marvell*. Two studies of the political aspects of Marvell's writings were highly recommended by the respondents: John M. Wallace's *Destiny His Choice: The Loyalism of Andrew Marvell*, which relates Marvell's independent stance to his providential beliefs; and Annabel M. Patterson's *Marvell and the Civic Crown*, which not only presents detailed analyses of the Cromwell poems and later satires but also attempts to resolve the split between the poems that fall into the different phases of Marvell's career.

The history of critical responses to Marvell until the early twentieth century is captured in Elizabeth Story Donno's *Andrew Marvell: The Critical Heritage*. The critical anthologies edited by John Carey and Michael Wilding, both titled *Andrew Marvell*, begin with seventeenth-century commentaries and thus overlap Donno's volume, but both contain substantial selections from the twentieth century that reflect the controversy over historical versus New Critical approaches to such poems as "An Horatian Ode" and "The Nymph Complaining for the Death of Her Fawn." The Twentieth-Century Views volume *Andrew Marvell*, edited by George deF. Lord, comprises ten essays. More recent collections of original essays on Marvell, prompted by the tercentenary of his death in 1978, are *Approaches to Marvell: The York Tercentenary Lectures*, edited by C. A. Patrides (fifteen essays); *Andrew Marvell: Essays on the Tercentenary of His Death*, edited by R. L. Brett (four essays); and *Tercentenary Essays in Honor of Andrew Marvell*, edited by Kenneth Friedenreich (thirteen essays).

Part Two

APPROACHES

INTRODUCTION

Teaching against the Tradition

Annabel Patterson

In the early 1980s, I greatly disconcerted a director of undergraduate studies at an Ivy League school by declaring, as a candidate for a job, that I would not teach their standard course in metaphysical poetry. Why not? Because, I asserted with tactless confidence, there was no such thing. Today my iconoclastic position on that issue has, if anything, hardened, fortified both by the attacks on New Criticism now commonplace in the profession (since it was the earlier New Critics in England who were chiefly responsible for creating a "school" of metaphysical poetry) and by the new historical work on Donne, Herbert, Marvell, and Cowley that depreciates style in favor of larger cultural determinants. Michel Foucault's *Order of Things: An Archaeology of the Human Sciences* proclaimed that "literary analysis . . . now takes as its unity, not the spirit or sensibility of a period, nor 'groups,' 'schools,' 'generations,' or 'movements,' . . . but . . . the particular structure of a given *oeuvre*, book, or text" (5). Foucault spoke from the perspective of a structuralism about to be displaced (for him) by a newly depersonalized historicism. But what he allowed us to see is that "metaphysical poetry" was already old-fashioned when it first became fashionable, that its governing premise of stylistic influence was finally incompatible with the central premise of New Criticism, that every text is self-determining and intelligible in terms of its own structure. It may seem peculiar to install an attack on metaphysical poetry at the front of a volume devoted to instantiating once more that venerable critical idea and extolling its pedagogy; yet my agreement to become a contributor was not entirely deconstructive in intent. The most problematic aspects of the metaphysical idea—its internal incoherences and its major exclusions—can render it an effective tool in the classroom, provided one teaches *against* the tradition.

Suppose we begin where many classroom teachers probably begin: with an attempt to define the term *metaphysical* (as Joan Bennett admitted, "not a happy term") to a group of young people supremely indifferent, in most instances, to the nice art of definition. Invariably, I find myself explaining to such an audience that by the term *metaphysical* we do not mean what we ought to mean, a philosophical perspective on the nature of the universe, of being, or of the relation between materiality and immateriality. A handful of poems do concern themselves with at least the last of those problems—Donne's "Ecstasy" and Marvell's "Dialogue between the Soul and Body"—but the majority of the texts conventionally incorporated under the metaphysical rubric are not connected by any philosophical agenda. Where, then, does the term come from, one's students can be encouraged to ask? The answer, if truthful, can cite only institutional history and its accidents. The term comes, I explain, from a chance remark by John Dryden in "A Discourse concerning the Original and Progress of Satire" in 1693, a remark that was applied solely to Donne and was intended to depreciate Donne's style in comparison with Dryden's. The extension of the term to a group of poets was first made by Dr. Johnson in his "Life of Cowley" (1779), where again the intention was primarily depreciatory, as the arbiter of neoclassical literary values assessed the limitations of earlier and different values. It was Dr. Johnson who observed that "the metaphysical poets were men of learning, and to shew their learning was their whole endeavour" (397), thereby directing the attention of subsequent critics to the Jacobean fashion for learned metaphors and "occult resemblances." It was therefore a late eighteenth-century emphasis on style, wit, and *discordia concors* as a disturbing kind of wit that informed Herbert Grierson's 1921 *Metaphysical Lyrics and Poems of the Seventeenth Century*. In Grierson's introduction to his anthology and in T. S. Eliot's review of it, the negative judgments of Dryden and Johnson were transformed by a modernist fascination with the difficult and the strange. The "shew [of] learning" became intellectuality and "passionate ratiocination," and Dryden and Johnson were themselves dismissed as a passing fashion that led to the decease of wit and the age of sentiment. "Great poetry," concluded Grierson, "is always metaphysical, born of men's passionate thinking about life and love and death" (lviii). Yet the influence of Johnson pervaded Grierson's influential essay, which emphasized the "fantastic" and "learned" quality of "Metaphysical" metaphorization (xv).

However familiar that genealogy may be to the readers of this volume, it makes strange listening for students, whose suspicion of authority can here be invoked to good effect. Rather than attempt—as did Barbara Kiefer Lewalski and Andrew J. Sabol in their anthology *Major Poets of the Earlier Seventeenth Century*—to rescue metaphysical poetry from its self-contradictions and to find a certain utility in a critical label "fixed by more than three centuries' use" (xix), I tend in the classroom to find another utility in its manifest unfixedness. Intelligent students can learn from this story, even before they tackle a single poem, that nothing in literary studies is written in stone, that much of our terminology is an imprecise working vocabulary to permit discussion to begin, and that our conventional categories are sometimes arbitrary beyond the systemic arbitrariness of language itself. Neatly conveyed here are the relations of three major "periods" in literary history, as well as the crucial fact that values alter. The concept of paradigm shift is made easily accessible, and the student is freed to decide independently what to make of Donne and his contemporaries. At the same time, the teacher is freed from the responsibility to demonstrate an absolute connection between the concept "metaphysical poetry" and a certain kind of wit or style. In my experience, wit is the hardest of all literary conditions to demonstrate to those who do not already perceive it; the notion that wit resides in excessive or gratuitous learning is all too easily connected with academic pedantry.

Before a single poem is read, the teacher can use the story of "how we got metaphysical poetry" to develop a healthy skepticism on the subject of the canon. The one thing that emerges from a candid examination of where the term came from is that nobody agrees about whom it should apply to. Dryden spoke only of Donne. And Johnson's group consists solely of Donne and Cowley, with Giambattista Marino as the primary influence. Grierson, however, extended the group considerably, including not only Edmund Waller and John Cleveland, whom Johnson had mentioned but then excluded from the "fashionable style," but also the religious poets Henry Vaughan, George Herbert, Thomas Traherne, and Richard Crashaw and the Cavalier poets Thomas Carew, Richard Lovelace, Thomas Stanley, and William Davenant. Implicit in Grierson's choices were certain beliefs whose secret influence has shaped our pedagogy ever since. The inclusion of Cavalier poets must be partly understood in terms of Grierson's statement that "the metaphysicals were all on the King's side . . . for they were on the side of the humanities" (xxix). That assertion is supposed to include Andrew Marvell, whose poems were selected accordingly, along with the recalcitrant parliamentarian John Hoskyns, represented by a single love poem, and Milton, represented by "Ode on the Morning of Christ's Nativity." Grierson insidiously suggests that the interesting poetry of the period was politically conservative.

Equally influential was Grierson's introduction of a sizable body of religious verse, a genre not considered by Dryden, who had been thinking only of Donne's satires and love poems, and not considered by Johnson, who had nowhere suggested that *metaphysical* carried that semantic content. Grierson shifted the concept of metaphysicality toward spirituality and allowed for a new principle of selection and definition. When Joan Bennett produced her 1934 study of the "tradition," it was entitled *Four Metaphysical Poets* and included only Donne, Herbert, Vaughan, and Crashaw. In 1964 she changed her mind and added Marvell, which somewhat rebalanced the argument in favor of the secular imagination. In 1936 Helen C. White's *Metaphysical Poets* selected only the religious poets. In 1960 Robert Ellrodt's *L'inspiration personelle et l'esprit du temps chez les poètes métaphysiques anglais* expanded the list to eight, deciding in favor of Marvell, whose uneasy status as a member of the group is itself worthy of analysis. The details of the scholarly history are obviously excessive for an introductory class, but I cannot responsibly refer students to those sources and resources without preparing them for what they will find or fail to find.

Students are acute on the subject of anthologizing and selection. They can become indignant if shown a text that has been excluded but that interests them, and they are remarkably discerning of bias and ideological constraints on their reading (including, of course, my own). And there is one further principle embedded in the tradition that is useful for them to grasp as a framework for their reading experience. In 1973 Lewalski and Sabol noted that in earlier discussions of metaphysical poetry the issue of group identity had been confused by "inadequate sampling" and the focus on "a relatively small and perhaps atypical assortment of apparently Donne-like poems" (xxiv). They decided therefore to offer their readers "generous" and "representative" selections of the five poets who in their view had "traditionally" been grouped as the metaphysical school— Donne, Herbert, Vaughan, Marvell, and "perhaps" Crashaw—and two representatives of the "classical" school, Ben Jonson and the strongest of his followers, Robert Herrick. Yet Lewalski and Sabol continued to beg the questions of canonicity and value by defining those writers as "the seven major lyric poets of the period" (xxvii). The selection was less telling than the premises silently spoken by the five words that reported it: *seven, major, lyric, poets,* and especially, *the.* Inextricably blended in that statement are both the idealism and the pragmatism that has marked our literary pedagogy from its origins: the privileging of poetry as the finest challenge to criticism and the practical recognition that lyric poetry is quantitatively manageable in the classroom.

The idealist premise is often the one that students find the hardest to swallow, whether or not it is made explicit. What is so special about poetry and about lyric poetry in particular that we should read it to the exclusion of other forms of discourse and with such minute attention to detail? What can it display about the seventeenth century that could not be better understood by reading Donne's letters to his friends, Thomas Hobbes's *Leviathan*, or the records of the parliament of 1628–29? And if the poetry has no historically specific message to bring us, why do we insist on our students' making acquaintance with that alien language, unless it be for the satisfaction of demonstrating that the texts contain mysteries only we can unlock, that special skills are required for success- ful access to them? The best answers to such questions (volunteered or elicited) are not those that attempt to essentialize poetry, an attempt that generally founders in the recognition of its own belated Romanticism. Courses in metaphysical poetry became and remained the standard intro- duction to seventeenth-century literature not because (there is no reason not to advise our students) the texts so selected are intrinsically more valuable than others but because they are convenient. Their brevity lends them to reasonably full discussion—a lyric or two for each class period— which can scarcely be managed with even a single book of *Paradise Lost*, let alone *Leviathan*; and their limitations as windows onto the world they came from permits intelligibility without extensive recourse to a library. Demystification at the beginning is the strongest incentive to students to enjoy what they are about to do, to lower their resistance (especially to poetry), and to give them confidence in their own analytic and evaluative instincts.

I offer the students a poem—one chosen to reinforce all the doubts just raised at the levels of procedure and theory (if that is not too grand a term) and chosen also to reverberate with the quaint story of how we got metaphysical poetry. I introduce them to Donne with "The Flea" and with Dryden's original observation that Donne

> affects the metaphysics, not only in his satires, but in his amorous verses, where nature only should reign; and perplexes the minds of the fair sex with nice speculations of philosophy, when he should engage their hearts, and entertain them with the softnesses of love.   (Clements 106)

I find that students are genuinely amused by the outrageousness of "The Flea" and that they are willing to name the quality that amuses them "wit." They do not associate wit with metaphysical imagery, and I doubt that they ever will, no matter how carefully instructed. They can also see instantly that there is nothing particularly learned or difficult or esoteric about it, that the central metaphor is, on the contrary, bodily and mundane. And they are easily encouraged to argue, with each other and with Dryden, about whether that wit is seductive. Naturally (or, rather, culturally) the women are indignant with the premise that a poem like "The Flea" would perplex them, rather than render its author attractive for his intelligence; the men are likely to be divided (by temperament and experience) between a Dryden-like preference for the airhead and a suspicion that sexuality is a head game. But almost all recognize and are startled to find themselves involved in the dangerous issues the poem engages with such bravado.

Those tensions can be put to good use in a corporate attempt to decide why the poem engages and divides its audience and in what its outrageousness consists. Students can easily detect both the intentional misfit between the randy associations ("It sucked me first, and now sucks thee" [3]) and sacramental claims ("yea more than married are" [11]) and the sudden shift in the male speaker's logic at the poem's conclusion. And all students are quick to observe that while the male speaker dominates the discourse, allowing his partner only reported speech, there is a real contest between them; male linguistic dexterity must shift its ground before female physical action: "Cruel and sudden, hast thou since / Purpled thy nail in blood of innocence?" (19–20). Nor does it escape a group engaged in matters close to themselves that the poem manages, at the point where the physical wins, a disturbing transference—enabling, if not requiring, them to see that the mention of cruelty, blood, and a nail makes the woman the violator in a drama of defloration of her own choosing, one that the male speaker (who had intended another defloration) is forced to articulate in the language of his own transgressive sacramentalism. All that without a single learned annotation; but it hardly escapes the students that the poem operates in one territory—sexuality—in which the relation between the physical and the conceptual is constantly being negotiated, that it is, in a sense they can understand, metaphysical. But we have not endorsed, after all, the idea of "metaphysical poetry," that peculiar aggregate of the stylistic, the devout, and the masculinist approach to literary value. The demonstration can be neatly rounded off by remarking that Grierson excluded "The Flea" from his original account of metaphysical poetry and by asking the students why they think he did so.

GENERAL DISCUSSIONS AND BACKGROUNDS

Vivifying the Historical Approach: Exercises in Teaching Seventeenth-Century Love Poetry

E. R. Gregory

When I was an undergraduate back in the nineteenth century, Professor Dryasdust always began his lectures on Donne's love poetry by telling us that, of course, we couldn't possibly understand Donne unless we understood Elizabethan love poetry, which, of course, we couldn't possibly understand unless we understood Petrarch and, more remotely, of course, Ovid, Catullus, Anacreon, and the Greek Anthologists. He gave us copious notes on Petrarch (1304–74), on the characteristics of Petrarchan love poetry—the lady was blonde, chaste, cruel; the lover was supposed to love for years on end, though his love be never consummated; the lady was always presented in an idealized and unrealistic way; and so on—and on the vogue of Petrarchan love poetry in England, beginning with Wyatt and Surrey, progressing through Spenser, and debouching (finally!) into our reading a few poems like "The Canonization" and "The Apparition." The poems seemed somehow separate from and overwhelmed by the background that had been presented.

Dear Professor Dryasdust. He is gone now these many years and the decades that have passed since his demise have seen the profession swept by approaches he never dreamed of—Marxism, feminism, deconstruction, and so forth. We who daily ponder the teaching of literature are grateful to them all; for, whether we embrace them or not, each at its best does shed new light on old works. My own approach, however, has been to salvage some of what Professor Dryasdust was trying to inculcate. After all, literary antecedents and approaches to composition practiced in the seventeenth century do have the power to illuminate works like "The Canonization," but any professor worthy of the name realizes that students today are not about to memorize large globs of information simply because the professor assures them that someday, somehow, the globs will help them understand the works at hand. I have tried, then, to develop exercises that bring such material alive for students possessed of good will and intellectual curiosity but little intellectual or methodological sophistication and less backbone when faced with the mastery of large quantities of desiccated data. The exercises are not conceived with scholarly rigor. They make generous use of analogy, which we all know is best used to illustrate, rather than to prove a point; and they all involve ignoring or slighting material that students must ultimately grapple with in making the poems their own. The exercises do, however, foster a genuine, if limited, understanding of the works taken up. More important, they underscore the point that literary history is a matter of concepts to work with as well as facts to memorize.

The exercises described below lead up to the students' writing Petrarchan sonnets in class. As is usual in classroom procedure, each exercise serves several functions at the same time. The writing of the sonnets serves not merely to reinforce the students' sense of what a sixteenth- or seventeenth-century love poem was like but also to give them a firsthand experience of how composition was then taught, an area with ramifications that extend far beyond the writing of just love poetry.

My first step is to encourage student awareness of how different the seventeenth century was from the present. They know in a general way that it was different, but they have never sorted out what they know or pondered how that knowledge affects their responses to the period. The first day I ask them to spend a few minutes in jotting down ways that the seventeenth century differed from our own time. Usually, they come up with the same items—no electricity, no running water, no rapid transportation, no mass communications, primitive medicine, a short life span. Seldom do they come up with the more profound differences in outlook toward society, astronomy, and theology, but the items they do come up with lend themselves to the imaginative efforts I then try to stimulate in them. I tell them to close their eyes and imagine themselves back in a world that differed radically from the one they are used to. Most of them quickly realize a few of the implications in their daily lives—waking hours lived more according to the sun than according to the clock, distances that created problems where none exist today, a greater knowledge of literature among the literate.

That exercise has real value. Never again do the students pick up their Kermode and Hollander or their Witherspoon and Warnke without some residual sense of caution warning them that, however flatteringly like us the writers seem to be, the possibility exists that, having lived in a different world, they may, in fact, be different. Some of the exercise's seeming drawbacks—that it insufficiently differentiates the collective experience of an American college classroom from one in a third-world country and that it creates a sense of superiority because of our own incomparable modernity—can be turned to good advantage in the next phase, when we begin to examine ways in which the writers of that time were as sophisticated and as knowledgeable as we are, possibly more so.

The area I concentrate on to make that point is schooling. We examine sixteenth- and seventeenth-century educational practices, do an exercise in *imitatio* ourselves, and then examine some poems in the light of that experience. In examining the educational system, we begin with Shakespeare's thumbnail description of "the schoolboy with his shining face / Creeping like snail unwillingly to school." Having noted that the response is common to all eras, we look at some reasons why the schoolboy of Shakespeare's day and Donne's and Milton's had substantive reasons for creeping unwillingly to school—eight-hour days, six-day weeks, few holidays, tremendous amounts of memorization, and the ever-present birch rod for encouragement as needed. Once again, those details, while not necessarily the most significant ones, are the ones that stick first in students' minds and prepare them for the profounder differences that then emerge. When we consider what was taught, for example, we note that much of what we regard as basic, like math and the natural sciences, was given short shrift; the arts of composition—prose and poetry, oral and written—were given full and overpowering treatment. The students soon realize that Shakespeare, the metaphysical poets, and Milton did not know as much about science and technology as we do, but they were far more sophisticated in language than all but a small minority of today's educated classes are. The endless exercises in translation, paraphrase, and composition provided a thorough working knowledge of language from the individual word to the lengthiest of epics and as surely affected the composing of love poetry as they did every other kind of writing.

We then put into practice what we have learned about composition as then taught and what we have been reading in sixteenth-century poetry. The resulting exercise is only a simulacrum of a seventeenth-century student's experience, but even one semiexercise in *imitatio* greatly clarifies for students the effects such exercises had on the writing of poetry. I assure them that *imitatio* had various meanings—anything from a painfully close paraphrase to a free re-creation of the spirit of the original. The exercise itself, however, convinces students that, even at its freest, *imitatio* fostered an awareness of models and a consciousness of craft far greater than they had considered necessary.

Later on, I show them that even in the twentieth century *imitatio* is not entirely dead or entirely irrelevant to the writing of poetry. I read from Robert Duncan's description of his own introduction to writing poetry:

> I discovered writing poetry . . . in high school when I'd fallen in love with a teacher. . . . What really got me there, though, was the practice of imitating poems in class. When we read Chaucer, we read the Prologue and then we wrote prologues ourselves to an imaginary pilgrimage poem. And then when we came to Robert Browning we wrote dramatic monologues, and there I discovered another thing that I had always loved, and that was "being" throughout the period of mankind. And Robert Browning suddenly showed you that you could go into words and be all sorts of people. And that was so exciting that then I knew I wasn't going to be an architect; I was going to be a poet. (Ginsberg 105–06)

For the moment, however, my hands are full in getting the students past the debased Wordsworthian poetic that an overwhelming majority of them embrace and that militates against their getting into the spirit of the exercise. As one of them so memorably put it: "Poetry to me is like you know a feeling." I assured her that seventeenth-century schoolmasters had a vastly different attitude and that, while Platonic theories of divine furor were by no means unknown, the more normative pedagogical attitude was summed up in John Brinsley's dictum that "the making of a verse is nothing but the turning of words forth of the Grammaticall order, into the Rhetoricall, in some kind of metre . . ." (192).

Doubts linger, however. Even after the students have been assured that the exercise will be ungraded, they are not keen on doing it. "We don't feel like doing this," they say, or "I'm no good at this sort of thing." All such comments, of course, amplify the purpose of the assignment. "Do you think," I ask, "that seventeenth-century schoolboys always wanted to write imitations of Ovid or Horace? Or do you think that all seventeenth-century schoolboys were gifted at that sort of thing? Imagine that you've got to do it and that, if you don't do the very best you can, I'm going to rap your knuckles with a birch rod." Then they usually settle down and within an hour's time have produced a genuine sonnet.

The students' reading for that assignment included a fair amount of Petrarchan poetry, a genre with obviously imitable features that engendered a number of seventeenth-century poems the students can check their work against. One of the advantages of John Hollander and Frank Kermode's *Literature of Renaissance England* is that it provides an ample background of Elizabethan materials that can be used in this assignment. We read fifteen sonnets by Wyatt, Surrey, Spenser, and Shakespeare and sometimes supplement them with handouts, including translations from Petrarch. Students quickly catch on to the stock imagery of eyebrows like Cupid's bows, so that Shakespeare's sonnet 130 is an immediate success; but it takes them longer, sometimes much longer, to see that a great writer like Spenser can work within rigid constraints and yet achieve originality.

Those complementary perceptions are reflected in the following sonnets, done as assignments in January 1986 and reproduced here with the students' permission. I gave the initial line, "My mistress' eyes are very like the sun."

1.

My mistress' eyes are very like the sun,
But not because they burn as bright, or warm,
Or e'en because they smile when free of storm;
It is, because, alas, she has just one.

My mistress' teeth are like unto rare pearls,
That in the depths of Neptune's sea do grow,
Arrang'd within her mouth, in row on row,
Yet crook'd are they, as are the grins of churls.

Her hair unto a gauze is like, so soft,
But thin, almost invisible, and pale,
That one might think it was not hair: a veil
So easily by gust tis borne aloft.

And if she read this calumny, I fear
She soon my heart, out from my breast will tear.

2.

My mistress' eyes are very like the sun,
Which follows me and warms my life each day
And clouds with tears if I must go away
But only close their light when day is done.

My mistress' lips are very like a rose,
Which slowly opens sending forth fresh scents
From petals soft and moist, which please my sense
The more when I do hold them near my nose.

> My mistress' voice is very like a song
> Played softly on a minstrel's flute or lyre
> With tones and words so sweet that I desire
> To dance to love's sweet calling all night long.
>
> And thus does she find likewise love in me;
> No other sphere has lovers such as we.

The first thing one notices about those exercises is that they are not very good, and that is to the point because it helps students understand that the training our seventeenth-century poets received does not "explain" the greatness of their work. For every Donne and Milton, there were countless Adam Martindales who looked back with genuine rue on their schoolboy efforts:

> Mine exercises were usually a piece of Latine . . . every day of the weeke, save Thursdays and Saturdays; and besides somewhat weekly as I rose in ability . . . an epistle wherin I was to follow Cicero, though (alas!) at a great distance.   (15)

We note that the instinctive response of many students is to parody, inspired doubtless by Shakespeare's example, but we also note that in a sense parody is the easy way out. If example 2 above is less successful than example 1, it is because the student has undertaken a more difficult task—to render sympathetically a genre and a mode of expression that most modern readers do not much care for.

When pressed, the author of the second example admitted that she had looked ahead in her assignments and had read some Donne, which explains the reference to "no other sphere" in the last line. Her action underscores the impossibility of making the exercise any more than a faint approximation of a seventeenth-century exercise; and yet it is still worthwhile. Having completed the exercise, the students come to Donne and are able to enter imaginatively into his anti-Petrarchan sentiments far more easily than if they had merely been told about educational practices or that Petrarchism had a vogue in the 1590s and then fell off sharply in popularity. It gives them an entrée into lines like "What merchants ships have my sighs drowned" ("The Canonization," line 11) and into whole poems like "The Apparition" that they otherwise would not have.

As the students grow in sophistication, they become aware that literary history does not explain everything about a work; they become aware, for example, that, while one can label the conversational tone of "The Canonization" as a reaction against the excessive formality of Petrarchan work like Spenser's *Amoretti*, that label does not adequately define the urgent quality of the poem's opening lines. Similarly, Donne's emphasis on the sex act as a part of the love experience, while rejecting the Petrarchan emphasis on unrequited love, embraces a variety of attitudes—reverent, jocular, hostile—not explicable merely as reactions against an established literary tradition.

The students need to have that awareness repeatedly heightened before it becomes a working part of their intellectual equipment, but in time it does. Consider the relation of George Herbert's "Vertue" to carpe diem. Helen Vendler writes, "We would, if we were sufficiently responsive, sense from the beginning that this poem could not possibly end with a call to gather the roses of today . . ." (11). The crux of the matter is who is included in the *we* she refers to. I have proved empirically that it does not include undergraduate readers at the University of Toledo. Having read a number of carpe diem poems, the students are given the first three stanzas of "Vertue" and are asked to write a conclusion. Invariably, they conclude it with an injunction to the imagined lady addressee to surrender herself to the male speaker of the poem. When shown the concluding stanza that Herbert wrote, they immediately grasp the cleverness of reversing carpe diem expectations; more important, they are now in a position to benefit from Vendler's subtle and persuasive demonstration that "the difference in tone between this poem and its erotic predecessors (a difference occurring not only at the end) seems to remove the poem almost entirely from its parent genre" (11).

Practical objections can be raised to the exercises sketched above: they inevitably involve an overlap with courses in Elizabethan poetry; they are prodigal in their use of class time; and, like all educational procedures, they are incomplete. If, however, the process of integrating the perceptions gained about seventeenth-century schooling and the popularity of long-dead genres is the work of a lifetime, at least the students have learned something about the active, not passive, nature of reading. Also, unlike students forced to memorize lists of Petrarchan characteristics, they don't forget. The comments that they make at the end of the quarter and, in a few instances, years later suggest that they think those exercises helped them develop a set of critical tools that were beneficial in any further literary study that they undertook.

Tottel's Miscellany
and the Metaphysical Poets

William A. Sessions

One of the advantages of comparing the texts of metaphysical poets with those of Thomas Wyatt, Henry Howard, Earl of Surrey, and the other poets in *Tottel's Miscellany* (Rollins) is that modern students directly enter into what was a central experience for any poet or reader of the Renaissance: a sense of the past. If in our time such a sense must be taught, the advantage of discovering how old and older texts relate in a symbiosis (a process students know well from other studies) has the further practical purpose for students of explaining the bewildering selections in anthologies like *The Norton Anthology of English Literature* (gen. ed. Abrams) or in a series of class textbooks. Not everything happened at once. All texts may be floating, but the modern student, especially the beginner, needs a context as a way to avoid the danger that contemporary criticism often passes down to students: abstract, forced labels that ironically (despite announced purposes) have little to do with the student's perception of reality. Intertexuality can help fill the need, for, as evidence of continuing life and as a continuing source for new origins, intertexuality offers the student generally unaware of history a perspective on time itself not only as an arbiter of taste but also as a matrix for new creation. Intertextuality helps students understand the relation of the metaphysical poets to the poets in Tottel's 1557 collection, the first anthology of modern English lyric verse.

With intertextuality as a basis, the modern student soon learns what Donne, Herbert, and Marvell knew: the sense of the past is never abstract; it is always a matter of text. The advantage for students here is that their immediate enjoyment can be the catalyst to a firsthand understanding of what a traditional culture was all about. In the Renaissance, tradition was central even to the revolution; for example, Erasmus's radical call *ad fontes* (to the sources) led to deeper traditions that acted as springs to English humanism and the Reformation itself. Poets understood that radical call, and an exercise helpful for fathoming the complexity of imitation is a comparison of John Donne's defiantly anti-Petrarchan poem "The Indifferent" with Wyatt's equally defiant English Petrarchan sonnet "Divers Doth Use" (both in the *Norton Anthology*). Students discover that, for sarcasm and cynicism about human love, Donne cannot match the ferocity of Wyatt, when expectations may have led them to think otherwise. Whereas Patricia Thomson may be correct about the greater complexity of Donne's art, students (in a written exercise, if necessary) can note similar qualities in those two texts. Thomson notes "immediacy, the conversational tones, informal openings, sense of situation, wit, logicality, and self-analysis" (143). At the same time, the comparison exercise teaches students something important about a "writerly text," to use Roland Barthes's term—namely, that in all writing of poems, from Donne to Dickinson to Ashbery, earlier texts echo and wait to be reshaped within the poet's unique experience.

Especially in the seventeenth century, with the general collapse of the old belief structures of society that Wyatt and Surrey had assumed in their own revolutionary time, that sense of the past was acute. It was not only a matter of seeing what was being lost but also a matter for Donne, Herbert, and Marvell of finding language for their time in order, as Eliot (translating Mallarmé) says in "Little Gidding," "To purify the dialect of the tribe" (2.74). Such has been the task for all poets, and for those not content with the old pieties but still with a sense of the past, "the age demanded an image," as Ezra Pound said in *Hugh Selwyn Mauberley* (see Bach, Sessions, and Walling 349); it demanded radical surgery that lyric poets from Sappho to Gerard Manley Hopkins heroically performed. For their own age, the metaphysical poets devised a particular textual strategy to deal with that acute sense of the past, a strategy of imitation generally marked by parody. If the term *parody* retains some of the simplicity of Rosemary Freeman's definition ("Parody") and the resonance of Rosemund Tuve's explorations of the term, especially her emphasis on music ("Sacred 'Parody' "), a student can observe, as in a laboratory, the transformation of elements from one text into another.

George Herbert is a good place to test the strategy. When Freeman defines *parody* as "based on literary examples, in which the aim is creating a meaning that is positive and constructive, not absurd," and in which the poet feels "the language which can best express his thought is a familiar language possibly spoilt by over-use but still more forceful than any idiom free from well-worn associations," the whole process hinges on the discovery of an appropriate degree of detachment, a term borrowed from Eliot's "Little Gidding" (Freeman 307–08). For Freeman, as for Tuve with her musical analogies, such a process will provide a means of understanding Herbert's "Parodie" and its meditative and contemplative center. In that poem Herbert takes a contemporary song with Petrarchan motifs such as first appeared in English in *Tottel's Miscellany* (see Surrey's "O Happy Dames" in the *Norton Anthology*) and transforms it, in his usual strategy, from profane to sacred. Students can easily apply Freeman's terms to that and other poems reprinted in the *Norton Anthology* as they discuss the strategy of parody. Used even more crucially, parody in Herbert's "Easter" focuses on his second stanza, which directly appropriates Wyatt's song "My Lute, Awake!" a text also appropriated by Donne in his "Valediction: Forbidding Mourning" and "A Hymn to God the Father." Wyatt had begun his sardonic lyric:

> My lute, awake! Perform the last
> Labor that thou and I shall waste,

> And end that I have now begun;
> For when this song is sung and past,
> My lute, be still, for I have done.

Herbert marks his parody with a musical base like Wyatt's:

> Awake, my lute, and struggle for thy part
> With all thy art.
> The cross taught all wood to resound his name
> Who bore the same.
> His stretched sinews taught all strings what key
> Is best to celebrate this most high day.

Wyatt's profane lyric, with its mocking style of *Petrarchismo* derived from Aquilano Serafino (1466–1500) rather than from Petrarch himself, is transformed into Herbert's complex semiliturgical meditation, as any student can note, through the swift metamorphoses of Wyatt's original lute into poem, cross, and, finally, the body of Christ, all within the musical frame. The transformation is a superb example of what Freeman means by appropriate detachment in parody, a term students may want to explore further in a longer writing exercise. Exploring further the technical, critical, and even philosophical dimensions of the strategy begins a process of understanding the methods of most metaphysical poets. Further along, the student may want to examine how Herbert, the master of intertexuality, became the source for the texts of Vaughan and Crashaw in endless echoes of a floating text, as his own book *The Temple* had flowed from earlier texts, not least those of his friend and master John Donne.

Donne is a good place to focus any comparison of the metaphysical poets and the early Tudor poets because he is the fountainhead of the style to which Dr. Johnson gave the name. Nowhere is such a style more evident than in Donne's language of meditation. Here *Tottel's Miscellany* can be particularly helpful. Appearing in June 1557, when, in the Victorian editor Edward Arber's phrase, "the martyrs' fires were luridly lighting up England" (Rollins 2: 86), *Tottel's Miscellany*, the first Renaissance collection of lyric verse, went back to the 1530s, when Wyatt and Surrey were composing their verse and when, under the influence of the humanist intellectuals, poets at the universities and at court were trying out new forms in imitation of Vergil, Horace, and other classical poets. Surrey, the only poet mentioned on the title page, was probably the best focal point for the collection, especially with its humanist purpose: "to the honor of the Englishe tong, and for profit of the studious of Englishe eloquence" (Rollins 1: 3). Surrey was certainly as Petrarchan as any of the other poets in the volume, and introducing Petrarch and *Petrarchismo* (already almost two centuries old) was one of the most revolutionary achievements of the book, although Chaucer had first translated Petrarch in *Troilus and Criseyde*, a text crucial for understanding Wyatt and Surrey. If Donne's strategy, especially in his religious poems, is to turn the Petrarchan strategy on its head, students reading the first poem in *Tottel's Miscellany*, Surrey's "The Sonne Hath Twise Brought Furth His Tender Grene," (an elegy worthy of being reproduced for class) recognize what does not change throughout the texts of all the metaphysical poets: the language of meditation.

Surrey's poem is a reflective *capitolo*, a three-line stanza form with an interlocking rhyming scheme *aba*, *bcb*, and so on, which had been brilliantly shaped by Petrarch from Dante's terza rima, and Surrey catches his master's blend of the elegiac and the erotic. What is more significant, he begins the topos, ubiquitous in the English Renaissance, of the melancholy lover reflecting, unlike Wyatt, on the pain of his love, the discontinuities of renewing nature and his own failed sexuality:

> The sonne hath twise brought furth his tender grene
> And clad the earth in liuely lustinesse:
> Ones haue the windes the trees despoiled clene,
> And new again begins their cruelnesse,
> Since I haue hid vnder my brest the harm
> That neuer shall recouer healthfulnesse.   (Rollins 1: 3)

If, as I argue elsewhere (102–03), such contrast of harmonious nature and the suffering lover is a topos that Petrarch and Surrey found in Dido's lament in book 4 of the *Aeneid* (522–53), Surrey's language was new and set a standard for the volume, whose popularity was echoed by Master Slender in *The Merry Wives of Windsor* and by the gravedigger in *Hamlet*, whose song with its same combination of eros and death is directly lifted from *Tottel's Miscellany*. More important, Philip Sidney and the later sonneteers imitated Surrey and his language; the admiration may be judged by Sidney's encomium to Surrey in his *Apology for Poetry* (Abrams 484). Thus, a student weaving through the immediate influences of Sidney and other Elizabethan texts on Donne's parodies can find in Tottel's origins what remained quintessentially metaphysical: the language of meditation, a dramatic voice in a style both colloquial and musical.

A good exercise at this point is to compare texts of Donne with three poems of Surrey (all in the *Norton Anthology*). The exercise focuses on the student's discovery of dramatic voice as a means of understanding the metaphysical lyric, a speaking voice in which "rhetoric becomes structural, not merely ornamental," a technique used to evoke emotion, as James

Anderson Winn notes about Monteverdi and *Petrarchismo* (136), or, as Arnold Stein remarks about Wyatt and Donne, "the extraordinary accomplishment of turning rhetorical emphases into the intimate and tender accents of the love lyric" (*Donne's Lyrics* 31). Surrey's poems "Love, That Doth Reign and Live within My Thought," "The Soote Season," and "Alas! So All Things Now Do Hold Their Peace" combine elements of *Petrarchismo* (most obviously the contrast of macrocosm and microcosm) and the meditative voice. The devices used are all easily identifiable, and a student listing them finds complex transformations in Donne, specifically the obvious parody of "The Flea"; the more reflective but still parodic "A Valediction: Forbidding Mourning," "The Extasie," and "The Canonization"; and the extraordinary hyperboles and parodic exaggerations of "A Nocturnall upon S. Lucy's Day," the *First Anniversary*, the sonnet "Batter my heart, three-personed God," and "Good Friday, 1613." A poem like the last may be a long way in rhythm, allusion, and theme from the first lyric in Tottel's text, but its structure is not.

That exercise serves the classroom purpose of relating and then discovering how the metaphysical poets remain English Petrarchans, with both terms operative. Thus, when a modern Herbert critic traces a literary genealogy that includes Wyatt, Sidney, and Donne and traces musical, thematic, and linguistic relationships (Bottrall 119), *Tottel's Miscellany* can be seen as more than a mere publishing event in 1557: it marks a central artifact in a revolution that continues through the metaphysical poets, blending, for example, their Augustinian base with that of Petrarch. Parody, with the appropriate degree of detachment, was the basis of the strategy. In fact, however much the metaphysical poets may have manipulated the decorative Petrarchan motifs and themes, the structural achievement of that central meditative voice, as begun in Tottel, never disappeared from their lyrics. That intimate voice is there in the persona who observes Teresa's "brim-filled bowls of fierce desire" in Crashaw ("The Flaming Heart," 99); in Vaughan (who read and annotated Petrarch) in his speaker who "saw Eternity the other night" ("The World," 1), his plain, direct accents anticipating Blake's; and in that probing voice in Marvell at whose back students have all heard "Time's wingéd chariot hurrying near" ("To His Coy Mistress," 22) within a panoply of parodies of Petrarch. With those and other poems discovered in reading, the student may do exercises of comparison to show the complex transformations.

That emphasis on parody as a basic strategy may provide an entry into the sense of the past integral to Renaissance poet and reader. It reminds us, however, of differences as well and thus allows us to focus on the unique structures that are metaphysical poems. Such awareness of differences is probably the catalyzing factor as the poet writes the text, for, even if Marvell's world still viewed the cosmos operating through correspondences, the universe of Wyatt and Surrey, cracking though its own communal and ideological assurances, had disappeared by the English revolution. The sense of abandonment dominates in many metaphysical texts, as their deepest structural mode—the individual seeking community—reveals itself. The difference between a poem by John Donne's grandfather John Heywood in the *Miscellany*—"Geue place you Ladies and be gon," a song probably about Queen Mary and filled with Petrarchan hyperbole—and Donne's own use of such motifs and techniques in his evolving panegryic of an idealized woman in the "Anniversaries" illustrates both a sense of the past and two forms of wit with radically different ideological bases. The inversion of the Petrarchan in all the metaphysical religious poems, from Donne to Crashaw and Vaughan, is itself indicative of the basic structural process that reveals the difference and unique experience of the metaphysical poets.

The student does well to examine, as a final exercise, what seems on the surface an unsystematic strategy of parody by Andrew Marvell, in a real sense the last English Petrarchan and the heir of *Tottel's Miscellany*. "To His Coy Mistress," a masterpiece of appropriation and detachment, rambles through its parody of Petrarchan seduction, dealing deathblows to whole civilizations, mockingly reducing all to an egoism as disdainful as Wyatt's, but with sinister Cartesian echoes. "The Garden" succinctly assaults *Petrarchismo* on all levels, even undermining the Neoplatonism of the Petrarchan Pietro Bembo for the text's own evolving myth. In each instance of parody, Marvell is probing language ironically for a means to uncover, if not construct, a true language of *civitas*, "to the honor of the Englishe tong" that Tottel had announced for his *Miscellany* in 1557, a hundred years before. That uncovered language reflected the reality to which Marvell gave his life after the Restoration, when his own lyric poetry ceased. In those lyrics, in a final special irony, Marvell's Petrarchan lover, whether in the dialogues or the mower poems, renders a complex and accurate representation of Petrarchan melancholy. In one such lyric, "The Definition of Love," Marvell's representation is rife with suppressed eroticism and is as elegiac in its lament as Surrey's text that began Tottel's collection. In fact, Marvell's ambiguity of closure fits the detached ambiguity of the whole enterprise of text and text:

> Therefore the love which us doth bind,
> But Fate so enviously debars,
> Is the conjunction of the mind,
> And opposition of the stars.

For such "conjunction" and "opposition" parody alone offered the poet the right strategy of combining a living sense of the past with the demands of an age. Only through the discovery of such language could the metaphysical poet continue the never-changing poetic task, "to purify the dialect of the tribe."

Teaching about the Religion
of the Metaphysical Poets

Gene Edward Veith, Jr.

I have taught metaphysical poetry in state institutions and church-related schools. In both, I have found that students, despite their lack of background, are strongly interested in the religious dimension of the metaphysical poets. By drawing on the religious pluralism of my students and by approaching the spirituality of the metaphysical poets historically and phenomenologically, I have found that the religion of the metaphysical poets need not be an obstacle for twentieth-century students; instead, it can be a bridge for them into the poetry.

We often think of the twentieth century as a secular or postreligious age. Although that is true in some circles, it scarcely applies to most of America and the world, nor does it apply to most students. According to a recent Gallup poll, more than ninety percent of college students believe in God; only fifteen percent said that religious beliefs were not important to them. Those statistics seem surprising for a postreligious age, but religion is a live issue for most college students. To be sure, their religious knowledge is often superficial, as that same Gallup poll indicates. Knowledge of the Bible and of theology is strikingly low, even among conservative believers, and fewer than forty percent of college students attend weekly religious services ("More Collegians"). Nevertheless, twentieth-century students, in their religious searchings and experiences, have more in common with seventeenth-century poets than they and we often realize.

E. D. Hirsch has shown that many students today lack the common references of vocabulary, story, and allusion necessary for a unified culture. That cultural illiteracy is a major problem in teaching the metaphysical poets. In discussing an allusion in a poem, I have to tell my college students the story of Noah and the ark. I am presently teaching in a Lutheran college; for us Lutherans, seventeenth-century theology is still a live issue. Still, even students with a traditional religious background, including conservative believers, often know little about theology, the Bible (polls continue to show that more people believe in the Bible than read it), and their own religious heritage. Studying the metaphysical poets can help students fill in those gaps, an important enterprise in itself, as Hirsch shows. Modern students are often acutely conscious of their cultural dislocation. Many students are not even aware that they have a spiritual heritage, and they are grateful for the discovery.

Though students lack the terminology, they often share the experiences. Everyone has experienced guilt, a dark night of the soul, the weight of responsibility, and the pressure of demands; everyone has had a taste of ecstasy and love. Everyone wants salvation. Those experiences and yearnings can find their "objective correlative" in metaphysical poetry.

Whatever the religious background of the students, my approach is not only to explain the poetry by means of the theology but also to explain the theology by means of the poetry. My research has led me to believe that it is not enough to use seventeenth-century theology to illuminate the poetry; in addition, the poetry illuminates the theology. For example, from the outside, Calvinism seems austere and forbidding; through the eyes of a Calvinist poet, however, that theology presents a different face, one that may be more relevant in understanding the effects of Calvinism. In teaching a poem, instead of using what may seem arcane religious concepts as background to explain a particular image or reference—a practice that can distance the student from both the religious tradition and the poem, making them seem historically remote—I often work from the other direction. One can begin with the poem—its emotion, its language, its form, its images. Close attention to the poem's aesthetic texture can lead to conclusions about the religious themes and the context of the poem, thus doing justice to both the aesthetic and the historical dimensions of the work.

Thus, Herbert's poem "The Collar" can be understood, at first, apart from its specifically religious references. Its basic emotional content is universal, even for people with little religious background. Everyone has felt the pressure of obligations and has yearned to escape. We have all "struck the board and cried, No more! / I will abroad!", whether in a job, a relationship, or any other routine that restricts us from being "free; free as the road" (lines 1–2, 4). In Herbert's poem, the speaker is bored and restless until he hears, behind the restrictions, the voice of one who loves him, the person for whom he is doing all that drudgery, whereupon the rebellion vanishes in love. I want my students to understand the emotional dynamics of the poem, the sense in which dissatisfaction can be transfigured when at the heart of the onerous responsibilities is a loving personal relationship. (Some examples help make the point: working at a miserable job for the sake of one's family, changing diapers for one's child, submitting to the sacrifices love always demands; students can supply a host of illustrations.)

I then go on to the theological level: Herbert believed that the human being's relationship with God is like that. The speaker of the poem is rebelling against the restrictions placed on him in his vocation as a priest and as a Christian. His feelings change, however, when he comes face to face with the love of God, a personal encounter that transforms his obligations and his self-understanding. Our discussion gets more and more technical, exploring the concept of God's grace, the idea of human sinfulness countered by the unconditional love of God, the relation between faith and good works, the various understandings of those ideas in seventeenth-century theology, and so on, not neglecting the formal crafting of the poem that images those themes precisely.

By beginning with the poem's particular emotional or aesthetic content and then explaining the religious concepts involved, rather than vice versa, a teacher can effectively present almost any religious poem, even to people who do not share the poet's religious vocabulary. "Love" (3), to use another example, can apply to any form of love that is always accepting, unconditional, and self-sacrificing. To be sure, some experiences in the poetry are alien to many students. That the contemporary mind has, to a certain extent, lost the sense of the sacred makes it difficult for some students to understand sacramental spirituality, the significance of ritual, and why Donne shakes with fear when he contemplates the face of Christ in the Holy Sonnet "This is my play's last scene" (see Kilpatrick 144–60). Still, I want my students, by means of the poetry, to experience vicariously the world of the writers, to know the poems from the inside. My approach, in other words, is phenomenological.

Metaphysical poems are often explicated as closed systems of images that bounce off each other in various complex and ironic permutations, apart from any reference to their historical and religious contexts. That sort of New Critical formalism always frustrated me when I was a student. I was not interested in the poems as jigsaw puzzles or as abstract art. I wanted to know what the poems mean: what they meant for the poet and what they may mean for me. Today, I do spend most of my time on the artfulness of the poems—on their form, metrics, craft, and aesthetic technique. I find, though, that students are more interested in the formal qualities of a poem when they are also seized by its significance. Attention to the biographical, theological, and historical significance of the poems can lead to students' finding personal significance in the poems in terms of their own beliefs and experiences.

Students come to the poems with more background and a wider range of religious experiences than we give them credit for. The problem is not that our classes divide themselves into believers and nonbelievers. Rather, our classrooms are richly pluralistic. There are Catholics, Baptists, Methodists, Mormons, Jews, Muslims, and possibly devotees of the guru Mahara Ji. Even among fundamentalists, major differences separate Baptists and charismatics. Evangelicals may be Calvinist or Arminian or some combination of the two. Even nonbelievers are diverse. Are they ex-Catholics or ex-Baptists? Which God do they not believe in? Are they right-wing atheist followers of Ayn Rand or left-wing atheist followers of Karl Marx? What do they put in the place of traditional religious beliefs—politics, psychology, new-consciousness mysticism?

I deal with that daunting pluralism by taking advantage of it. In my view, the metaphysical poets themselves are pluralistic. Although they are all seventeenth-century Christians with many similarities, they represent a wide range of spiritual styles that students, in all their variety, can learn to recognize and relate to.

I present Herbert as an example of divine monergism, the view that God accomplishes everything necessary for salvation, that God is the active partner and the initiator in the relationship between human beings and God. That idea was the major emphasis of the Reformation—uniting Lutherans, Calvinists, and early Anglicans—and can also be found in Augustinian Roman Catholics. The speaker in Herbert's poem is typically lost, running in the wrong direction, until God intervenes, breaking into the poem to initiate a relationship.

The monergism of the early Reformation was soon challenged by Arminian synergism, which taught that the human will must choose to accept and to cooperate with the grace of God, resulting in a different kind of Protestant spirituality, exemplified by John Donne. Donne depicts a soul on the knife-edge of salvation or damnation, torn between the choice of sin and the choice of God. Whereas monergism stresses that salvation does not depend on good works, synergism reintroduces the need for moral perfection. Donne's introspection, the wrenchings of the will, the violent conflicts, and his uncertainty make for dynamic, complex religious verse.

In discussing Herbert and Donne, I like to draw out my conservative Christian students, who are sometimes startled to find their ideas taken seriously by their professor—a simple measure that does more to open up such students to literature and to the intellectual enterprise than almost anything else. I ask the students to explain the experiences those writers are referring to. Often, the different religious factions on campuses tie in to the different theologies reflected in the poets. A hotly debated issue for evangelical groups is the doctrine of eternal security—whether a believer can lose salvation. Most students have no idea that the controversy goes back to that between John Calvin and Jacobus Arminius; in debating the issue, the students find insights into the struggles and assumptions of Herbert and Donne. Evangelicals are impressed with the biblicism of the poets. A good assignment is to trace the biblical images and allusions in the manner of Chana Bloch's excellent book on Herbert. Donne's conversion from libertine to preacher fascinates students and is a point of contact for those who have also experienced a radical conversion. Those students can feel a kinship with Donne and often, if allowed to, can illuminate the struggles Donne is describing. The spirituality of Donne and Herbert is more complex than that of many of our students, but, as they study the poets more deeply, they often find themselves realizing that their own religious tradition is richer, more complex, and more intellectually open than they had dreamed.

Crashaw reflects the spirituality of Counter-Reformation Catholicism. Crashaw blends otherworldliness and sensuality, reflecting a mysticism grounded in the Incarnation and the transubstantiation of the Sacrament. The physicality of Crashaw's religion is startling to most students, but the possibilities are provocative to them. I use the visual arts—baroque paintings and religious iconography—to help students understand Crashaw's imagination. I ask Catholic students to explain devotional practices, such as the adoration of the Sacred Heart and other meditations and sacramentals. This is sometimes a problem for post-Vatican II Catholics, who often find themselves starting to understand their heritage for the first time.

Discussing the Counter-Reformation is a good way to introduce Ignatius Loyola's techniques for meditation as applied to seventeenth-century poetry by Louis L. Martz (*Poetry of Meditation*). (First, imagine a scene from the Bible, engaging each of your senses; then analyze it with your understanding, reflecting on what the scene means; then enter into it with your will, speaking to the subject of your meditation). That threefold meditative pattern is designed to engage all the faculties of the mind. As such, it makes for excellent writing assignments, integrating description, analysis, and personal address. Since meditations can begin with practically any imagined scene, I use Loyola in my writing classes, even when I am not teaching metaphysical poetry.

Vaughan's Neoplatonism illustrates the spirituality of transcendence, of flying up from this "darksome" world into the "pure and endless light" of eternity ("The World," 16, 2). Although Vaughan is a Christian, the mysticism of transcendence is not limited to Christianity. Herbert's emphasis on the grace of God, Donne's struggle with sin and salvation, and Crashaw's incarnational spirituality are distinctly Christian. The patterns of ascent and the dichotomy of material and spiritual in Vaughan's poetry depict a mysticism also found in pre-Christian writers, such as Plato and Plotinus, and, in a different way, in Eastern religions.

In class I like to contrast the transcendent focus of Vaughan with the downward, incarnational focus of Donne, Herbert, and Crashaw. We discuss the difference between Eastern meditation, which some of the students are familiar with, and the meditation of Loyola. Eastern meditation is a process of negating the senses, which bind us to the material world. Loyola's meditation, by contrast, engages the senses as a way to make contact with the incarnate God. Vaughan's depiction of eternity as "a great *Ring* of pure and endless light" ("The World," 2) far above the world of matter is very different from the incarnational spirituality found in Herbert, Donne, and Crashaw. And yet, the breadth of Christian doctrine and the Western spiritual tradition can encompass both expressions.

Marvell seems to be at the other extreme from Vaughan. Whereas

Vaughan is otherworldly, Marvell seems this-worldly. Marvell illustrates one of the major results of the Reformation: the religious sanction of secularism. The doctrine of the priesthood of all believers, the rejection of religious art in favor of portraits and landscapes, and the affirmation of commerce and public service led to the secularization of art and culture. Biblical allusions and the themes of paradise, inwardness, and apocalypse are still present in Marvell, but they are displaced into ostensibly nonreligious terms. Nevertheless, the secularism of Marvell is a religious statement: the ordinary world is charged with spiritual significance. Teaching the religion of Marvell involves challenging the students' stereotypes about what religion is. Challenging their stereotypes about Puritans is a good place to begin. ("Do you think it unusual that 'To His Coy Mistress' was written by a Puritan? Why? What do you think a Puritan is?") The political struggle of the Commonwealth is also interesting to students. I present the Commonwealth not only as a theocratic experiment but also as the beginning of political liberalism. Marvell in that sense, though engaged with the inward and solitary, is a model of the Puritan activist.

My approach throughout is to affirm the student's own religious understanding and to help the student understand the spirituality of others. In doing so, I do not violate the separation of church and state. Robert N. Minor and Robert D. Baird, both professors of religious studies at state universities, have developed a rigorous distinction between teaching religion, which is forbidden, and teaching *about* religion, which is essential to a full understanding of human beings and, therefore, to a liberal arts education. According to Minor and Baird, a professor should neither discriminate against nor advocate any religion in the classroom. To do either, to say a religion is true or to say a religion is not true, would be to teach religion (69). Learning about the religious traditions and beliefs that have been important to our culture and to people's lives is essential. Any educated person should know what Catholics, Protestants, Jews, Muslims, Hindus, and Buddhists believe. Without a knowledge of religions, any historical, philosophical, or social understanding of human beings is glaringly incomplete (71–72).

Minor and Baird recommend a historical approach, "treating as heuristically true the variety of views available, to provide understanding" of the real people, past and present, who have held those views (72). Religious ideas should be presented in a spirit of rigorous objectivity and tolerance. Minor and Baird reject the practice of professors who proselytyze for their own religious views, whether these views support or attack traditional religions. Both proselytizing and persecution violate students' constitutional rights.

Students who are religiously conservative may sometimes be maddeningly closed-minded. Everyone has horror stories. ("When did Herbert go up at the altar call and accept Jesus Christ as his Lord and personal Savior?" "If Bunyan was such a good Christian, why didn't he pray in faith, so that the Lord would release him from prison?" "I don't feel that the Lord wants me to read Donne's 'Elegy.' ") The best strategy for dealing with such students is not to try to expand their minds by attacking their beliefs or by ridiculing them for being fundamentalists, a term that is generally pejorative and abusive. Colleagues who would never dream of making racist, sexist, or anti-Semitic comments are abusively creedist, to coin a term, savagely attacking and unfairly stereotyping people from conservative religious backgrounds. The way to get through to a defensive student is to accept that student, beliefs and all. When a professor realizes that the born-again student in the back row is probably closer to the worldview and the experiences of John Donne than are most secularist scholars, the two can start to understand each other.

Iconographic Perspectives on
Seventeenth-Century Religious Poetry

Albert C. Labriola

In his "Life of Cowley" Samuel Johnson comments that metaphysical poetry is distinguished by "the combination of dissimilar images" or by "occult resemblances in things apparently unlike" (470), a critical outlook that prevails into the twentieth century. Thus, a modern critic such as William Empson in *Seven Types of Ambiguity* (256–63) extols what he considers ingenious images in George Herbert's poem "The Sacrifice" and admires even passages that remain obscure to him. The predominant critical outlook that metaphysical wit is ingenious or obscure is challenged by Rosemond Tuve, who in *A Reading of George Herbert* (21–24) contends that the imagery of seventeenth-century religious poetry is conventional, if not commonplace.

The conventional images and their meanings are from an inveterate tradition charted by Tuve, a tradition ingrained in the consciousnesses and the sensibilities of medieval, Renaissance, and seventeenth-century authors and their audiences. The tradition emerged from a typological perspective on Scripture, whereby persons, objects, and episodes from the Old Testament are viewed as prefigurations of the new dispensation, usually of Christ's redemptive ministry. Christ himself encouraged typological interpretations of his ministry; an example occurs in John 3:14–15, when he likens his imminent Crucifixion to the episode in which Moses elevated the brazen serpent on a pole (Num. 21:6–9).

In addition to the Gospels, Paul's Epistles are laden with typological interpretation, which is also characteristic of the commentaries of the Church Fathers. At times, Paul and the Church Fathers stress contrasts, as well as similarities, between Old Testament and New Testament persons, objects, and events: between Adam as the old man (*vetus homo*) and Christ as the new man (*novus homo*), Eve and the Virgin Mary, and the tree of knowledge of good and evil and the Cross. Nevertheless, Christ's redemptive ministry, the means by which sanctification is offered to fallen humanity, remains the focus.

Typology underlies scriptural interpretation, liturgical celebration (communal prayer, hymns, and antiphons), readings at canonical hours, and services during Holy Week. It also distinguishes Christian iconography and the visual arts, notably stained glass, illuminated manuscripts, wood carvings, book illustrations, paintings, frescoes, sculpture, and emblem books. Because typological interpretation is the basis of the tradition charted by Tuve, my students examine iconography to regain the sensibility of the Middle Ages, the Renaissance, and the seventeenth century. Visual analogues provide the context and establish the outlook for interpreting the poetry of John Donne, George Herbert, and Richard Crashaw, all of whom I teach in an interdisciplinary course called Christian Literature and Art. My students perceive that the foregoing poets have used conventional, rather than obscure, imagery. By relating literary imagery to visual analogues, moreover, my students highlight contrasts between Protestant and Catholic influences in seventeenth-century poetry and aesthetics.

Using the visual arts, we analyze a single poem, poems by one author, or works by various poets. The most effective projects are (1) long or short papers that append photocopies of visual analogues to which reference is made as the poetry is explicated and (2) presentations by individual students or small groups who use either color slides or illustrated books and an opaque projector. Having previewed the slides available in the library, which includes a multimedia resource center, I direct the students to particular iconography. Because the course interrelates literature and the visual arts, it is cross-listed in English and art history, a department through which more slides are available. Team teaching is also possible, and, if music becomes a third component in the course, an interdisciplinary emphasis on aesthetic experience may be developed.

Many students rely on the opaque projector to introduce into the classroom the resources of our library, particularly the books illustrating works by major artists, including Donatello, Michelangelo, Raphael, Leonardo da Vinci, Titian, Bernini, Botticelli, Cimabue, Giotto, Fra Angelico, Bellini, Ghiberti, Giovanni Pisano, Masaccio, Caravaggio, El Greco, Velásquez, Stefano da Zevio, Bosch, Pieter Brueghel, Dürer, Grünewald, Jan van Eyck, Rogier van der Weyden, and the Master of Flémalle. Books with numerous diverse illustrations are also used: Gertrud Schiller's *Iconography of Christian Art*, Adolphe Napoléon Didron's *Christian Iconography*, Louis Réau's *Iconographie de l'art chrétien*, Robert Hughes's *Heaven and Hell in Western Art*, Edith Rothe's *Medieval Book Illumination in Europe*, Emile Mâle's *Gothic Image: Religious Art in France of the Thirteenth Century*, Marina Warner's *Alone of All Her Sex: The Myth and Cult of the Virgin Mary*, André Grabar's *Christian Iconography: A Study of Its Origins*, F. P. Pickering's *Literature and Art in the Middle Ages*, Walter Lowrie's *Art in the Early Church*, James Strachan's *Early Bible Illustrations*, facsimile editions of books of hours (*The Hours of Catherine of Cleves* [Plummer], *The Visconti Hours* [Meiss and Kirsch], *The* Très Riches Heures *of Jean, Duke of Berry* [Longnon and Cazelles; see also Rorimer]) and of block books (*Biblia pauperum* and *Speculum humanae salvationis* [Berjeau]). To contrast Catholic and Protestant influences in art and literature, my students inevitably analyze the emblems in Barbara Kiefer Lewalski's *Protestant Poetics and the Seventeenth-Century Religious Lyric*. That exercise leads, in turn, to a comparative study of Catholic and Protestant emblem books, of Crashaw's poems and the works of Donne and Herbert, and, more subtly, of the interaction of Catholic and Protestant influences in selected poems by Donne and Herbert. In what follows, however, I stress the broader framework of the course, without discriminating between Catholic and Protestant influences in art and literature.

In the course I proceed systematically by studying Christ's redemptive ministry and its Old Testament prefigurations in three separate, sequential stages: the Incarnation, the Crucifixion, the Resurrection. Iconography dramatizes the Incarnation as the voluntary descent of the Son, who assumes human nature as part of the providential plan of salvation. At the Annunciation, the moment when the Virgin Mary conceived Christ, his human nature begins to be emphasized, usually by his appearance as a babe, which suggests voluntary humiliation and subjection to finite space and the temporal condition. In the Mérode Altarpiece by the Master of Flémalle, the infant Jesus descends headlong on beams of light toward Mary. In the crook of his left arm and on his left shoulder is a fiery cross, signifying his fervent love of humanity and imminent self-sacrifice as fulfillment of the burnt offerings of the old dispensation.

My students then identify and interpret other details in the Mérode Altarpiece: the rising smoke from a recently extinguished taper, which rests on the table at which the Virgin is seated, symbolizes burnt offerings; the extinguished flame, Christ's entrance into the darkness of human nature. When I encourage them to compare the Annunciation with the Nativity, the iconography of which often shows the Christ child in a cave, my students focus on the darkness within the enclosure and on the light radiating from the infant, a striking contrast that they interpret as a Christianized adaptation of Plato's allegory of the cave. They next identify pertinent Old Testament prophecies of the coming of Christ, including Isaiah 9:2—"The people that walked in darkness have seen a great light: they that dwell in the land of the shadow of death, upon them hath the light shined." The God of the Old Testament is omnipotent and omnipresent, attributes depicted in his appearance in the iconography of the Annunciation and the Nativity, where his face and torso are seen in a cloud or the sun. Sometimes the Father—wearing a crown, holding a scepter and orb, and attended by angels—is seated on a throne in Heaven or in the firmament. Accordingly, the accommodation of the Deity's attributes to human nature is an essential paradox of the Incarnation and a recurrent feature in scenes of the Annunciation.

Having interpreted visual details of the Annunciation and the Nativity, we proceed to analyze poetic imagery. In Donne's "Annunciation," one of the sonnets of *La Corona*, Platonic symbolism, Old Testament prophecies of the coming of Christ, and his entrance into the darkness of human nature are simultaneously stressed as the Virgin is apostrophized: "Thou'hast light in darke" (line 27). Inside the Virgin, Christ, who "will weare / Taken from thence, flesh . . . " (21–22), paradoxically harmonizes his divine attributes with human nature: "*Immensity cloystered in thy deare wombe*" (28). Similar imagery occurs in Donne's *Holy Sonnets* ("Spit in my face yee Jewes" and "Why are wee by all creatures waited on?"), *A Litanie* ("The Virgin Mary"), and "The Annuntiation and Passion"; in Herbert's "Anagram of the Virgin Marie," "The Bag," and "The Sacrifice"; and in Crashaw's sacred poems translated into English from Latin and Italian, including "O Gloriosa Domina."

A central image that can be explicated chiefly by reference to the iconography of the Annunciation occurs in Donne's "Spit in my face yee Jewes," which develops an ironic contrast between Christ and Jacob:

> And *Jacob* came cloth'd in vile harsh attire
> But to supplant, and with gainfull intent:
> God cloth'd himselfe in vile mans flesh, that so
> Hee might be weake enough to suffer woe.   (11–14)

The etymology of Jacob's name (to deceive or supplant) highlights self-interest. Invested with the raiment of Esau, his brother, and wearing goatskins to seem hirsute, Jacob gulls his blind father, Isaac, into conferring on him the blessing and the birthright intended for Esau. But Christ, against his self-interest, is attired in flesh to advance the cause of fallen humanity. In Genesis 27 Jacob's collaborator is his mother, Rebekah, who clothes him like Esau and proposes the ruse of the goatskins. At the Annunciation the Virgin Mary, in whom Christ is invested with flesh, may be said to participate in a benign deception of the Father, who exacts from Christ, whom he perceives as human, the penalty of death laid on humankind at the Fall.

When the speaker in the poem perceives the immensity of Christ's sacrifice, he acknowledges his own sinfulness and ingratitude. My students also discern the speaker's guilt. Whereas the Jews "kill'd once an inglorious man" (7), the speaker crucifies "him daily, being now glorified" (8). Christ after his glorification or Resurrection is made to suffer repeatedly, as if he were recrucified by the speaker, who himself was offered glorification or sanctification because of Christ's sacrifice. What may at first seem to be an anti-Semitic poem becomes finally a harsh rebuke of the Christian speaker, who seeks to alleviate his guilt and to atone for his sinfulness and ingratitude by pleading to undergo Christ's suffering.

Poems such as Donne's *Holy Sonnets*, emphasizing the weakness and the woe of the Son after he has assumed human nature, anticipate the bloodshed of the Crucifixion. The paradoxical adaptation of the Deity's omnipotence to the self-sacrifice of the Son occurs when Donne uses *might* in "O my blacke Soule!": "Christ's blood . . . hath this might / That being red, it dyes red soules to white" (13–14). The Savior's blood is likened to a tincture that has the "might" to transform the soul's red condition of sinfulness to whiteness or purity, a transformation described in Scripture: Isaiah 1.16–18 and Revelation 7.14. Iconography of the Crucifixion more vividly depicts the paradoxical union of divine and human natures in the Son and the power of his blood to impart life to fallen humanity. In illustrated Bibles, books of hours, paintings, frescoes, and stained glass, the blood of the crucified Christ drops onto the earth, where the skull and bones of Adam were exhumed, as the legends of the Cross recount. In sequential iconographic depictions Adam, at times, acquires flesh; he rises; and he collects in a vessel the effusion of water and blood from Christ's side, an elixir of life that he imbibes. By juxtaposing iconography of the creation of Adam and the Crucifixion, my students perceive the reconciliation of Old and New Testament conceptions of the Deity. In illustrated Bibles, for example, God the Father breathes life into Adam, whose name (from the Hebrew word *adamah*) signifies red earth. At the redemption, analogously, Christ's blood reddens the earth; like a tincture on the bones of Adam, it has the "might" to re-create humanity.

With such a context and outlook, we then interpret a central image in Donne's "Good Friday, 1613. Riding Westward"—the power of Christ's blood to "make durt of dust" (27). Herein my students perceive God the Creator as an artificer who molds Adam from the red earth, a conception harmonized with Christ the Redeemer, who re-creates fallen humanity by an outpouring of blood, thus changing dust into pliable dirt. Old and New Testament conceptions of the Deity are also reconciled in Herbert's sonnet "Redemption," the octave of which depicts the speaker journeying to Heaven to communicate with the God of the Old Testament; in the sestet he returns to earth to find the incarnate Deity at the Crucifixion. In Donne's "Good Friday, 1613. Riding Westward" a similar accommodation is evident when the speaker first envisions God the Creator, whose hands encompass the cosmos; then God the Redeemer, whose hands outstretched on the Cross are "pierc'd with . . . holes" (23). Each of the foregoing poetic images has an iconographic analogue, including depictions in illustrated Bibles and books of hours of the Creator—immense and omnipotent, his stature extending through the entire universe—or visual images of the crucified Lord outstretched across the cosmos, so that the base of the Cross is implanted on the convex exterior of the earth, onto which his blood spills.

By recognizing that depictions of the Resurrection adapt the iconographic details of the Crucifixion, my students discover relations between poems that at first seem dissimilar, poems about Christ's suffering and death, on the one hand, and his Resurrection, on the other. The Cross of suffering, reddened by Christ's blood, becomes the Cross of triumph in iconography of the Resurrection. The triumphal Cross resembles a lance, which Christ deploys against the Devil. On its small transverse beam flies a pennon, emblazoned with a red cross. Holding the triumphal Cross, Christ rises from the tomb, cave, or sarcophagus in which he was interred. Surrounded by an aureole of light more resplendent than the sun, he is attired in white and gold, though the red wounds of his Crucifixion are sometimes still evident. In place of the crown of thorns is a garland of triumph. Christ's Resurrection is prefigured by Old Testament liberators, notably David and Samson, on whom my students focus their attention, citing, among other details, the Herculean attitude of Michelangelo's *David*, the resemblance of Donatello's bronze *David* to the young Mercury, and Samson's overpowering strength (visualized in the *Biblia pauperum* and elsewhere) as he pries apart the jaws of the lion or unhinges the gates of Gaza.

We use the preceding iconographic details to explicate literary images in numerous poems on the Resurrection by Donne (the *Holy Sonnets*, "Resurrection" in *La Corona*, "Resurrection, imperfect," and "Hymne to God My God, in My Sicknesse") and by Herbert ("Sunday," "Easter," "Easter-Wings," and "The Dawning"). In one of the *Holy Sonnets* ("Wilt thou love God, as he thee!"), Donne describes how the "Sonne of glory came downe, and was slaine" in order to "unbinde" humanity from the power of Satan, an allusion to the liberating effect of Christ's Resurrection on all people. A specific reference to "hels wide mouth" occurs in another of the *Holy Sonnets*: "If faithfull soules be alike glorifi'd." Like the tincture of Christ's blood, which restores life to all human beings, the sunlike, radiance and the golden appearance of Christ transform "sinfull flesh" (16) in "Resurrection, Imperfect" to a "glorified" state (81) in "Resurrection" of *La Corona*, a process likened to alchemy. In "Hymne to God My God, in My Sicknesse" the speaker pleads with the Father: "By these his thornes give me his other Crowne" (27), an allusion to the garland of the resurrected Christ, the victorious counterpart of the crown of suffering. Herbert's poems on the Resurrection, including "Sunday," allude to Old Testament prefigurations of the triumphant Christ:

> As Sampson bore the doores away,
> Christs hands, though nail'd, wrought our salvation,
> And did unhinge that day.   (47–49)

"Easter-Wings" emphasizes flight, suggesting to some students the fluttering pennon often visualized as a pair of wings, even in Protestant emblem books, or the Roman eagle on the triumphal Cross. Crowned with a garland and holding aloft the Cross, Christ becomes the New Testament counterpart of the kingly Father of the Old Testament.

Typological correlations depicted or implied in iconography provide the context and the outlook that enable us to identify and explicate the imagery of seventeenth-century religious poetry. Far from being obscure, the imagery of metaphysical poetry is perceived as traditional—indeed, conventional. My students conclude that the ingenuity of such poetry is attributable to the synthesis and the interrelation of conventional images, resulting in an enlarged range of associations and a multiplicity of meanings.

Discovering the Old World: The Renaissance Emblem Book as Cultural Artifact

Huston Diehl

How can we help our students imagine the past? More specifically, how can we help our students read metaphysical poetry with a deep awareness of the cultural assumptions that informed its creation and of the different assumptions that inform their own reading of it? When I teach metaphysical poetry, I spend about a week early in the semester addressing that issue. I use as my text the Renaissance emblem, a literary form that, conveniently, originated in the early sixteenth century, enjoyed immense popularity throughout the seventeenth century, and then died out. It is, in other words, a genre that appealed strongly to readers in the age of Donne and Herbert but not to readers in other eras. As such, it may provide insights into what is unique and distinctive about seventeenth-century culture and what may, if unrecognized, separate us from that culture's art and artifacts. Instead of emphasizing what is universal in the literature of seventeenth-century England, I choose for that week to focus on what is different, what students find odd, quaint, remote, and alienating. I have found that, by acknowledging and even dramatizing those cultural differences, rather than ignoring and denying them, students develop a strong historical imagination, one that can liberate them from the parochialism of their thinking, even as it deepens a sense of their cultural identifications.

Because I want my students to acknowledge and examine their culture-bound assumptions, as well as the seventeenth-century assumptions that inform metaphysical poetry, I begin not with the unfamiliar genre of the emblem but with the familiar genre of the local newspaper, an artifact that not only is central to their lives but also, like the Renaissance emblem book, expresses central truths about its culture. So familiar is the newspaper that the students have given it little thought, and they are surprised to realize how much an item that they have taken for granted reveals about their time and place, including their assumptions about language, knowledge, and experience. I use an archaeological metaphor: suppose you knew nothing about twentieth-century America, nothing about life in, say, Iowa in 1990. On an archaeological dig 350 years from now, you unearth a newspaper—I produce the morning edition of the local newspaper—and, from it, try to infer something about the way those alien people thought. How, I ask, does this artifact use language? How does it select, organize, and process information? How does it engage its readers? What expectations about words, pictures, facts, narratives, and ideas does it attempt to satisfy? Finally, I ask, what can you infer from this artifact about the way people in that culture interpreted and knew their world?

As my students examine the newspaper before them, trying to see themselves as someone from a different culture might see them, they begin to recognize that assumptions and expectations they had believed universal are culturally determined. They see how they are influenced by industrialization, mass production, mass literacy, democracy; how they value efficiency, immediacy, direct apprehension; how they apply political, scientific, and psychological paradigms but not theological or philosophical paradigms to the world; how they are grounded in the phenomenological world and assume that reality is based in sense impressions and physical facts. They quickly see how the newspaper defines the past as yesterday, foregrounds the immediate, and assumes that the reader has only a few moments to read. Those and other discoveries evolve naturally in an energetic and lively discussion. Because the newspaper is familiar and rooted in their own culture, the students easily learn how to infer something about culture from a single artifact, a single form of printed material.

Once they have learned my method and have begun to think about their cultural assumptions, I introduce the emblem book, again asking my students to imagine themselves archaeologists. I begin by showing them a facsimile of Henry Peacham's *Minerva Britanna* and telling them nothing. You discover this artifact, I say; the title page tells you it was published in England in 1612; what, I challenge my students, can you infer about the culture that produced this? I suggest that they begin with simple description, and I encourage them to consider whatever strikes them, looks odd, violates their expectations, or seems significant. They observe, among other details, that the book consists of separate poems, each accompanied by a picture and headed by a Latin phrase; that the pictures present symbolic images that the poems explicate; that decorative borders and additional marginalia give quotations in Latin and cite biblical, classical, and medieval sources. The pictures seem oddly schematic and unrealistic to them, the poems wooden and static.

After explaining the immense popularity of the emblem book among literate men and women of this era, I ask students to consider what the nature of the genre's appeal may have been. I give them time to examine emblem books as diverse as those by George Wither, Otto Van Veen, and Francis Quarles. I urge them to consider the ways in which the emblem differs in its assumptions and its appeal from the newspapers of their day, and I encourage them to contrast the rhetoric of the emblem with that of the newspaper and to think about the relation between form and culture. Together, we develop their inferences about seventeenth-century culture, attempting to imagine the ways people in the seventeenth century read and interpreted texts, knew and experienced the world. Much of what the students observe helps them understand and appreciate aspects of metaphysical poetry that had seemed alien and puzzling to them, and those observations are the ones I summarize here.

Picture and Word

One of the first features of the emblem book that my students want to discuss is the way the emblems combine pictures and words. I ask the students to compare the function of photographs printed in modern newspapers with the function of those emblematic engravings and to think about the different ways the two types of pictures engage the viewer. I introduce the concept of iconography and show how emblem writers use symbolic images from a received and shared tradition. When the students understand that emblematic images carry culturally determined meaning, they begin to see how those images function as a kind of language and to entertain the Renaissance assumption that "Pictures . . . are silent Poesies, and Poesies speaking pictures" (H. A., "Translatour's Epistle Dedicatorie," *Parthenia Sacra* A2v). I point out that the mottoes, the pictures, the epigrams, and the glosses in the margins all reiterate the same central idea, and we try to imagine an epistemology that makes no distinctions between pictures and words, one that assumes everything—books, pictures, objects in the world—is to be read and interpreted. Using Francis Quarles's defense of emblems—"before the knowledge of letters God was knowne by *Hieroglyphicks*; And, indeed, what are the Heavens, the Earth, nay every creature, but *Hieroglyphicks* and *Emblemes* of His Glory?" ("To the Reader," A3)—I introduce the Renaissance trope of the book of nature and discuss the belief in a "buried kinship between things," a kinship revealed through signs (Foucault 49).

I use Geoffrey Whitney's emblem depicting the image of a sheaf of hay (217) to illustrate the Renaissance habit of interpreting images, of knowing through resemblance, and of discovering hidden relations among things. But I also suggest that the earlier way of knowing was in the seventeenth century giving way to a different way of knowing, one that does not see images as evidence of a divine order but, rather, as arbitrary signs invested with meaning by the men and women who use them and clearly serving as substitutes for something they are not (Foucault 17–165). In contrast to the Whitney emblem, an anti–Catholic emblem by Thomas Jenner features a tavern signs to caution against a naive assumption that the sign is the thing it signifies to make the point that an image is only a man-made sign for something not present (F6v–F8; no. 28). Through the illustrations I suggest to my students that the culture they are studying is undergoing radical changes and that its truths are neither simple nor universal. The emblem book reveals some of the conflicts that era was experiencing, and different emblems resolve the conflicts in different ways.

As my students and I talk about those issues, we speculate on possible reasons why that culture invented a literary form that attempts to bring pictures and words into an equivalent relation. I suggest two major events that may inform that impulse—the Protestant Reformation and the invention of the printing press—and I encourage my students to think about the different ways those two events may have influenced the way people used and responded to pictures and words. We discuss the reformers' hostility toward pictures, considering their theological defense of iconoclasm and their privileging the word over external aids to devotion, and we look at ways some Protestant emblem writers defend their use of pictures by citing Biblical parables and metaphors (see Lewalski, *Protestant Poetics*; Gilman, "Word and Image"; Diehl). We look closely at emblematic pictures, and the students begin to see that the qualities of those icons that seem most unattractive to them—their unrealistic, schematized, and symbolic nature— may have made them acceptable to a people who feared the abuse of images and who destroyed images that they believed inspired idolatry, veneration, and superstition.

At the same time that Protestantism was creating a general mistrust of the visual image, print was replacing the spoken word; through the new technology of the printing press, the visual activity of reading was taking precedence over the aural activity of listening (Ong, "From Allegory to Diagram"; Eisenstein). My students and I discuss some possible ramifications of that shift from an oral culture to a print culture: experimentation with spatial relationships, the substitution of private means of apprehension for public listening, spatial rather than temporal organization, mass production. The students see how the emblem is a product of the printing press, and they appreciate elements of the emblem, including the static quality and the use of space to define parts and to communicate relationships, that had previously baffled or annoyed them. As the students analyze the relation between technological advances and literary forms, they begin to see how their habits of reading and thinking, like those of seventeenth-century readers, are shaped by technology.

That discussion provides a context in which to consider the relation of visual and verbal elements in metaphysical poetry. Aware of the interaction of word and image in the emblem, the students are eager to analyze the relation between pictorial shape and language in such pattern poems as Herbert's "Altar" and "Easter-Wings." They are able to appreciate the way Herbert simultaneously creates in "The Altar" a visual and aural experience of "reares" (that is, builds), "cut," and "broken," to perceive Herbert's impulse to internalize the image of the altar through the analogies of the communion table and the heart, and to connect that form to central issues in Reformation theology. Introduced to the culture's epistemological concerns about the function of visual images, the students are sensitive to the anxiety about visual perception, knowledge, and faith—expressed, for example, in Donne's "Good Friday, 1613. Riding Westward" and Herbert's "Mattens,"

"Sinne" (2), and "Even-Song." Attentive to shifts in attitudes toward signs, the students formulate questions about the function of the metaphysical conceit, including whether the relation between image and meaning is rhetorical, man-made and arbitrary, or natural, found within a divinely ordered universe. They consider the so-called dissociation of sensibility within a cultural context. Familiar with Renaissance iconography and aware that images in metaphysical poetry may have culturally understood meaning, the students develop their interpretations of such images as the fly and the taper, the eagle, the dove, and the phoenix in Donne's "The Canonization" in the context of received traditions, and they have access to a primary source for those images.

Enigma and Discovery

When I ask my students to discuss the aim of the emblem, they give what seem to be contradictory explanations. Some focus on the way the emblem resembles a riddle, representing an aphoristic motto, usually in Latin, and a symbolic picture that has no obvious relation to the motto. Those students argue that the emblem is a puzzle, presenting an enigma and engaging the reader in solving it. But others note that the poems tend to be didactic, giving detailed and explicit explanations of the pictures that, for them, nullify any potential enigma. I encourage them to think about those two different impulses—the enigmatic and the didactic, the hidden and the revealed—as related. Why, I ask, if your aim was to teach or show, would you initially conceal your meaning or puzzle your readers? What is the experience of the readers as they move from the enigmatic motto to the seemingly unrelated and puzzling picture to the detailed explanation?

As my students and I talk about the process of reading the emblem, they begin to appreciate the appeal of the riddle and the pleasure of discovering an explanation for what had at first seemed baffling. They see how the enigmatic motto and the picture engage the readers, activating their imaginations, stimulating them to seek an explanation or a relationship, and rewarding them with an answer. I emphasize the process of interpretation and the aesthetic pleasure of discovering a relationship where none seemed to exist, and I read statements by writers like Jacob Cats, who writes that his emblems, based on proverbs,

> are particularly attractive, thanks to a mysterious something, and while they appear to be one thing, in reality they contain another, of which the reader, having in due time seized the exact meaning and intention, experiences wondrous pleasure in his soul; not unlike one, who, after some search, finds a beautiful bunch of grapes under thick leaves.

Experience teaches us that many things gain by not being completely seen, but somewhat veiled and concealed. (Qtd. in Praz, *Studies* 87).

As we discuss that aspect of the emblem, I ask my students to compare the experience of reading an emblem with that of reading a newspaper, and I encourage them to imagine a literary form that incorporates mystery, requires interpretation, and privileges discovery. I also locate that tendency in both the humanist movement, with its interest in hermetic philosophy and hieroglyphics on the one hand and its commitment to teaching on the other, and the reform movement, with its dual emphasis on the hidden God and the revealed God.

Insight into the era's impulses toward enigma and discovery enable my students to appreciate the value and the pleasure of metaphysical wit and to recognize a process of interpretation that begins in mystery, requires mental effort, uses logic and analogy, and ends in discovery. When they understand that seventeenth-century culture valued riddles and particularly enjoyed the pleasure of interpreting the obscure, the enigmatic, and the esoteric, they are willing to enter into the spirit of poems like Herbert's "Anagram" and "Coloss. 3.3." Attention to the emblem genre also deepens the students' understanding of the metaphysical conceit, its challenges, its pleasures, and its effects in the poems. The students learn to relinquish their expectations of clarity, directness, and simplicity and, instead, to expect and to engage the enigmatic, the indirect, and the difficult.

Past and Present

My students raise questions about the way emblems combine Latin mottoes and vernacular poems, quotations from the past, and an original poem that often cites current events and contemporary people. Agreeing that it is an intriguing aspect of the emblem, I point out that the English emblems often use images from classical, biblical, medieval, and Jesuit traditions but give contemporary, personal, or Protestant interpretations of those images. We begin to discern a tension within the emblem between the authority of the past and new ways of seeing things. What at first appear to be conventional and standard images are, in fact, often original, personal reinterpretations: the pelican serves no longer as an image of Christ but as an image of a particular man in his role as father; the rebirth of the phoenix signifies not spiritual resurrection but, rather, the rebuilding of the town of Namwiche after a fire (Whitney 177, 157).

I encourage my students to imagine the seventeenth-century reader's experience of those reinterpretations of familiar stories and motifs. They see how the emblems may play on the reader's expectations, surprising with personal applications or shocking with new interpretations, examining images from received tradition in fresh ways, perhaps criticizing and even subverting the original. At the same time, the students agree, the emblems carry an implicit respect for authority and tradition that is less evident in their own culture. The emblems seem to revere the old, even as they challenge and transform it. I suggest two possible sources for the impulse to adopt and transform the past—humanism and the Protestant Reformation— and mention humanist philology, translations, education, and Reformation insistence on the vernacular Bible and the habit of finding personal relevance in scriptural narratives. I emphasize the dual impulses in both humanism and Protestantism, each movement turning for inspiration to an earlier age (classical Greece and Rome, the primitive church) and, paradoxically, each helping to forge what we have come to call the early modern age.

Acknowledgment of the era's felt tensions between past and present, authority and originality, Latin and vernacular languages helps the students to understand the way metaphysical poets adopt, parody, and subvert earlier generic forms like the Petrarchan sonnet, the Renaissance pastoral, and the Catholic meditation and the ways the poets use well-known iconographic motifs like the heart, the winepress, the tear, the coin, and the drop of dew in new or shocking ways. When they see how the emblem writers apply images from the past to their own time and place, the students become sensitive to the way Donne adapts conventional images to personal experience, uses erotic images in sacred poetry, and plays with images drawn from his contemporary world. They are better able to recognize and appreciate the subtle ways Herbert and Marvell alter traditional material, shifting perspectives, undercutting conventional meanings, and violating expectations. They become more attuned to the way metaphysical poets use and allude to central biblical tropes and parables in their religious poetry. And such a discussion provides an opportunity to discuss why English poets such as Crashaw also wrote Latin verse.

By using the emblem book to introduce seventeenth-century culture, I teach my students to imagine ways of knowing, interpreting, and experiencing quite different from their own. My emphasis on habits of reading and thinking is designed to deepen the students' responses to metaphysical poetry through their imaginative identifications with the readers of a different era and their acknowledged, keenly felt separation from that older world. After studying the emblem and comparing it with an artifact of their own day, my students are able to read in a way very different from the one they use when they read the morning newspaper. They are less apt to impose their own assumptions onto the poetry of another age and are more able to enter into the spirit of another culture.

On Altering the Present to Fit the Past

P. G. Stanwood

> Duty and discipline are all very well, but they must start from joy. Only the obsessed by literature can impart it, and then quite as much by osmosis as by analytical pedagogy. (Warren, "True and False Shepherds" 52)

In his essay "Tradition and the Individual Talent," T. S. Eliot wrote of the "historical sense" that the writer must struggle to perceive, a perception that involves not only "the pastness of the past, but of its presence." Writers change the existing order, although only slightly; thus, "the past [is] altered by the present as much as the present is directed by the past" (4–5).

Eliot himself had a lively sense of tradition, of preserving and sustaining a literary culture that may be carried across the ages. Hence, tradition is not, he implies, simply an inheritance passed down from one generation to another, like a chest full of relics and old keepsakes. Understanding tradition in that way, we can't fundamentally alter the present because it is part of the past; but we can see the meaning of the present by finding its parts, which must necessarily include Homer, Margaret Atwood, and Robertson Davies.

The challenge facing us all every day of our professional lives is to develop, both in ourselves and in our students, that historical sense about which Eliot writes. I doubt if many undergraduates study early literature with a belief that they are going to learn more about what is later or contemporary, nor do they approach what is new to discover what lives on from the past. Yet the knowledge, hard and strenuously learned, that the present is made up of the past and the past of the present is surely basic to literary study and to the educated imagination.

Altering the present to fit the past means changing our convictions about the past to regain or even to own for the first time the mysterious truth that Eliot advanced. Such an alteration helps root out the notion that the study of the past is unrelated to the present. This function is not the same as making an old condition relevant in a present context; it is the much more difficult task of seeing the relationship of all conditions in a timeless present.

One's approach to literature rests on certain assumptions, whether consciously expressed or not. My own approach is firmly historical in the widest sense (reflecting also what Eliot is saying), blended with a desire to let the texts speak for themselves. My lineage, which helps account for my predilections, goes back to 1950s Michigan, where I was taught by G. B. Harrison, the Shakespeare scholar and editor who, as a young man, had collaborated with Harley Granville-Barker by joining Elizabethan and Jacobean history to the modern theater in *A Companion to Shakespeare Studies* (1934); by Frank Huntley, who published elegant works on Thomas Browne, John Donne, and Jeremy Taylor; by Louis Bredvold, whose pioneering *Intellectual Milieu of John Dryden: Studies in Some Aspects of Seventeenth-Century Thought* (1934) remains a model of historical scholarship; and especially by Austin Warren, who, as a theorist, wrote *Theory of Literature* with René Wellek (1949) and, as a critic, wrote such memorable books as *Richard Crashaw: A Study in Baroque Sensibility* (1939). Warren—along with Robert Penn Warren, Cleanth Brooks, and Allen Tate—was a member of the New Critics literary movement; all anchored their studies in close reading. But the shadows of Harvard were also long, especially of such historically oriented Renaissance scholars as Herschel Baker and Douglas Bush and, to an earlier generation, of legendary figures like the great neohumanist Irving Babbitt, who had been Warren's teacher.

Freshly graduated from Michigan, I went to Tufts University, where I was given the freedom to develop the seventeenth-century course, which I wanted to design along the historical-textual lines I had learned. As in most such courses, the metaphysical poets occupied an important place, but they had to share time with the great prose writers and with Jonson and other poets not usually considered metaphysical. There I began to address the great issues of the century that Donne and his school considered. Some of those questions still focus one's attention on perennial concerns: What or where is authority in religion, in the state, in personal life? How is society constituted? What is the role and the significance of natural law, of science and philosophy and education? What are the connections between literature and the other arts? Can we trace the development of the heroic couplet and of prose style?

Those are the questions that I thought the students should ask, but I was wrong to think that students would necessarily be excited by them or that they would like my tentative way of offering more questions, instead of good answers. Students mostly want straightforward solutions to complex problems, to have the period analyzed, systematized, and put together again. They also want uncomplicated descriptions of literature that avoid posing new problems. I remember my hour on Donne's "Goodfriday, 1613. Riding Westward"; I gave a subtle analysis—so I supposed—only to field a question at the end: "Could you tell us what Good Friday means and why Donne is so upset about it?"

To convey a sense of history and an understanding of the text itself are the two principal goals of my teaching. To achieve those ends, I resolved that the students should first be able to understand the meaning of the words on the page. They need also to have a sense of chronology, so that Herbert does not become a contemporary of Chaucer, and Shakespeare does not become an Old English poet. One way of beginning a course is to ask the students to identify or explain the words, phrases, and ideas in a metaphysical poem, such as "The Canonization" or one of the *Holy Sonnets*. That informal exercise helps me learn how to address the students in a meaningful and encouraging way. At the same time, the students become fascinated by the often unfamiliar language and the ideas it conveys; soon they are eagerly discussing the poetry and its context, making intelligent use of their new knowledge.

The seventeenth-century survey course at the University of British Columbia, where I now teach, is an introduction to the period. In such a course one always needs to select and emphasize, to fit the material into the time available, to speak to the capacities of the students, and to make use of one's own interests. The survey course is an idea that comes from an earlier time, but my students know that Donne and the metaphysical poets are generously featured. Yet I always begin with a general view of the period by asking the old, important, and large questions that point to the special concerns of the writers; I refer to the aesthetic, philosophical, and critical traditions, as well as to the historical context of a century that influenced the world view and literature of our own time. Then I start at once with Donne. His wittiness, perverse logic, and reasonableness strike students most of all. Once I found that the erotic elegies intrigued people, but they no longer seem to fascinate as once they did—perhaps the use of double entendre seems too sly or even unnecessarily obscure, or perhaps Donne's strongly masculine voice is offensive and grotesque to some. "Satyre 3," however, is good for showing Donne's reasoning and his troubled mind at work, and it is good also for pointing up some of the religious issues of his time and for showing how seriously Donne took them.

I divide the course into six unequal parts: (1) Donne and the metaphysical poets (Crashaw, Herbert, Vaughan); (2) science and philosophy (Bacon, Browne, Burton); (3) Jonson and the line of classical wit (Herrick, Suckling, Lovelace, and Marvell—the wittiest poet of all); (4) the Spenserians and the epic writers: changing poetic fashions (the Fletchers, Davenant, Hobbes, Cowley, the early Dryden, Denham); (5) an age in transition (selections from the prose of Donne and Andrewes, and of Bunyan and Walton); (6) the Restoration (Dryden's "MacFlecknoe" and *Absalom and Achitophel*).

The study of Marvell gives me a good chance to look back to Donne and Jonson. We try to see what is unique in all the writers, for I believe in worrying about their differences to stem the notion that any one of them could belong to a corporation that moves with a single will. The last part of the course gives me an opportunity to discuss the development of wit and the metaphysical style. That is where Dr. Johnson's comments about Cowley are useful, along with some samples of Cowley's poetry. By that time, the students are beginning to see what metaphysical means in terms of wit and metaphor; and Dryden's lamentable elegy "Upon the Death of Lord Hastings" is a good example of what Donne usually avoided. John Cleveland's "Rebel Scot" is another egregiously unsuccessful poem that tells volumes about metaphysical poetry, and it forces everyone to recognize one of the principal themes of the course—the historical process that changes language and style.

My students do more than listen to lectures; they participate in the class study of texts, especially at the beginning of the course, when I keep asking about the meaning of a poem until everyone has a good sense of what is happening in it. Individual class reports on poems or topics are usually dull and do not involve enough people or engage universal attention. Small group reports work best, and they are the liveliest, especially late in the course, when the students know one another. Furthermore, the essay assignments reflect and complement the growth in textual and period awareness that I stimulate. First, I ask for a short *explication de texte*, of about a thousand words, of a single poem. I issue certain admonitions: Avoid large or universal judgments, such as, "Donne is a metaphysical poet who reconciles the opposing forces of body and soul," and "Crashaw is a baroque artist who responds to the mood of the Council of Trent"; I explain that a better statement is, "Donne gives meaning to 'interanimate' in 'The Extasie' and makes that sense fundamental to the poem," or "Crashaw brings tears to life in 'The Weeper.'" My topics also suggest, for example, that one compare "Loves Deitie" with "A Nocturnall upon S. Lucies Day" or "Elegie 16" ("By our first strange and fatall interview") with "The Canonization" to demonstrate how Donne reveals different attitudes toward love. Or one may show to what extent Carew successfully describes Donne's poetic program in his elegy on the death of Donne ("Can we not force from widdowed Poetry . . ."). An additional possibility asks for an explication of lines 171–218 of Donne's *First Anniversarie* (in which the poet complains that "new Philosophy cals all in doubt" [line 205]), requesting also an explanation of what that section contributes to the whole poem.

For the second essay (about 1,500 words), I ask the students to bring two writers together in a useful comparison. As with the first essay, the second one needs little or no familiarity with secondary sources. Since I believe that students learn to read best by developing confidence in their own critical abilities, I discourage reading in the secondary literature; nor do I believe that they can offer generalizations about the period before reading deeply and widely in the primary texts. The text must, first of all, form the primary focus of whatever is said: "Your critical response is what must be of interest—not what others have said," I maintain; "you should be reading texts carefully and sympathetically and not necessarily as a springboard for developing a critical theory." Many of my students do wish to study critical theory for its own sake, but that is not the purpose of my course; they are, however, learning a critical approach that may later allow them to analyze the theoretical basis of their study. A sample topic for the second assignment is the following: "It is said that Donne is a much smaller and in some ways less complex poet than Herbert. . . . How far do you agree with that judgment? Examine several poems by each poet." Or I may ask that the poetry of Herbert and Vaughan be carefully distinguished or that one of Crashaw's long poems be compared with one of Donne's devotional lyrics. Sometimes I give students the two versions of Crashaw's "Letter to the Countess of Denbigh" (1653) and ask them to comment on the nature and the success of the changes; then we discuss the characteristic features of tone and manner in Crashaw. Or I may ask how Donne, who neither founded a school nor originated metaphysical poetry, is distinctive of the poets we have so far studied.

The final essay of the course (a negotiable 2,500 words or so) is a critical study of one or more writers, but it may also raise historical or intellectual issues requiring some knowledge of secondary sources. Nevertheless, I still prefer the kind of topic that also gets students to read more of the literature of the period or to focus on one figure: "Discover the significance and discuss the literary or other influences of Richard Hooker, Nicholas Ferrar, William Chillingworth, Henry More, or Benjamin Whichcote. Or describe the variety and evaluate the importance of topographical poetry, noting especially John Beaumont, Ben Jonson, John Denham, Andrew Marvell." Or "What was the contribution to seventeenth-century aesthetic theory of Bacon and/or Jonson, Hobbes, Dryden?" An interest in comparative literature, which I promote during the course, offers some students an excellent chance to write on metaphysical poetry as an international movement; they can refer to French, Italian, or another Continental literature and bring together such writers as Donne and Jean de Sponde or Crashaw and Giambattista Marino, among many possibilities.

An interest in such comparative topics has sometimes led to an attempt to fill in other contexts, especially art, architecture, and music of the earlier seventeenth century. Peter Paul Rubens and Anthony Van Dyck provide many striking examples of portraiture and other paintings, and they lead easily into a discussion of baroque art and design in Stuart England, with such notable examples as the Banqueting House, Whitehall, by Inigo Jones (1622) and the ceiling painting by Rubens, with its principal subject the apotheosis of James (1634). That the English baroque period coincides with a time of extraordinary political, ecclesiastical, and economic changes and upheavals is a helpful point of departure for illustrating some concerns of the literature. An hour or two devoted to politics and art, with perhaps another hour of musical examples from Henry Lawes and contemporary composers gives students an awareness of the cultural setting of the poetry and makes them sensitive readers.

The climax of the course is the feast. All thirty or so students who enroll in the course know that they are also joining the Seventeenth-Century Club, whose sole function is to plan and enjoy a period entertainment. Begun eighteen years ago by a student who wanted to do a project and not an essay (she ended by doing both) and now firmly settled into the course, no matter who teaches it, the idea is to provide a chance for everyone in the class and many friends to cook, dress, make music, and offer readings and dramatic interludes in a way that re-creates an evening in a great house of about 1630. The first of the occasions offered a menu in four "removes" that kept fifty or more persons occupied from late one Saturday afternoon until early the next morning. Three removes are really enough: a goose for one, a suckling pig for another, a salmon for the last. Other feasts have also provided venison, rabbit, duck, quail, and an assortment of secret pies (for disguising vegetables), with coriander and cinnamon and other spices common to the time, huge pans of sweets with tops that look like hedgehogs, and tall cakes decorated with candied bumblebees, huge flies, and tiny birds—all in motionless flight. Sometimes one or two students make wine, which becomes a snapdragon punch of hippocras, or they brew beer for the event or, as a last resort, bring some local "Rhenish" wine.

Most students come in appropriate costume, some with help from the theater department. On one occasion, a student presented a style show with the help of her friends, displaying and explaining the features of dress from about 1620 down to the Restoration. Between removes, students sing madrigals or airs or play harpsichord music. Some students recite their favorite poems, and some read scenes from plays by Jonson, Marston, or others. Nothing about the occasion happens without considerable planning and organization, but the results are worthwhile; most of the students are learning to live in the seventeenth century, to know and to enjoy it as a social, historical, and literary epoch. The texts are meaningful in that culture, but they speak also to ours, as all joyfully discover what Ben Jonson calls "the mysteries of manners, armes, and arts" ("To Penshurst," line 98).

I began by discussing tradition, inspired by Eliot's puzzling remarks, whose obscurity speaks clearly enough to me. What I learned from my teachers about literary history has little to do with the dull business of canon and chronology. What I gained from them and mean to pass on to others is akin to what Eliot felt in his bones: the acute consciousness of one's own place in time. Austin Warren left me to think of those thoughts with his own interpretation of them: "The teacher of literature must not only represent tradition, but also engage in the constant revision of it" ("True and False Shepherds" 51).

"New-found-land": Teaching Metaphysical Poetry from the Other Side

Ann Baynes Coiro

I began my teaching career at an old liberal arts college that had recently and painfully gone coed. When I was interviewed for that job, the faculty members wanted to know how I would teach metaphysical poetry to the young women who were appearing in their classrooms so angry with the sexual assumptions of some seventeenth-century poetry (John Donne's "Elegy 19" and Thomas Carew's "Rapture" had precipitated the conflict) that they argued such stuff should no longer be read by politically correct people. Both the faculty members' astonishment at the anger and the anger itself were impulses behind the ways I began to teach seventeenth-century poetry.

In the classroom now we are all caught in the middle of change. Anthology indexes include new names for which no ready-made critical pronouncements exist. Feminist critical theory has grown in the last few years in many directions, some of them in conflict with one another. The question of what characteristics women share across class and across history remains. Certainly, the idea of a politically correct position, of one unified and righteous front, has begun to look stultifying at best and, at worst, frightening. Instead, a feminist perspective can bring to an undergraduate classroom the plurality, the diversity, the questions and tensions and possibilities of the last twenty years—indeed, the possibility of change itself.

As part of a discussion of the five metaphysical poets on whom this volume focuses, it is illuminating to look with our students around the edges of this constellation and determine what is excluded, a strategy we have learned from feminist procedures. Students should understand the line of criticism that T. S. Eliot's essay on the metaphysical poets helped engender and should see the irony in Eliot's praise of the metaphysical poets as men who succeeded in creating a unified poetry out of all the physical and intellectual elements of their particular experiences. The irony lies in the effects of Eliot's musings, musings whose intentions may have been to place early seventeenth-century poetry in a historical context but whose effects resulted in the close reading strategies of New Criticism, which "disassociated" the metaphysical poems from their historical moment, styling them disembodied voices of intellectual wit. We must not read seventeenth-century poetry out of history and in a timeless realm of close reading; and we must not isolate the poetry in a timely realm of any one feminist theory.

At the beginning of every semester I make my own position as clear as possible to my students. As a scholar, a teacher, and a feminist, I read and teach seventeenth-century poems in a context as richly political—that is, historical and cultural—as possible. Early in the course, for example, I talk about the fact that under the critical rubric of metaphysical the five central poets—Donne, Herbert, Crashaw, Vaughan, and Marvell—are all men. If we do not address that starkly obvious situation at once, our students may assume that women in the seventeenth century had no talent or no desire to write and, therefore, no place in the received canon. Even in the most recent *Norton Anthology*, which had an explicit mandate to include women writers, the editors can find only one seventeenth-century woman poet, Lady Mary Wroth (in the *Norton Anthology*, 5th ed.). In my class we do read that lone and moving voice, a voice always threatening to collapse in upon itself in silence. The disturbing alienation of her poems is important for students to hear while they are reading the shared dialogue of Donne, Herbert, Vaughan, Crashaw, and Marvell, for she is clearly only on the margin of that dialogue. Wroth's poems are punctuated largely by question marks and are structured by metaphors of entrapment. Her repeated image patterns of self-blinding, self-silencing, infanticide, and love poetry itself as a labyrinth with no exit make students confront the difficult question of how a woman can speak without using a language already shaped by men, a language in which she is an object.

There were, of course, powerful, intelligent, creative women living and working in the seventeenth century. Most of them, however, were not writing lyric poetry for public view. Nevertheless, women played a significant role in the production of seventeenth-century poems. Lucy Harrington, Countess of Bedford, for example, was a crucial power broker at the court of James I, and John Donne addressed a number of verse epistles to her and probably several lyrics as well. As part of an argument for the coterie nature of Donne's poetry, Arthur Marotti reconstructs the groups to which Donne was specifically directing his poems, including both a male coterie and a female coterie of court women like Lucy, Countess of Bedford. But Marotti argues further that, in writing for a woman like Lady Bedford, Donne was conscious of a second, male audience, one that both read the poem and "read" the Countess of Bedford reading it. However, Marotti seems to underestimate the sophistication of Donne's female coterie. I suggest that, in those poems addressed primarily to his male friends, Donne was conscious of a female audience reading the poems, reading the men reading the poems, and aware that Donne was aware the women were there.

Donne's verse epistles are rarely placed on an undergraduate reading list, but the inclusion of at least one epistle to the Countess of Bedford allows students to watch Donne squirm uneasily under the need to flatter a powerful woman. Once they have perceived, in what seems to be abundant praise, Donne's discomfort and satiric undertone, the verse epistle puts new light on the aggressive male posturing of many of his lyrics. In conjunction with Donne's verse epistles, Ben Jonson's epigrams to Lady Bedford give a sense of how social status affects poetic decorum. The verse epistles also allow students to consider poetry as a partly autobiographical gesture, instead of an artifact with no human agency, and allow students to wrestle with the idea of patronage before they read "The Anatomy of the World."

The Countess of Bedford is one among many women present in the work of the metaphysical poets. In striking contrast to Lady Bedford's sometimes frustrating flesh and blood presence in Donne's life, there is the numinous presence of Elizabeth Drury, dead at the age of fourteen, a girl Donne never met. There is Ann More, Donne's wife, who was a member of a family of generations of educated women and, as Ilona Bell points out, was quite capable of being Donne's intellectual companion and audience for his poems. There is Magdalen Herbert, the mediating presence in the poetry of Donne and behind the poetry of Herbert, who was both actually present and worthy of praise. Andrew Marvell's repeated imagining throughout his poetry of the voice and the presence of a girl must surely rest in part on his experience as tutor to Maria Fairfax, named as the pivot of "Upon Appleton House." That Marvell was hired as the tutor for a young woman is itself a historical corrective to the bleak picture sometimes painted of the status of seventeenth-century women.

Certainly, Henrietta Maria, queen consort of Charles I, had, for good and for ill, political and artistic influence. Both George Herbert and Henry Vaughan conceived of their poetic practices as deliberate rejections of the vogue of love poetry the queen encouraged. Richard Crashaw, by contrast, took refuge in the queen's orbit after he abandoned Cambridge in anticipation of his ejection. Crashaw dedicated *Carmen Deo Nostro* to the Countess of Denbigh, mistress of the queen's bedchamber and the specific audience of the extraordinary erotic wooing "To the Noblest & Best of Ladyes, the Countess of Denbigh." In real and complicated ways, women were much more than the subjects of metaphysical poems; they literally authorized them.

Attention to the women who surround seventeenth-century poetry is a significant departure from New Criticism, but a departure we must make if we are going to "read it right." Once students recognize the forming pressures of seventeenth-century women as readers, as subjects, as patrons, and as new and resented sources of social and political power, the students can begin to recognize themselves as readers and to recognize the power of that position.

The poems of John Donne, the quintessential metaphysical poet, are ideally suited to teaching a number of key literary principles, especially the concept of persona. "The Good-Morrow," "The Flea," "Batter my heart"— all those poems are handy pedagogical tools to show our students how a poem can portray with remarkable economy the voice and the character of its dramatic speaker. However, an uncritical first reading of persona in Donne and many other seventeenth-century poets can—indeed, should—alienate the current generation of students, who are beginning to be alert to the male bias of the canon. In fact, the metaphysical persona is not a simple literary trick that a student masters so as not to appear a naive child in the teacher's eyes. We have begun to think about how we have read back into history the subjectivity we privilege, the preeminent *I*. Such questioning makes us cautious about the assumptions we impose on our students. Moreover, some metaphysical poems are easily turned into one-sided sexual jokes, and probably most of us have felt uneasy, even as we laughed. I imagine that at least every woman reading this essay can remember from her undergraduate education the leering, elbow-in-the-ribs reading of seventeenth-century poems. Do such attitudes still persist in the classroom? When we teach "Elegy 19" or Carew's "Rapture" or even Marvell's "To His Coy Mistress," do we smugly attribute the students' unease to their lack of literary sophistication, to their inability to disengage themselves from the text, to their unsophisticated notion that somehow both poet and reader are responsible for the attitudes producing that unease? The students' unease and ours should not, however, be displaced onto a persona and neatly contained in critical conventions. We need to talk with our students about the gender of any persona, about how we as readers form the persona's gender, about how the gender forms the poem, and about the implied but silent other who is also shaped by the gender of the speaker and by us.

For the same reasons that New Criticism privileged metaphysical poems—the complex tensions and the play of language involved in their "wit"—the metaphysical poets are ideally suited to a classroom where student and teacher are on a relatively equal footing, since the reader's wit can be as important as learned background knowledge. I teach a pair of classes on Donne in which I draw on all the students' native shrewdness and acquired skills as poetry readers. The first class we spend on "The Good-Morrow." We read the poem together and establish the speaker, the auditor, the scene, the situation. Then I give the students ten minutes to read it alone. To get them going, I list on the board some ways into a poem we have used before: the rhyme pattern, the variations in the rhyme, the meter and its interruptions, the use of enjambment and caesura. Ten minutes later we open up the discussion again. I usually begin the discussion by having each student contribute something in turn. The students at the far end of the room are always sure they will have nothing left to say, but they discover that they have more to say, since they can refine or disagree with what has gone before. The strategy gives each student a chance to be the speaker and to take a position to defend or build on for the rest of the class. At the end of the class the students see how their stances as active readers engage them with the poem and make each one a collaborator with every other member of the class and put each one just slightly at odds with everyone else. Meanwhile, all the technical details I've listed on the board and the students themselves have brought us back to the powerful *I/we* of the poem and to the bed. We all leave the classroom that day feeling successful and competent. In the next class, we read together—we confident and triumphant readers—"Break of Day."

The students see at once that the aubade is similar to "The Good-Morrow," that the two poems from their titles on share important features but that "Break of Day" is spoken by a woman to a silent man and that the movement of the poem is not toward the bed but away from it. Once we have established that together, I ask the students to do what they did in the previous class, to spend ten minutes applying all their shrewdness and training to the poem before we discuss it together. What they discover is that "Break of Day" is the flat convention against which the antiaubade of "The Good-Morrow," with its witty denial that time passes and love ends, is constructed. What the students usually decide is that "Break of Day" is a poor poem—a liberating discovery for those who assume that anything they read in school must be great, even if they can't always see why.

On the surface the two poems are so remarkably similar and their effects so remarkably different that together they become an exemplary unit on "bad poetry and good." But the source of the difference lies in the gender of the persona. If "Break of Day" is bad, it seems intentionally bad, intentionally a failure as dense, compelling poetry because the speaker is a woman. The two poems are more than a lesson in imagery and structure. Students need to face the critical question of intention. They may begin with the endearing student version of historicism (and a standard professorial argument against feminist quibbles)—in those days they didn't know any better, so we must humor the foibles of those old boys and read their poems as curious artifacts. The students are not completely wrong, of course, but I insist that they think about the implications of their argument. How free is any person? To what extent is each of us a product of culture? Then I ask them to consider the other possibility, that "Break of Day" is intentionally mocking. Which scenario is more frightening—Donne's deliberately mocking women or Donne's inability to imagine a woman speaking in any other way? (The second is the more appalling, but the first seems to me closer to the truth.) By the end of the class I hope that my students are uneasy and unsure, and I hope that they retain that unease throughout the semester.

John Donne intended to shock, and he does shock and anger students. I don't want to deny their anger or even allay it but to use it to make them examine their own assumptions and the assumptions and gender constructions of Donne and all the other metaphysical poets. The eroticism of seventeenth-century religious poetry, for example, is shocking for students. Donne delivers the first shock and becomes their reference point. Donne draws clear sexual lines and usually talks to his God as one aggressive guy to another. The most complete self-abnegation that he can imagine is, in "Batter my heart," to place himself before God as a woman, a woman begging to be raped. When we read Herbert's poetry, the students can see that it too is clearly sexual. For one thing, Herbert explicitly appropriates the language of sexual love and places it in the service of God. But in Herbert's poems the gender of the lovers, speaker and God, seems to shift and ultimately disappear. In "Church-Monuments" part of Herbert's dissolution of all human pretensions is the dissolution of gender division. When at the end of "Church-Monuments" all human constructs are dissolved before God, the traditional dialectic of female soul and male body with which the poem began has also dissolved. When in "Jordan" (1) Herbert extends the reach of poetry beyond human sexual impulses by asking, "Who says that fictions only and false hair / Become a verse?" (lines 1–2), one of the "fictions" is the rigid sexual roles such poetry can perpetuate.

A course taught with a feminist view must reconsider emphases and shortcuts that have become traditional in seventeenth-century poetry courses. Difficult as it is, "The Anatomy of the World" cannot be omitted. And Richard Crashaw cannot be read as an amusing exception to everything "really English." The fifth edition of the *Norton Anthology* (gen. ed. Abrams) still tells students that "there is really no other English poet who is much like him" (1355), an axiom rejected by most recent scholarship. Crashaw's marginalization seems yet another neat political excision, in his case for his Catholicism and the exaggerated sexuality of his poetry, but the costs of his excision are a radical skewing of the historical circumstances of seventeenth-century England and the loss of a poet who centered his writing and his life on women and who offers an important site for any consideration of gender in the Renaissance. In "The Flaming Heart" Crashaw directs his readers to "transpose the picture quite / And spell it wrong to read it right; / Read *him* for *her* and *her* for *him*" (9–11). "The Flaming Heart" is a disturbing deconstruction of the portrayal of male and female in art. Extraordinarily sophisticated and highly charged, Crashaw should not be placed in demeaning parentheses in any seventeenth-century poetry course and certainly not in one with a feminist emphasis.

If the sexes are elided in Herbert's poetry and put through a series of dizzying switches in Crashaw's, in Henry Vaughan's poetry they are often predated in an attempted escape from sexuality. Vaughan's persona in "The Retreat," for example, apostrophizes "those early days" so close to the "first love," before the child falls into language and every other "sin" of the senses (lines 1, 8, 18). And yet, "The Retreat" offers proof that we are all sexual beings from infancy on; the poem ends with a powerful wish to conflate tomb and womb, beginning and end, God and Mother.

In Andrew Marvell's poetry, female figures stand somewhere between the childhood of Vaughan and the erotic adulthood of Donne and Crashaw. By the time my students read Marvell, they have already read Milton's *Comus* and at least one Shakespeare comedy and have become fascinated with the Renaissance idea of a girl on the edge of womanhood. Throughout Marvell's poems the figure of a girl appears in the garden—"Little T. C. in a Prospect of Flowers," Maria Fairfax in the center of her father's estate, or the wild garden itself as unspoiled female sexuality in "The Mower against Gardens"—but the girl is trembling on the edge of eroticism. "The Nymph Complaining for the Death of Her Fawn" is the strangest and most moving of those poems, a poem for which I have no easy explanation; for that reason it is a wonderful poem to discuss toward the end of a semester, when the students are bolder about exploring their ideas. In English Renaissance poetry, nymphs and fawns were a shorthand for woman to the point of cliché. What Marvell has done in "The Nymph Complaining" is take the trivialized object of a poetic tradition and give her a voice. I don't want to romanticize the poem. As Jonathan Goldberg shows, it ends in death and silence (*Voice* 32–37). But the power of the poem's nihilism and utter sadness lies in the gender of its voice, a young woman's voice.

A semester on the metaphysical poets begins with seduction. Donne's "Elegy 19" seduces us all, since we can read into its dramatic scene our own desires and experiences. Possible readings of "Elegy 19" have expanded significantly since women entered the classroom in great numbers and influence. Because "Elegy 19" is flamboyantly masculine and apparently masterful; because the young man in the back row wakes up for the first time when we get to that poem; because, as layers of allusion are peeled away, the poem makes women students angry, "Elegy 19" has been reread in recent years from the perspective of the woman addressed. When the metaphors of licensing and colonialization are considered from her position, the dramatic situation can become one of mutual erotic play or can be read as an eroti-cized metaphor for the power of women in the Renaissance, able to grant a license for the new-found-land—and, one presumes, to revoke it.

A semester on the metaphysical poets also ends with seduction. But Marvell's "To His Coy Mistress" allows us little room to enter into dramatic play. The coy mistress has none of the rounded actuality of the women playing between the lines of Donne's poems. In "An Horatian Ode," Marvell had sustained an inscrutable ambivalence about "the forcèd power" of Cromwell's erected sword (line 66). But "To His Coy Mistress" is about the end of ambivalence, and the forced power of its language drives us all toward its consummation. It ends the semester with a stunning warning.

I have been largely silent about an important area of sexual difference, and that is, at least in coeducational schools, the classroom itself. For most students, feminism is not, on the face if it, revolutionary but is just another cultural given, already in place before they were born. It doesn't take more than a session or two on Donne, however, to charge a classroom with debate that breaks down pretty consistently along gender lines (no male student at my small college had complained about having to read "Elegy 19"). It is the strength of the poetry that it is able to cause such a rift and the resulting dialogue. As one gender reads, the other gender reads them reading. The flea, alive or dead, can always serve for another hit; there is never a last word. We, women and men, multiply the audience, multiply the game. About one thing the New Criticism was certainly wrong. Poems do not close off neatly in self-enclosed units, and neither do good classes. They open out in every direction, and they change us all.

COURSE CONTEXTS

Ben Jonson and the Metaphysical Poets: Continuity in a Survey Course

Robert H. Ray

Presenting the metaphysical poets in English literature survey courses challenges the teacher to simplify. Most critical and classroom approaches simplify by separating the metaphysical poets from Ben Jonson and his followers. To distinguish too sharply, however, may imply a discontinuity in English literature, with poets after John Donne and Ben Jonson dividing into two enemy camps. Many teachers, given limited time and the overriding popularity of Donne and the other metaphysical poets, choose to exclude Jonson. One should perhaps teach the metaphysical poets by covering Jonson early (preferably just after Donne), both because he is biographically tied to Donne and because many elements in later metaphysical poetry derive directly from Jonson. So, in a survey course I believe in simplification by categorizing but not to the extent of distortion.

My own classroom approach ties Jonson to several metaphysical poets and encompasses many poems. In this essay I propose a core of writers, works, points to be made, and order of study abbreviated from my classroom practice. My potential readers here, I assume, are primarily those who are nonspecialists faced with teaching the metaphysical poets in English literature survey courses, perhaps on the sophomore level. Specialists, though, may adapt and fill out this framework for an advanced survey of seventeenth-century poetry. For convenience, all references and quotations in this essay, unless otherwise indicated, are from volume 1 of *The Norton Anthology of English Literature* (gen. ed. Abrams).

I first assign Donne's poetry to engage the interest of the class and to provide the essence of metaphysical characteristics. The students also read the excerpt from Dr. Johnson's "Life of Cowley" (2418–20) that comments on Donne and the metaphysical poets. (At that point the teacher should distinguish between Samuel Johnson and Ben Jonson.) To begin our first class period on Donne, I list some of the major characteristics of metaphysical poetry and mention that we shall test them inductively as we look at Donne's poetry. The following is a selected list, and several can be tied to Johnson's statements: (1) metaphysical conceit—a brief definition suffices, including Johnson's designations of "farfetched," "combination of dissimilar images," "heterogeneous ideas yoked by violence together"; (2) complexity or obscurity; (3) paradox; (4) exaggeration—Johnson's "hyperbole"; (5) rebellion against Petrarchan and Elizabethan poetic conventions; (6) colloquial language; (7) natural speech rhythms or extreme distortions of metrical patterns—Johnson's "modulation . . . so imperfect that they were only found to be verses by counting the syllables"; (8) irregular lines and stanzas; and (9) argumentative form and content. Such a list has the virtue of simplicity and provides strands that students can trace through succeeding metaphysical poets.

Teachers have their own favorite poems to illustrate the qualities of Donne and metaphysical poetry. Table 1 presents some that I have found useful.

Immediately after Donne, the class proceeds to Jonson. I emphasize that he is the other major poet of the early seventeenth century and is generally regarded as the important classical exemplar, comparable to Donne in the metaphysical genre. If the textbook contains excerpts from Jonson's conversations with William Drummond of Hawthornden, the students read Jonson's famous comments on Donne. Or I provide them. Unfortunately, the *Norton Anthology* prints only two of Jonson's statements (1062); but all the important ones are in the text edited by Witherspoon and Warnke, used in many advanced courses, and I quote the following samples from it. In class I first stress Jonson's disagreement with some metaphysical qualities: "Donne, for not keeping of accent, deserved hanging" (127) and "Donne himself, for not being understood, would perish" (128). But also Jonson "esteemeth John Donne the first poet in the world in some things" (128). Students should be told that Donne and Jonson were exact contemporaries (both born in 1572), were personal friends, and shared a patroness (the Countess of Bedford). Merely remarking on those matters prevents the misconception that they were opposed to each other in every way and begins to establish subtle bonds that suggest cohesiveness in our survey.

At that point I simplify, in a way parallel to the first period on Donne, and focus on characteristics generally regarded as typical of Jonson and classical

Table 1. Characteristics of Sample Donne Poems

Poem	*Norton Anthology* pages	Major Metaphysical Characteristics
"The Indifferent"	1066–67	Rebellious (anti-Petrarchan, anti-Spenserian); colloquial (esp. lines 6–7); irregular in metrics and lines
"The Flea"	1071–72	Paradox; exaggeration; rebellion; colloquialism; natural speech; metaphysical conceit (flea as sexual consummation, pregnancy, marriage, marriage bed, marriage temple: relate to Johnson's comments); argumentation
"A Valediction: Forbidding Mourning"	1075–76	Colloquialism; intellectual complexity; argumentation; paradox; rebellion (anti-Petrarchan in lines 5–8); metaphysical conceit (four major ones: stanzas 1–2, 3–5, 6, and the most famous in 7–9—effectively illustrated point by point in class with a draftsman's compass)
Holy Sonnet 10	1099	Paradox (esp. lines 1–2, 3–4, 5–6, 9–10, 14); irregular metrics (esp. lines 1–2, 8, 9–10, 13–14); argumentation
"A Hymn to Christ"	1102–03	Metaphysical conceit (esp. the journey from England to Germany as a voyage from Earth to Heaven, combined with the analogy of Christ as the speaker's true lover); paradox (esp. lines 19–21, 26, 27, 28); argumentation

poetry. I propose to the students a list illustrated with Jonson poems. Here is a selected list: (1) balance, parallelism, symmetry in style and structure; (2) careful organization and progression; (3) general metrical regularity; (4) frequent use of couplets and caesuras; (5) formal, polite, courtly diction and tone; (6) restraint of emotion; (7) emphasis on classical themes and forms, such as complimentary verses, carpe diem verses, praises of country life and of good food and drink; and (8) presentation of a poet in a public role and as a social, moral, ethical critic.

Table 2 offers an approach to Ben Jonson.

Of the poems in table 2 "Still to Be Neat" most succinctly illustrates the classical style. The parallelism, balance, symmetry, and careful organization are epitomized in such a line as "Still to be neat, still to be dressed" (line 1). Students see how the placement of stress, caesura, and alliteration enforce parallel words, phrases, and syntax. Jonson emphasizes the neatness of his style as it corresponds to the excessive neatness of the lady in stanza 1, but he breaks the parallels and art in stanza 2 as he describes "sweet neglect."

Table 2. Characteristics of Sample Jonson Poems

Poem	Norton Anthology pages	Major Classical Characteristics
Song ("Come, my Celia, let us prove") from *Volpone*	1163–64	Carpe diem theme; couplets
"Still to Be Neat"	1226	Balance, parallelism; octosyllabic couplets and caesuras; polite, courtly diction and tone
Stanza 7 (lines 65–74) of the "Ode" on Lucius Cary and Henry Morison	1223	Classical theme and form; careful organization and progression (large size in 65–66, length of life in 67–68, small size in 69–70, short life in 71–72, small size in 73, and short life in 74)
No. 4 ("Her Triumph") in *A Celebration of Charis*	Not in Norton; 765–66 in Witherspoon and Warnke	Balance, parallelism, symmetry; metrical order and harmony; careful organization and progression (esp. in last stanza: specific images of things white, soft, and sweet, leading to the last line, summarizing the qualities in that same order)
"To William Camden"	1209	Complimentary verse; balance, parallelism (in words, phrases, lines, metrics, and alliteration); heroic couplets; caesuras
"To Penshurst"	1215–17	Classical allusions and themes of country life, good food and drink; poet in public role and as social, moral, ethical critic; couplets; formal diction and tone; careful organization and progression (esp. from building to grounds to animals and fruits to tenants, guests, lord and lady, and back to building)

Such techniques, used and broken to correspond with feeling, are central in a metaphysical poet like Herbert. Also, Jonson's "Lady, it is to be presumed" (line 4) embodies polite diction and tone, followed by a critical slap two lines later, elements in some of Marvell's work.

To complete Jonson, the class studies "To John Donne" (1210–11). Heroic couplets lend the poem a typically Jonsonian aura. But Jonson also uses some Donne characteristics—striking metrical variations and enough elision to verge on obscurity. In fact, Jonson is matching Donne's irony, wit, and compact statement with his own ambiguity, since practically every statement is double-edged, easily interpreted as either compliment or criticism. Jonson is particularly on Donne's ground in the ambiguous assertion that he "cannot" praise Donne as he "should"—an ending close to that in Donne's ironic poem "Upon Mr. Thomas Coryat's Crudities," where Donne (supposedly humble), rather than read Coryat's book in full, "would read none" (line 76 in Shawcross). "To John Donne" must be taken as a friendly joke between Jonson and Donne, as well as a compliment, assuming imitation as flattery. (For a helpful reading of the double meanings, see Wiersma.) The poem reveals some interesting connections in wittiness and friendship between Donne and Jonson. Students also see that, if a classical poet like Jonson borrows metaphysical qualities for his purposes, then metaphysical followers of Donne may similarly borrow Jonson's classical qualities.

Such a follower appears in George Herbert. I begin the first class on Herbert by indicating that he is traditionally categorized as a metaphysical poet, his mother was an important patroness and friend of Donne, he probably grew up reading Donne's poetry, and Donne gave Herbert a ring and a poem about it. But we begin with "Virtue" (1343–44). I ask the class what previous poet seems the primary influence on Herbert's style and structure in that poem. Although some students naturally indicate Donne, others say Jonson. They specify as classical the impressive symmetry, balance, and parallelism of the first three stanzas ("Sweet day," "Sweet rose," "Sweet spring"), enforced by the repetition of both words and metrical patterns. Similarly, parallels and the regular metrical pattern in line 1 ("Sweet day, so cool, so calm, so bright"), giving the feeling of delightful harmony and admiration, compare to Jonson's techniques in line 30 of "Her Triumph" ("O so white, O so soft, O so sweet is she!"): in both Herbert and Jonson four stresses fall on three adjectives and the modified noun (in Herbert) or pronoun (in Jonson), conveying the desired fusion of perfect characteristics in an entity of ordered beauty. That comparison leads us into the other Jonsonian parallels in the refrain, into the classical organization and progression from "day" to "rose" to "spring," and consequently from three elements of mortal worth to one of spiritual worth in the final stanza. Perceptive students see the patterns of symmetry and expectation in the first three stanzas violated in the last—a device underlining the soul's uniqueness: form embodies content in a way similar to Jonson's "Still to Be Neat." A few students connect Herbert's "rose" with Jonson's "lily" in the "Ode" on Cary and Morison (line 69). We then focus on what is Donne-like and metaphysical, and we conclude that primarily it is the use of such conceits as the spring analogous to a box of perfumes and the soul compared to seasoned wood. Herbert, then, fuses Jonsonian style and structure with Donnean conceits and seems as much influenced here by the classical as by the metaphysical.

To see why Herbert is primarily metaphysical, the students proceed to many poems that undeniably carry the marks of Donne: "The Collar" (1349–50) with its implied conceits, colloquial outbursts, and irregular metrics and lines that convey the disoriented mind of the speaker; "The Pulley" (1350) with the ingenious conceit of rest as the pulley; and "Prayer" (1) (1340) with its paradoxes and "heterogeneous ideas yoked by violence together." However, treating a poem such as "The Windows" (1342) near the end of the

Herbert sample again reminds the students of the metaphysical and classical combination in Herbert. The metaphysical conceit of a holy preacher analogous to a stained-glass window is embodied in a classically restrained form of equal stanzas, parallel line lengths, and symmetry to both the eye and the ear (repetition of syllables, echoes of sounds, and rhymes increase with each successive stanza). The Jonsonian line beginning the third stanza ("Doctrine and life, colors and light, in one") gathers the content from the two previous stanzas and uses parallel style to reflect the balance of qualities in the holy preacher who lives what he speaks.

Despite my insistence that Andrew Marvell is another metaphysical poet, the class is now alert to the classical mode. "To His Coy Mistress" (1387–88) is ideal to examine first, since it mingles much of Donne and Jonson. In fact, students recognize the carpe diem theme from Jonson's song to Celia in *Volpone*. Additional links between the followers of Donne and the followers of Jonson appear by relating Marvell's poem to Robert Herrick's carpe diem "Corinna's Going A-Maying" (1324–26) and "To the Virgins to Make Much of Time" (1327). Another obvious classical quality in "To His Coy Mistress" is the use of octosyllabic couplets. The polite, courtly formality and compliment (followed by some blunt criticism) of both line 2 ("This coyness, Lady, were no crime") and line 19 ("For, Lady, you deserve this state") are reminiscent of Jonson's "Lady, it is to be presumed." The symmetry of line 1 ("Had we but world enough, and time") with its generally regular metrics and carefully placed and heavily stressed "world" and "time" ending each half-line is also Jonsonian. But suddenly in the second couplet the Donne-like violation of smooth metrics radically slows the movement. Other metaphysical qualities can be probed: witty exaggeration, argumentative progression, and colloquial language.

For further classical stylistics in Marvell, we observe couplets in all four "Mower" poems, "The Garden," and "An Horation Ode" (1390–1401). The regular, symmetrical lines and stanzas (with their polish, repetition, parallels, contrasts, and careful organization) are more classical than metaphysical (see "The Mower to the Glow-Worms": line 1, "Ye living lamps"; line 5, "Ye country comets"; line 9, "Ye glow-worms"). "The Garden" and "Upon Appleton House" (the latter not in *Norton Anthology*) derive mainly from the tradition of the country house poem begun with Jonson's "To Penshurst." Thus, colloquial language, obscurity, witty exaggeration, and paradox abound in Marvell, but many of his classical forms, tones, and themes are inherited from Jonson.

The essentially dual nature of the period's poetry appears in varying degrees in other writers. Henry Vaughan's "Rhapsody" (1368–70) is redolent of Jonson and parallel to Herrick. Also, the strict couplets of "The Retreat" (1372–73) and the balanced phrasing and placement of stresses in some lines of "The World" (1375–76) suggest a Jonsonian influence in poems that echo both Donne and Herbert in conceits and colloquialisms. Richard Crashaw's couplets, rhymes, and parallels in "The Flaming Heart" (1364–66) have a touch of the classical, even beneath the esoteric metaphysical magnificence. The mingling of strains explains why critics have disagreed on the classification of someone such as Thomas Carew. His "Elegy upon the Death of . . . Donne" (1640–42) and "To Ben Jonson" (1642–43) eloquently represent the admiration of both great figures by many younger poets and provide an excellent climax for our integrative approach in the classroom. In fact, detailed student explications of those poems and Carew's third "Epitaph on the Lady Mary Villiers" (not in the *Norton Anthology*) reveal the joined metaphysical and classical influences.

Practicing the foregoing approach that first separates for simplicity and then combines for perspective convinces me that students who read metaphysical poetry without knowing Jonson do not really understand all the components of that poetry. To remedy such deficiency and discontinuity should surely be the aim of all teachers of the metaphysical poets.

Metaphysical, Mannerist, Baroque: A Seminar for Undergraduates

Faye Pauli Whitaker

When my university bookstore called with the information that Wylie Sypher's *Four Stages of Renaissance Style: Transformations in Art and Literature 1400–1700* was out of print and would not be available for my seminar in the fall term, I felt a sense of panic. I had planned a course, awkwardly titled Metaphysical and Baroque, that would focus on the study of the metaphysical poets in the context of the larger issues of aesthetics and cultural history. Sypher's book was to provide the structure for the discussion. The seminar would enroll ten to fifteen undergraduates, mainly English majors nearing the completion of their undergraduate work. Even at that point in their studies, I could not assume that they had studied any Renaissance writers other than Shakespeare, and I could assume that few had done more than sample lyric poetry in survey courses. I wished to have students study the poetry in some depth, to acquaint them with significant issues in aesthetic and intellectual history, and to help them understand some theoretical and philosophical issues involved in literary and cultural history.

When I proposed the course in 1980, I was well aware of the limitations of Sypher's impressionistic methods, his confusion of chronology, and his failure to separate features of style from issues of content and theme. He had taken a roasting from many—William K. Wimsatt and Monroe C. Beardsley, René Wellek, and Alastair Fowler to name a few. The Tillyard-style history of ideas was already in ill repute in 1980. Nonetheless, Sypher's work seemed to provide a critical statement comprehensible to inexperienced undergraduates, and certainly Sypher provided an example of the critical minefield encountered when one makes generalizations. We could, in fact, catch him and his text committing critical sins and yet not abandon the generally compelling notion of intellectual and aesthetic history. As it happened, Sypher was not to be our common text, and that fact opened greater possibilities for our study.

The course that ultimately developed and that has been repeated because of its success provides students with a productive context for constructing interpretations in which theoretical questions can emerge—questions of ideology, period style, interart analogies, and poetic schools. Beginning with the close reading of texts, I arrange the course to proceed inductively, asking students to generalize at every stage of the process. At the end of the course they have come to grips with the terms metaphysical, mannerism, and baroque, and they have a sense of literary history as an investigation involving the analysis of individual texts, the assessment of a cross section of a given literary moment, and the consideration of that moment in the context of other artistic expressions. What follows is a description of the way the course proceeds. Its success is attributable to the students' dutiful and thoughtful responses to the daily assignments. Their responses have been enthusiastic. They come to class prepared to discuss the material and eager to contribute. The weak student has the success of close-reading the texts, and abler students get not only a profitable study of the metaphysical poets but also an introduction to many theoretical questions involved in the study of literary history.

We begin the course by reading John Donne's *Songs and Sonets* in full. An analysis of two poems reveals the range of Donne's attitudes toward love and fundamental issues concerning style. "The Flea" and "A Valediction: Forbidding Mourning" work well for that purpose, as they provide a balance of serious and ribald wit, incorporate traditional elements handled in an original way, and express two attitudes toward love. Further, each speaks out of a dramatic situation in which both the persona and the person addressed are clearly imagined. Each poem represents a moment in an ongoing relationship in which the persona tries to shape the future by controlling the response of the person addressed. In "The Flea" Donne gives the Ovidian seduction poem a lively and dramatic realization. At the end of each stanza we consider the literal response of the woman addressed; her action in the white space following the stanza provides the occasion for the logical argument of the subsequent stanzas. One student is asked to read a stanza, and another student must perform the response—first the gesture threatening the life of the flea and then the impurpling of the nail. Students easily understand how the poem builds on the imagined action of a second party. The response following the final stanza is, however, left undefined, a situation that requires the student to speculate on the parameters of the poem and how the conclusion is to be interpreted. In the "Valediction" the person addressed, the other, is characterized by the speaker's opposition to her. A comparison of the two poems shows similarities of style and poetic techniques as surely as they reveal differences.

I ask the students to keep notes that summarize the arguments of the remaining poems, taking into account the tone of the poem, the attitude and character of the persona, and, most significantly, the rhetorical strategies used. Ultimately, they are asked to draw some generalizations about the collection as a whole. Near the end of their study of the poems, I provide them with a sampling of sonnets by Shakespeare, Philip Sidney, and Edmund Spenser—new to many of them—to compare structure, style, and tone. Just as the process of defining a period style involves looking at the cohesive aspects of the style represented in an author or a school, it also involves contrasting it with the style that stands at the margin, a style that incorporates different conventions. The order and the symmetry of the Elizabethan sonnet offer that point of contrast. To conclude the study of

Donne, we turn to the religious sonnets and "Goodfriday, 1613. Riding Westward" to consider the extent to which the techniques used in the *Songs and Sonets* are confined to the treatment of secular love and the extent to which subject matter is the controlling force in the structure of Donne's poems. Recently, I have asked students to read critical studies by Alan Sinfield and by David Aers, Bob Hodge, and Gunther Kress to consider the effects of religious, economic, and biographical contexts in shaping the rhetoric of the poems.

Next, we turn to George Herbert, who presents new problems for students who have just become confident and enthusiastic readers of Donne. My method here is the same as that used in the analysis of Donne—close reading, note taking, working toward the development of general statements about the norms and the continuities found in Herbert's poetic work. Several issues are new, and I find that, while the students have difficulty with Donne's syntax, they often find Herbert's frame of reference even more foreign. Since I am most concerned that the students come to grips with Herbert's style, the nature of his voice, and the presentation of his identity, I supply the students with the needed information from the Bible and other sources in the Christian tradition, minimizing the theological complexities as much as possible. Though the students are immediately interested in the pattern poems (given the later emphasis in the course on visual matters, I find it hard not to cultivate that interest), I delay the discussion of them until after we examine in detail four poems more typical of *The Temple.* "The Collar" picks up the dramatic features of Donne's poems, including the idea of an individually defined persona and the utterance of the poem as representing the process of discovery of his self, often in opposition to his world and his God. The poem also allows for a discussion of its theatrical element and the positioning of the reader as an observer of the persona's "dialogue of one" ("The Exstasie," line 79) with God. "The Pulley" introduces the students to Herbert's justification of divine providence and his unusual use of titles to complicate the metaphorical dimensions of the poem. It provides a clear example of Herbert's practice of creating narrative demonstrations of theological issues. "Josephs Coat" illustrates Herbert's understanding of the Bible and his experimentation with form. "The Sacrifice" brings the traditional, biblical, and liturgical elements together with Herbert's characteristic dramatization of his theology. Ultimately, the students want to discuss the pattern poems, and, by the time we have examined in detail the four poems I selected for classroom analysis, they see that, though the pattern poems seem to be dominated by the ingenuity of contrived line length, they are much more. Herbert's concern with spiritual conflict and theological paradoxes is apparent here as well. As in the case of Donne, I ask the students to draw some generalizations, considering rhetorical figures, characterizations of the persona, narrative strategies, and the place of the reader, noting when the reader is addressed and when the reader is positioned as audience in a theatre, viewing a drama enacted between the Lord and the poet.

Richard Crashaw, Thomas Traherne, and Henry Vaughan occupy a smaller part of the course, though the process of analysis remains the same. After assigning many poems and discussing selected poems in class, I ask the students to consider what general statements can be made about each author. Those poets try the students' patience somewhat more than Donne or Herbert, since the students find them repetitious and less earthbound (conventionally mimetic texts carrying a positive literary value). Few anthologies, including the one I use, Mario A. Di Cesare's *George Herbert and the Seventeenth-Century Religious Poets*, reproduce the emblems with Crashaw's poems, and it is important that they be provided for "The Weeper" and "A Hymn to the Name and Honor of the Admirable Saint Teresa" so that those poems and others may be examined in the light of the concept of meditation and so that the role of the visual arts in religious contemplation may be considered. Both Vaughan and Traherne, as they reflect on the potential of the human spirit and the glorious rewards of heavenly visions, illustrate the extent to which fantasy, subjectivity, and a sense of spiritual release are poetic preoccupations of the metaphysical poets.

Finally, we turn to Andrew Marvell and the presentation of both secular and religious ideals. Though "To His Coy Mistress" is easily read by the now-experienced readers (the *Songs and Sonets* are still a lively background for class discussions), the students are perplexed by the seeming triviality of such poems as "On a Drop of Dew" and "The Nymph Complaining for the Death of Her Fawn." Many students, in fact, prefer Traherne's surging imagination to Marvell's hyperbole. Marvell's poems, however, suitably climax our study because they combine concerns present in the other poets—dramatic intensity, exaggeration, paradox, self-realization, and a quest for spiritual experience. The discussion of Marvell's work takes place in the context of the work of the other poets, developing the idea of a poetic school. At that point I ask the students to read some critical statements in which readers identify the group as metaphysical poets, a title now so well established that it makes a volume of this kind possible and understandable. The students read selected critical materials in the Norton Critical Edition of John Donne (ed. Clements), including commentaries by John Dryden, Samuel Johnson, T. S. Eliot, and Joseph Mazzeo. For a midterm essay I ask them to discuss the presence of Donne in the work of each of the five poets. I summarize the matters reported in their essays on a handout, and we spend a class session examining which elements unique to a poem or to a poet are ignored when we construct a set of stylistic norms.

From that point on the course focuses on the problems and the issues involved in defining literary schools and periods in literary history and the consequences of those issues for the understanding of literary history. The visual arts now enter our study, and my approach provides the opportunity to evaluate the relations between visual and literary arts in several ways: (1) to consider referential relations between specific poems and specific visual traditions or specific works of art, (2) to consider the interaction between visual and literary arts in emblem literature, and (3) to consider the possible analogies that can be made regarding the selection of subjects and features of common style. I described the pertinent elements of traditional Christian iconography while we studied individual poems, and now I add to that an examination of specific examples from emblem literature. So that we may discuss the possibilities of period style involving both literary and visual arts, I ask the students to read two slim volumes summarizing the major issues in sixteenth- and seventeenth-century art, the Cambridge Introduction to the History of Art, volumes 3 (Letts) and 4 (Mainstone and Mainstone). We spend several class periods not only examining the material in the texts but also considering the descriptive statements that art historians make in the discussion of artifacts. The students compare those statements about style in the visual arts with the statements about style that we have just made about the metaphysical poets—descriptions of single poems, generalizations about the work of a given poet, statements delineating a poetic movement or a school, and comments about the ideological context of the work. The students take quickly to that kind of critical-interpretative work, and, perhaps even more than in literary criticism, they see how the accumulation of critical statements enlivens their perceptions and understanding of a work. As an ancillary benefit, they learn conventional terminology and an awareness of significant artistic achievements of the past.

Each student is asked to select a visual "author" and to present a brief report to the class that focuses, as did our study of the poets, on significant features of that artist's style. Many students in their enthusiasm for the new subject matter have difficulty concerning themselves with the art itself because the material conditions of the visual arts are interesting in themselves. Class discussion now forms around the terms from art history—mannerism and baroque. I provide background information on the history of the terms and some examples from critical writings that consider baroque poetry. We examine the meanings of the terms as they are used in the Cambridge histories they have read. Our descriptions of the metaphysical poets now come into play. What can be made of such statements if they are applied to the visual arts? What can be made of the terms mannerism and baroque if they are applied to the poetry we have read? Though caution is important in responding to those questions, the study of the various art forms in the context of a historical period succeeds if it allows for the examination of issues that the reader does not encounter when the arts are seen in isolation. A particularly useful bibliography, "Recent Studies of Literature and Painting in the English Renaissance" by Clark Hulse, can be found in *English Literary Renaissance.*

The concluding section of the course takes up the study of period style from another literary angle—that of the theater. In the theater the visual dimension of the literary object is essential, but it cannot be fixed concretely, since each performance constitutes its own fleeting image. The theater shares with the visual arts a concern for space and place, and it shares with lyric poetry a concern for personality, emotion, and private experience. It extends narrative beyond the generic possibilities of both the visual arts and the lyric poem.

We begin with Shakespeare's *Hamlet* because students usually bring some knowledge of the play with them and because questions of the realization of the individual and the metaphor of the theater, central to seventeenth-century thinking, are in the foreground of the play. The comparison with Donne's work can easily be made, as Hamlet (like Donne's varied personae) is an uncertain interpreter of a fleeting and unstable world. Style alone is not the defining principle in either metaphysical poetry or mannerist art; thus, *Hamlet* promotes a discussion of how the themes and the issues that come to the fore at that historical moment extend beyond genre boundaries. Emotional disruption is found in Hamlet himself in the several poses he assumes—he resists stasis, his world is in a state of flux and he is not at home in it.

John Webster's *Duchess of Malfi* and John Ford's *'Tis Pity She's a Whore* are the final readings in the course and provide the students with a further sense of the concerns of the period beset by spiritual turmoil, when the desires of the heart were confounded by a world reflecting the rule of uncontrolled passions, madness, and violent death. The passive heroism of Hamlet, the Duchess, and Annabella stands against a grotesque, aggressive, and incoherent world. Order and understanding are sought in another world more real than this one. The power of desire in the confrontation is also found within the work of the metaphysical poets—in Donne's love affair with death, in Herbert's reclusive trust in his God, in Crashaw's paradoxical desire to transcend the body with the senses, in Vaughan's nostalgia for an innocence no longer available to him, and in Traherne's grasping for a mystical world more vivid and more pure than that of the here and now.

A course of this sort may need defense on sheer critical grounds, given the anxieties that currently surround the study of literary history. The limitations of the historical study of literature are well-known and need not be recited here, but the values of pursuing such a study with undergraduates far outweigh the dangers involved. Arguments that the individual text is obscured, even lost, in the development of generalizations are not validated in classroom practice. Our students, in fact, because they lack a sense of the forces shaping the history of Western culture, approach the work of the metaphysical poets with an open mind and labor to discern the poetic of the early seventeenth century from the evidence found in the texts. They are less likely than many of us behind the lectern to fall in line with impressionistic generalizations without reference to the texts that modify and limit such pronouncements. Yet the act of generalizing, of naming similarities, is a powerful intellectual tool that students are rarely called on to use in a curriculum that still emphasizes the close reading of texts in relative isolation from one another. In literature courses at my university the students are frequently asked to analyze themes and characters, even to compare two texts, but they are seldom encouraged to consider large aesthetic matters. Students are well aware that seventeenth-century texts are not in their idiom, but they are not well equipped to interpret and describe the distinguishing features of that era. That is where the study of literary history should begin.

Teaching in the School of Donne:
Metaphysical Poetry and English Composition

Steven Marx

What is the practical application of metaphysical wit? Can Donne, Herbert, and Marvell help students learn to write? Is there a place for seventeenth-century poetry in the composition curriculum? A number of years ago those questions would have been supererogatory. Teachers of college writing courses assigned essays on literary works of their own preference, assuming that exercise in critical analysis would eventually improve their students' reading, writing, and thinking skills. The metaphysical poets ranked high on the list of subjects for English composition because, in addition to affording aesthetic gratification, they provided unequaled opportunities to display mental gymnastics.

However, since the emergence of composition and rhetoric as an independent, fully articulated discipline, the metaphysical poets rarely make an appearance in the freshman-English classroom. In contrast to the classic essay, the modern short story, or even yesterday's newspaper editorial, abstruse lyric poetry doesn't seem to fit into the standard writing curriculum. I would suggest, however, at least one element of the curriculum, the subject of diction and style, is uniquely enriched by the study of metaphysical poetry. And I would further argue that an approach to literary interpretation through the rhetorical topics of diction and the use of the dictionary can lead students to original critical insights, specifically into the metaphysical poets and into other literature as well.

I came to that conclusion after designing materials for a program that integrates two first-year requirements at Stanford: a writing course and an introduction to literature, philosophy, and the arts in Western culture. Our approach to these familiar requirements is distinguished by an emphasis on mutually reinforcing objectives. To improve the quality of writing, we provide appropriate subject matter, and, to improve the quality of reading, we demand continual written responses. Classes and assignments are organized around those objectives. Students attend formal lectures about the Western culture on Monday, Tuesday, and Wednesday mornings. On Wednesday afternoons they divide into small groups to discuss the lectures and readings. On Thursday and Friday mornings they meet with their discussion group leaders for composition classes centered on assignments dealing with the week's Western culture text. In each assignment we stress a specific rhetorical topic—one that fits into an overall sequence of skill development and that correlates with a feature of the week's reading. For example, students focus on the topic of invention by comparing and contrasting Hebrew and Greek versions of creation; they model personal essays on

Augustine's *Confessions*; they uncover hidden assumptions and rationalizations in the process of writing appeals of Dante's last judgments.

According to the sequence prescribed by standard rhetoric curricula, after students become familiar with the large-scale elements of English composition—thesis, paragraph construction, and essay organization—they review sentence structure, grammar, and punctuation. Then, before tackling the analysis of persuasive language and the production of a research paper, they examine the microlevel of linguistic organization—diction and style. The purpose of such study is to purge prolixity and vagueness and to teach concision. Under diction and style, we classify the topics of semantics, figurative language, the interplay between sound and sense, denotation and connotation, etymology, and the use of the dictionary.

Through a happy coincidence, our composition course reaches those topics at the same time that the Western culture survey arrives at the seventeenth century. The week's lectures treat aspects of baroque style. One lecture analyzes a Bach cantata, another compares Rembrandt and Bernini, the third contrasts the plain style of Ben Jonson's poetry with the aureate mannerism of John Donne. Discussion groups synthesize the three lectures, relating forms of emotional expression to Renaissance, Reformation, and Counter-Reformation attitudes. We consider style itself as a function of changing social fashion and as a means of expressing personal identity through the display of posture and ornament. The class analyzes individual poems—Donne's "Canonization" and "Batter my heart, three-person'd God" and Herbert's "Paradise"—primarily with reference to stylistic effects produced by diction: puns, conceits, tone shifts, imagery, sound effects, hieroglyphic devices.

The following day's composition class draws student writing into the discussion of metaphysical diction and style. We choose examples from the poetry for several practical applications:

1. The examples demonstrate that selecting the right word conveys precise denotative and appropriate connotative meanings. I contrast examples of inexact or vague diction from student papers with Donne's use of *litigious* in the phrase "Lawyers find out still / Litigious men" ("The Canonization," lines 17–18) to illustrate the power of the *mot juste*. After searching for synonyms, the students realize that the only denotative alternative would be some awkward circumlocution lacking the wrangling and niggling connotations evoked by the sound of *litigious*.

2. The poetry examples differentiate the virtues from the vices of ambiguity. To elucidate the richness of a line like "Contemplate, what you will, approve" ("The Canonization," 8), I ask the students to delineate its multiple meanings with unambiguous paraphrases.

3. The examples supply models of writing with stylistic flair. After the

students analyze some devices of metaphysical wit, they are willing to play and experiment in their own prose. Having been drilled in the virtues of the plain style throughout their writing course, they are encouraged to use puns (if only in their titles), figurative language, and analogies.

4. The examples occasion the creative use of the dictionary. To achieve even surface comprehension of metaphysical poetry, the students must look up unfamiliar words and usages. That activity can become a rewarding exploration, rather than an onerous routine.

I introduce these applications of the metaphysical poets to English composition with a one-page handout. At its center is a reproduction of the title and final stanza of "The Canonization":

> And thus invoke us: You whom reverend love
> Made one anothers hermitage;
> You, to whom love was peace, that now is rage;
> Who did the whole world's soule contract, and drove
> Into the glasses of your eyes
> (So made such mirrors, and such spies,
> That they did all to you epitomize,)
> Countries, Townes, Courts: Beg from above
> A patterne of your love!   (37–45)

Surrounding it like a scriptural commentary are three columns of minuscule print photocopied from the *Oxford English Dictionary's* entries for *pattern* and *patron*. I circle the word *patterne* in the last line of the poem with a dark handwritten loop from which ten arrows extend in different directions, targeting specific locations in the nest of gloss. The arrow that leads to the upper left part of the page points to the etymology of *pattern*:

> [ME. *patron*, a., F. *patron*, which still means both "patron" and "pattern." In 16th c., *pa*tron*, with shifted accent, evidently began to be pronounced (pa*t′rn) as in *apron* and spelt *patarne, paterne, pattern*. By 1700 the original form ceased to be used of things, and *patron* and *pattern* became differentiated in form and sense.]

The arrow leading to the upper right part of the page points to the etymology of *patron*. The remaining arrows lead to distinct definitions of both *pattern* and *patron* relevant to a reading of the poem. At the bottom of the handout appears the instruction, "See also entries for *canonization, canon, mystery, phoenix, epitomize, glasse*." At the top appear the course title, the paper topic, the number of words required, and the date due.

When the students first see the handout, with its multiple typefaces, its mysterious abbreviations, and its strange spellings, they are as bewildered by it as by a recondite Donnean conceit. Deciphering its dense code of information serves as a vehicle for discussion and an in-class start on a writing assignment; it works as an introduction to the *OED* and as an explication of part of a poem; and it initiates students into the methods and the rewards of literary scholarship.

After explaining the connection between *patterne*'s seventeenth-century double meaning and the Neoplatonic and feudal backgrounds of the poem, I ask the students to discover how the listed variant meanings affect the denotation and the connotations of the concluding line. If everything goes according to plan, they end up marveling at the way each referent—founder of a religious order, protector, advocate, guardian saint, exemplar, paradigm, and specimen—amplifies the speaker's compliment and alludes to a previous image in the poem. The next day the class meets in the reference section of the library. The students bring several key words to look up from the poems they have chosen to write about. Working in pairs and consulting with me or a librarian for help, they carry out their detective work in the *OED* and in slang dictionaries, reporting their findings to the whole class at the end of the hour. Though their papers need not center on lexical research, the requirement that students include at least three citations from a dictionary virtually eliminates the problem of plagiarism while encouraging the experience of original scholarly discovery. One sort of discovery concerns the iconographical allusions of key words, as in this paper about Herbert's "Easter-Wings":

> As the second section begins, the narrator prays for his soul to "rise as larks" in harmony with God. The lark image is symbolic of man's soul, for *lark* is defined in the *OED* as "with allusion to the lark's habits; e.g. early song and the height it attains in contrast with the low position of its nest." The soul, like the lark, has a low nest—earth, and the ability to fly much higher than its nest into heaven. Also, in the next line, the narrator wishes to become one with Christ and to sing praises as the lark sings.

The *OED*'s terse enumeration of the word's connotative reference sheds light on the poem and allows the student credit for a primary find. Further dictionary research leads to a deeper discovery:

> The last five-line section is another plea to Christ. The narrator desires to become one with Him by "imp[ing] my wing on thine." *Imp* is defined in the *OED* as "to engraft feathers in the wing of a bird so as to make good losses or deficiencies and thus restore or improve the

powers of flight." Accordingly, the narrator attempts to improve his powers of flight by having his wings incorporated by Christ's. . . . Herbert carries the imping method one step further by actually grafting key words and phrases from one set of wings to the other. Examples are *victories* and *the flight in me*. It is as if he were imping the first pair of wings onto the second in order to create unity between the two.   (Kelly Kodama)

Finding the meaning of an obscure word has not only explicated an image but revealed a distinctive feature of metaphysical style—the imitative form, which displays the correspondence between signifier and signfied. The structure of the poem, both verbal and visual, embodies its central action of "imping." Metaphor metamorphoses first into icon and then into concept. Herbert's trick inspires the student, who imps his own figure of speech— grafting key words—on the poet's.

Attention to connotation can also unearth a poem's patterns of organization. Here a student outlines the arrangement of contraries created by connotative diction in Donne's "The Flea":

A tension between greatness and littleness prevails throughout the poem. The title itself, "The Flea," has an alternative explicit meaning of "a type of anything small or contemptible" (*OED* 4: 305). Mingling three bloods (Donne's, his mistress', and the flea's), the tiny flea "swells" or tends "to magnify . . . exalt" their love (*OED* 10: 317). Despite its greatness as the embodiment of their love, this blood can be belittled for its "innocence," its "harmlessness, innocuousness" (*OED* 5: 312). Finally the "drop," as "the smallest quantity of liquid that falls or detaches itself," (*OED* 3: 678) indicates minuteness. Yet it is this minute drop of blood that Donne aggrandizes as his marriage with his mistress. The contrast between great and small . . . gives rise to the underlying strain of tension throughout the poem; though Donne is constantly playful, he is at the same time unrelenting in his determination to gain dominance over his lover.

Her investigation of Donne's microscopic subtlety inspires the student to compose with analogous precision. Using few words, she elaborates a complex design, adduces examples, and incorporates citations in antithetically balanced sentences that mirror the paradoxes of her model. Her own exercise in diction and style concludes with a fittingly mannered arabesque:

Thus, Donne adheres strictly to the unconventional conventions of the metaphysical poets in "The Flea." Through style, he maintains the

> metaphysical conceit, comparing his love with a flea. Through paradox, he shocks with the novelty of his comparison. Through diction, he juxtaposes sex and religion. Through structure, he frames his carpe diem appeal with a battle between her honor and his hankering. Throughout, he trifles, exhorts, besieges and assails, determined to conquer.   (Elaine Lu)

Having completed that unit on diction and style, I pass from the four applications mentioned earlier to subsequent topics in English composition that also dovetail with metaphysical poetry. Newly heightened awareness of the emotional effects of verbal connotation prepares the students to analyze and practice persuasive rhetoric. The seduction poems of Donne, Marvell, and Carew supply skilled examples of the use and the abuse of wit to manipulate a reader. Juxtaposing those examples with modern seductive advertisements makes for a provocative inquiry into the language of exploitation. And the metaphysical poets are excellent subjects for projects in library research, to which the students have been introduced through their etymological investigations.

In addition to preparing the ground for subsequent lessons in composition, the exercise has yielded fruit in unexpected contexts:

> The first paragraph of *Great Expectations* is devoted solely to introducing the story's narrator and principal character, Pip. As Pip states his full name, Phillip Pirrip, and traces his family background, we become aware that he is trying to establish an identity for himself. Pip's sense of his own insignificance is marked by one meaning of the word *pip*, "a spot or a speck." (*OED* 7: 892) Pip's attempt to find his place in the world is much like a young bird's first attempt at flight. Just as a young bird is hesitant to fly until he is sure of his surroundings, Pip fears entering the world without a sure knowledge of who he is. This bird imagery is reflected in Pip's name. Not only does Pirrip sound like the chirp of a small bird, but "Pip" means "to chirp as a young bird" (*OED* 7: 893) and Philip is "a name formerly given to a sparrow" (*OED* 7: 775).   (Gretchen Rodkey)

Dense textual analysis, rich critical insight, concise yet elegant style—that is what one hopes for toward the end of the freshman year. Getting it suggests to me that students learn something from analyzing metaphysical diction that they can put to use long after their requirements have been fulfilled.

Teaching the Metaphysical Poets in a Two-Year College

Mark Reynolds

Teaching poetry in a two-year college challenges most instructors because the students often come with little experience or interest in reading literature. With only a few exceptions, they take a British literature survey course because their majors require it. Most have never been poetry readers, making metaphysical poetry with its inherent difficulties—elaborate conceits, syntactic complexities, intellectualism—even more challenging to teach.

To meet the challenge in survey courses, I ask each student to keep a reader's journal, a spiral notebook in which the student responds in writing to course readings. With all authors, the metaphysical poets especially, I use a variety of brief poem-specific prereading, reading, and postreading written exercises to force an encounter between the student and the text in the informal and private arena of the reader's journal. Varying from poem to poem and author to author, many exercises elicit specific responses to a particular poem; other exercises are general and work with any poem. The students contribute to class discussions what they discover about a poem from the exercises, or they develop some journal writings into more formal short papers. What follows is a description of the journal exercises and other activities that have proved successful with the metaphysical poets.

For each author studied in the survey course, I begin by having a student give a brief oral biographical report to the class. Letting the students relate what they find interesting about an author's life allows me to see how best to introduce the writer or where to place an emphasis so that they will want to read the works. Our text is the first volume of *The Norton Anthology of English Literature* (gen. ed. Abrams), and our study of the metaphysical poets begins with John Donne. The biographical report on Donne invariably emphasizes the dual nature of the poet's life: early rogue and composer of love poetry, later devout preacher and writer of religious poetry. Sometimes as a lead-in to Donne, I ask the students to locate both a love poem and a religious poem that they like by other authors and bring copies to class. Their examples range from "Roses Are Red" to Rod McKuen and the Twenty-Third Psalm to Helen Steiner Rice. After the students share their poems in class, we determine the characteristics of love poetry and of religious poetry. Once we have read and discussed Donne's poetry, I ask the students to compare and contrast in their journals the poems they had brought to class with two poems of Donne's. Nothing helps them see the complexity of Donne's thought and syntax better.

For individual Donne poems I use a number of specific journal writing exercises. "Song" ("Go and catch a falling star") is an excellent poem for students to model in its entirety in their journals. Imitating a poem forces students to study it carefully. For modeling, I pick poems the students find least difficult, and I do not expect too much. Rather than have them share their models with the whole class, I find it less threatening to group them and let them discuss their efforts with only a few other students. Group discussions often lead to fruitful and serious considerations of the original poem that surface in the subsequent general class discussion. For another activity with "Song" I tell the students to list in their journals seven impossibilities and use them as Donne does to suggest a truism about the opposite sex. They usually want to share those efforts with the entire class. Sometimes I have them counter Donne's argument that "No where / Lives a woman true, and fair" (lines 17–18). Another time I have the students write a brief prose summary of "Song."

"The Indifferent" is another poem the students can model, especially the first stanza. Here again, I ask the students to write a counter to Donne's argument against fidelity or suggest a curse (Hera's perhaps) on unfaithful lovers. Before discussing a poem in class, I sometimes assign a stanza each to particular students, asking the students to become experts on their stanzas. The students must look up all unfamiliar words, write line-by-line prose summaries in their journals, and relate their stanzas to those that precede and follow. The exercise works well with both "The Indifferent" and "The Canonization."

An excellent poem for students to imitate is "The Flea." I have had some ingenious models using mosquitoes, horseflies, snakes, hornets, and even poison ivy ("Mark but this vine . . . / Me it rubbed first, and now rubs thee / And on this leaf, our two skins mingled be"). I sometimes have the students write prose paraphrases of "The Flea," discuss their paraphrases and the poem's meaning in groups, and then report to the class—all before I say anything about the poem. Because many of Donne's poems are dramatic, a student can write a scenario for a particular poem or produce a dialogue based on the poem. Both activities work well with "The Flea," particularly dialoguing, in which both the speaker and his mistress can be assigned lines. Some students even suggest lines for the flea.

I also assign scenarios and dialogues for "A Valediction: Forbidding Mourning." For a prereading journal exercise, I sometimes bring to class a mathematical compass and ask the students to observe it closely and list in their journals all its characteristics. Then I tell them that Donne wrote a love poem to his wife using the compass image, and I ask them to speculate in their journals on what he may have said. At the next class meeting we discuss first their journal writings. Afterward, I read the poem aloud, and together we explicate it. Their writings inevitably aid their understanding of the poem. Most effective with the poem is drawing a circle with a compass during the class and relating the poem to the activity. As a postreading exercise, I often have the students write brief commentaries on the effectiveness of Donne's conceit or compare their prereading journal exercises with Donne's poem.

For any of the *Holy Sonnets* the students write prose summaries or summarize the arguments of the sonnets assigned. Sometimes I group students and assign each group a sonnet to explicate and then explain to the rest of the class. As a prereading journal exercise for "Death be not proud," I may ask the students to list everything they can think of that imitates the state of death or to express briefly their views of death. When we discuss the sonnet in class, they can usually relate ideas from their journals to the discussion. For a postreading journal exercise, the students compare Donne's views of death with their own.

As a preliminary to "Batter my heart," I have the students look up the word *paradox* in a dictionary and define it fully in their own words. Then I have them read the sonnet and list and explain in their journals all the paradoxes in the poem. The poem often proves difficult for students, so it is helpful for them to define unfamiliar terms in the poem, such as *usurped, viceroy, fain, enthrall*. Even after the class discussion, I have the students write short prose synopses in their journals, then compare them in groups to be sure the poem is clear.

After a brief look at Donne's religious poems, we move on to George Herbert. An easy way into Herbert's poetry is through his shaped verse. That a poem's shape can reflect its subject matter and meaning intrigues students. As an introduction to Herbert's shaped verse, I often use the section on shaped verse in *The Heath Guide to Poetry* (Bergman and Epstein), which contains some excellent examples. As a journal exercise for "The Altar" and "Easter-Wings," I ask the students to explain how each poem's shape affects its content and meaning, and we discuss their analyses in class. I often have them suggest other possibilities for shaped verse, secular or religious. Sometimes I have them try producing a shaped poem. Crosses are common, but stars, stables, and fish are all possible shapes for religious poems; secular examples include tennis rackets, skateboards, and guns. Their efforts give the students more appreciation for Herbert's shaped verse.

Students also respond well to "Prayer" (1) when asked to write out and explain all the comparisons Herbert uses for prayer. With "The Pulley," I have them draw a pulley and try labeling it to suggest the poem's meaning or draw a rough pictograph to illustrate the meaning. Usually I have the students write postreading journal commentaries on their responses to Herbert's conceit. A good prereading exercise for "The Flower" is for students to list all the similarities between a flower and a human being. They often discover some of the same parallels Herbert uses in his poem.

I usually have time for only one of Crashaw's poems, "On Our Crucified

Lord, Naked and Bloody." I ask the students to explain in their journals with line-by-line prose paraphrases what Crashaw is saying in the poem. Then I have them list all the connotations they have for the phrase *purple wardrobe*. I let them discuss in groups what they have written. They generally work out the conceit without difficulty. In a subsequent class discussion, I can say enough about Crashaw's style and subject matter for a survey course.

If time does permit, I seek some volunteers with access to church hymnals and have them search for references to Christ's wounds in hymn lyrics. They report their findings to the class and relate them to Crashaw's poem. Sometimes I give the class copies of "Rock of Ages" and have the students relate its lyrics to Crashaw's poem. The connections between hymns and metaphysical poetry are also fruitful areas for formal papers, as are the connections between the devotionals, meditations, and sermons produced throughout the period. Although substantial work in those areas is beyond the scope of many two-year college students, some students can research seventeenth-century English religious literature and write short papers relating it to metaphysical poetry.

With Henry Vaughan, I normally assign "The Retreat." I introduce the students to the idea of childhood innocence as a means of spiritual insight and to the idea of preexistence, hoping they will recall the exposure later, when they study William Blake's *Songs of Innocence and of Experience* and William Wordsworth's "Ode: Intimations of Immortality." As a prereading journal exercise, I have the students list all the good qualities they associate with childhood or speculate on the notion of growing younger toward death, instead of older. I also extract certain phrases from the poem and ask students to respond to them in free association fashion in their journals: "angel infancy," "a white, celestial thought," "first love," "black art," "th'enlightened spirit," "a forward motion." After the students read the poem, they can explain or define those phrases in the context of the poem. As another postreading activity, I ask the students to argue for or against Vaughan's "retreat."

For Marvell, I assign "To His Coy Mistress," along with several activities. Because I want the students to understand the carpe diem theme, as a prereading exercise I have them comment on the "Grab for all the gusto you can get" philosophy and, after reading the poem, relate it to the carpe diem theme. If earlier in the course the students have read Christopher Marlowe's "Passionate Shepherd" and Robert Herrick's "To the Virgins," I assign a postreading exercise to compare and contrast the three poems. In another good postreading exercise, the students write a reply (not necessarily poetic—the best have been Dear John letters) for Marvell's mistress. I often have students write prose summaries of the argument because the poem's "Had I [if] . . . But . . . therefore . . ." pattern illustrates well the structure of argument, and it is good for students to see the pattern work poetically. Because the poem contains many vivid images, I also ask the students to illustrate it. Those who claim no artistic ability I ask to describe how the poem should be illustrated or to use pictures from magazines. One or two have used pictures cut from magazines to make collages that demonstrated well their comprehension of Marvell's poem.

Those short written exercises in journals and the related activities have helped motivate students to read poetry closely. As a result, class discussions have been lively and thoughtful. Most important, the activities have helped make even the difficult poetry of the metaphysical poets accessible and appealing to students who are neither literature majors nor sophisticated readers.

Poetic Affinities:
Metaphysical and Modern Poets

Bridget Gellert Lyons

I recently devised a course for senior honors majors in English that paired major poets of the seventeenth century with twentieth-century poets. The emphasis was more on the seventeenth-century poets, but my assumption was that a selective use of modern works for comparison and contrast would help make the older poetry more available to students who (at least at my university) find modern literature more interesting and challenging than anything early. I tried to focus on poetic concerns common to both groups: their attitudes toward inherited traditions and forms and the tensions in writers between the expression of personal, authentic feeling and the need to write for a public audience (a tension felt even by those earlier poets circulating their poems in manuscript). At the same time, the poetic pairings involved contrasts, because all literary subjects—the specific forms that religious and philosophical issues took, for example—were governed by particular historical circumstances. The course was organized around four pairs of poets: Donne and Eliot, Jonson and Yeats, Herbert and Frost, and Marvell and Stevens. I concentrate here on the two pairings treated most extensively in the class: Donne and Eliot, Herbert and Frost.

The first and most obvious pairing, Donne and Eliot, set itself up because of Eliot's admiring comments on Donne. Both poets were philosophical, learned, and difficult; both depended on a literary tradition that they thought to be exhausted in many respects; both felt strong attractions to drama. In the class we began by reading and discussing Eliot's 1921 essay on the metaphysical poets, in which he defined the "dissociation of sensibility" that set in after Donne's time and praised Donne's poetry for its fusion of thought and feeling. It became clear to the class that, when a writer expressed such strong preferences and dislikes about earlier poets, he was defining his own poetic ambitions and problems as well. For Eliot, as the essay shows, the poetry of his own time needed to be written partly in response to what he felt were the false elevations of Victorian poetic language and to express accurately the fragmentation and the alienation of modern consciousness.

After the essay had provided us with useful terms for Eliot's attitudes, we went on to consider some of his poems in detail, especially "Preludes," "Rhapsody on a Windy Night," and "The Love Song of J. Alfred Prufrock." We discussed the poems' relations to the essay in their assimilation of disparate experiences and their avoidance of traditional poetic situations. ("Preludes" with its evocation of bad smells and dirty feet and its conscious image making was a useful beginning.) In our two classes on "Prufrock" I raised issues that would be relevant to our later discussion of Donne: What is our sense of the speaker's personality? How is he characterized by diverse cultural associations and his attitude toward them? What is the relationship (if any) between the speaker and the beloved? In what sense is it a love song?

When we turned to Donne's poems, I first proposed that he, too, was a poetic innovator in his time, one who felt that poetic language needed to be revitalized and who was both praised by contemporaries for his originality and blamed for his obscurity. "The Good-Morrow" and "The Sun Rising," with their dramatic sense of time and place and their real—as opposed to poetical—speech, were good openers. (Before discussing those poems, I asked the students to define their preconceptions of what a love poem should include; the answers suggested a romantic atmosphere created by elevated diction, and compliments to the beloved. The students were made to understand, by means of selected Elizabethan sonnets, that many of Donne's contemporaries felt the same way.) Other poems—"The Apparition," "The Flea," "The Bait," "The Relic"—offered good examples of Donne's wit in reanimating earlier models, his immediacy, and his capacity to shock.

After my students' attention was caught by the vividness and energy of Donne's poetic situations and language, I introduced two related topics that had been important in our consideration of Eliot: the presentation of a dramatic self in the poems and their learnedness or difficulty. We had discussed whether Eliot's weary and erudite speakers in "Prufrock," "Gerontion," and "La Figlia che Piange" were differentiated from each other or were all the same character; the same question proved fruitful in discussing Donne's assertive voices in "The Canonization," "The Sun Rising," and the religious sonnet "Batter my heart." The comparison of Donne's speakers with Eliot's characteristic voice was especially useful when we talked about the gloomier of the *Songs and Sonnets*, such as "Twickenham Garden" and "A Nocturnal upon St. Lucy's Day." I have always had trouble teaching those poems to undergraduates because so much class work has to go into explicating the allusions. The comparative method enabled us to focus more easily on the dramatic and self-expressive energies of the poems: To what extent did Donne and Eliot have occasions for their feelings? Did their moods change within particular poems? If so, why? To what extent were women represented as the cause or the scapegoats for the speakers' melancholy? Eliot, whose speakers' exhaustion and pessimism are related to their sense of the futility of image making, provided points of contrast with the way Donne tried to give new life to stock poetic subjects through his learned conceits. We discussed the metaphysical imagery in the two most famous valediction poems ("A Valediction: Of Weeping" and "A Valediction: Forbidding Mourning"), "The Good-Morrow," and several other poems. I asked the students whether and how Donne's range of references and his extended elaborations gave precision and energy to such worn subjects as "I can't live without you" and "I wasn't alive till I met you."

Only after close readings of several Donne poems did we consider larger issues: the placement of Donne and Eliot within their cultural situations and literary histories. Eliot was seen as a self-consciously late poet, burdened (as he shows in numerous passages) with the difficulties of writing, one who found the writers of the past less a source of energy than a sign of the cultural disadvantages of the present. For Donne, the past provided sources of imagery and disputation—scientific, theological, philosophical—that were useful to him rhetorically, whether or not he was committed to them intellectually.

The students had to write a long comparative paper at the end of the unit, so I encouraged them to focus on large issues in specific texts. One suggested topic was Donne's first "Anniversary" poem as an expression of cultural malaise, with selected sections of "The Waste Land" and "Prufrock" as contrast. Another suggested topic was a comparison of Eliot and Donne as dramatic poets, focusing on the Eliot monologue "Portrait of a Lady" and on specific details of tone and context in at least one of the *Songs and Sonnets*. One topic concerned the two writers as religious poets. The students read Eliot's essay on Lancelot Andrewes, which explained his preference for Andrewes over Donne as a sermon writer, for a comparison of Eliot's "Journey of the Magi" with one or two of Donne's religious poems. Those challenging assignments were productive because they grew out of class discussions.

The course's second major pairing, Herbert and Frost, allowed us to consider two poetic sensibilities radically different from Eliot's and Donne's: not consciously difficult but direct and ostensibly simple. Because both Herbert and Frost favored short lyric forms, manageable in their entirety in class discussions, and because they show even closer affinities of poetic temperament and practice than did our first pair, I used a larger number of Frost's poems to compare directly with Herbert's.

My first concern was to make the students appreciate that simple does not mean naive or simpleminded, that colloquial everyday diction can express profound thoughts and feelings—in short, that a great deal is going on in the poems. I began by showing that both poets were dramatic, even in their most lyrical and private moments: creating voices (or contrasting voices within poems) with artfulness. I first asked the students to discuss Frost's remarks from one of his prefaces:

> Everything written is as good as it is dramatic. It need not declare itself in form, but it is drama or nothing. . . . Sentences are not different enough to hold the attention unless they are dramatic. No ingenuity of varying structure will do. All that can save them is the speaking tone of voice somehow entangled in the words and fastened to the page for the ear of the imagination.   (Cox and Lathem 13)

The easiest way to elaborate and apply Frost's point was to begin with poems with contrasting voices, poems in which the poet uses dialogue to differentiate between two characters or to show a relationship between them. "Home Burial" is a particularly available example, with its highly charged dialogue between husband and wife, but there are many other examples, including "Mending Wall," in which the poet's "I" engages in conversation with a respondent. For Herbert, explicit dialogue was equally important, the poet's interlocutor more often being God or an unidentified "One" who speaks for him. The students considered such famous examples as "Love" (3), "Dialogue," and "The Collar," discussing the contrasts between the voices within a poem and Herbert's capacity to create tension between a resistant speaker and his interlocutor.

After that introduction it was easier for the students to respond to the subdued dramatic qualities of poems written for a single voice, poems in which the drama was one of discovery: Herbert's "Virtue," "Hope," "Life," and "The Flower" and Frost's "Desert Places" and "The Need of Being Versed in Country Things" were among several possible examples. It was important to make the students aware that the speaker in Herbert's poems, even in those that are not overtly dialogues, is a persona, sometimes a limited and fallible one, rather than the poet instructing his readers. Because Herbert's poems were religious and remote in time, that notion was not as obvious to students as it was in Frost's poems. Herbert's "Thanksgiving" was a useful example because its speaker, with his false crescendos and overconfident intentions both to lead a good life and to write good verse, is treated with pointed irony.

Once the class had got used to talking about both Frost's and Herbert's lyric poems as representations of interior dramas of discovery, rather than as lessons for the reader, the students found it easier to respond to the simple, colloquial diction that both poets favored. Such diction could be as resonant with meaning as the more difficult, obscure, and allusive language in our earlier pairing. We read several of Herbert's poems that discuss language explicitly (the "Jordan" poems, "The Forerunners," "A True Hymne"), showing in his ambivalence about the ornate phrases he decries that the issue of language is a moral one for him. The problem of the sophisticated religious poet, for whom submission and self-effacement are moral imperatives at odds with the self-display inherent in poetic virtuosity, is worth discussing because it was articulated also by some of Herbert's contemporaries and successors (Donne, Marvell) and because in its secular form it is implicit in such poems as Frost's "Mowing" and "They Were Welcome to Their Belief."

I waited until late in the unit to discuss poetic form directly, even though Herbert and Frost are both poets for whom that is an important consideration. Students generally seem to be too ready to learn prosodic and stanzaic definitions as ends in themselves, rather than listening to voice, tone, and movement, as we tried to do earlier on. Since both Herbert and Frost typically expressed themselves in a variety of tight poetic forms—see Frost's comment that writing free verse is like playing tennis without a net (Wintle and Kenin 308)—they offered good opportunities for discussions of the formal aspects of verse. Herbert's intricate stanzas and the illusion he wished to create that he was struggling to achieve prosodic regularity and rhyme within a poem were not formal issues only (I left the question open in a few poems, like the shaped ones, that have never worked for me); he aimed to reflect in verse his speaker's spiritual struggles and resolutions.

As I wanted the students to perceive formal devices in relation to their expressive values, the two poets provided affinities and contrasts of tempera- ment. In both, tightly constructed forms were allied to ambivalence about freedom (travel, "ranging"), as opposed to the security but the potential confinement of home—a universal conflict. Any number of Frost poems could be chosen to illustrate his complicated juxtapositions of indoor with outdoor, wide spaces with small and well-defined areas ("An Old Man's Winter Night," "Stopping by Woods on a Snowy Evening," "The Lockless Door," "Desert Places," "Come In"). Herbert's formal arrangements were often designed to reflect a world infused with divinity, but, while he tended to be on the side of humility and formal restriction, he, too, was ambivalent about the loose freedom of large spaces and the confinement of small ones; "The Temper," "The Size," "The Collar," "Content," "Affliction" (1), or even the speaker's resistance to the invitation to enter in "Love" (3) are examples.

Comparative paper topics for the unit were based not only on the subjects described above (such as the use of dialogue by the two poets) but also on contrasting responses to nature; different strategies with poetic forms, such as the sonnet (a form both poets used in innovative ways: Herbert's "Prayer" (1), "Joseph's Coat," and "Redemption"; Frost's "Design," "Putting in the Seed," "The Oven Bird"); and comparisons of poetic voices. I got good responses to one of the suggested topics on voice: the representation of childhood by each poet and the moral and stylistic values that concept had for each.

While my course centered on the two pairings described above, we touched on others as well. Jonson and Yeats—poets who assumed public voices to praise and blame; whose interest in the past was ethical, rather than religious or philosophical; and who shared some ambivalence about the idea of aristocracy—provided another interesting comparison. Marvell and Wallace Stevens suggested themselves as witty, philosophical poets con- cerned with the mind's relation to reality and with the imaginative possi- bilities and limits of poetry. Both poets played with spatial and mental perspectives (with conflations of inner mental states and outer landscapes and, correspondingly, of literal and figurative language), and some of my best students were challenged and intrigued by the comparison between Marvell's pastoral and architectural poems and the even more radical self-consciousness of Stevens's "Anecdote of the Jar" and "Six Significant Landscapes," among many other possibilities. For a change of pace from extended contrasts of poetic figures, I introduced in one or two classes some modern poets often labeled metaphysical, such as William Empson and Allen Tate, so that the students could discuss what they had in common with the earlier poetry.

Whatever its precise focus, the comparative format had the virtue of heightening the students' awareness of literary history and locating some issues of style and self-presentation common to the two periods. The focus on comparisons produced better writing than did close readings of poems I had assigned in other courses; the students were more attentive to the texts and better able to relate details to general statements when they concentrated on similarities and differences than when they used close readings. Finally, the students seemed to like the comparisons course, as their evaluations at the end showed.

APPROACHES TO SPECIFIC POETS

Teaching Donne through Performance

Nicholas Jones

A novice reader of Donne faces many blocks in reading a newly encountered poem: distant historical and social contexts, unfamiliar literary conventions, and severe perplexities of language. I am concerned here not with mastering context and convention but with helping the student get a grasp on Donne's wonderful and idiosyncratic language. To do so, I borrow a method used widely by teachers of Shakespeare: classroom performance. By performing Donne's poems, with or without extensive preparation, a student can learn to overcome the initial difficulties of syntax, meter, and semantics; can explore their rich poetic structure, discovering possibilities for otherwise-ignored turns of phrase and changes of tone; and can present to the class a finished reading that vividly plants the words of the poem in the ears and the minds of all in the class.

Some of us may have less than pleasant memories of classroom performance methods in our ninth-grade encounters with Shakespeare: having sat through twenty-six reluctant renditions of "The quality of mercy is not strained" is not likely to encourage us to use class recitation as a teaching method. In recent years, however, in college and high school, close performance-oriented studies of Shakespeare have gained widespread interest and validity. In large part, that interest is due to the combination of the text-as-script emphasis in Shakespeare studies, particularly in the work of

John Russell Brown and J. L. Styan, and the concurrent influence of the Royal Shakespeare Company on Shakespeare pedagogy. Royal Shakespeare actors have regularly trained and rehearsed with close attention to the nuances of rhetoric, figure, and versification, treating them as cues for attitude, position, movement, and voice treatment. Although the Royal Shakespeare techniques are ultimately geared toward the production and the understanding of full-length plays, the actors often work extensively with lyric poems, especially with Shakespeare's sonnets. Through visits to college campuses and a widely marketed series of videotapes, the Royal Shakespeare method and its derivatives have become part of many Shakespeare classes.

Donne's lyrics have even more dramatic elements than Shakespeare's sonnets, giving the performer strong—if ambiguous—implications for characterized voice, action, interchange, and situation; as Heather Dubrow points out, the sonnets of Shakespeare do not meet those criteria. With the obvious literary differences between the metaphysical lyric and the Elizabethan theater and the equally obvious structural and functional differences between the academic classroom and the repertory theater company, I am far from claiming performance as the only or even the main activity of a section on Donne. But I believe that, within reasonable limits, performance is an appropriate and effective introduction to Donne.

One of the first blocks to understanding a Donne lyric is the strong line— mystifying texture, ragged diction, strange syntax, and emphatic meter. In introducing a Donne lyric, I assume that the students have done some preparatory work on the poems outside class, but I find that, in fact, the language is so strange that their out-of-class work doesn't bear much fruit. Reading "Love's Growth," for example, many students lack the patience and the skill to sort out on their own the syntax of the first stanza:

> I scarce believe my love to be so pure
>   As I had thought it was,
>   Because it doth endure
> Vicissitude, and season, as the grass;
> Methinks I lied all winter, when I swore
> My love was infinite, if spring make it more.

It is tempting and wrong to read line 3 alone, as if it meant that love simply endures. The temptation to focus on separable phrases like "it doth endure" gives a feeling of easy conquest, leading the student to ignore any element, even the essential context of syntax, that may lead to a richer and more complex reading. In this case, we must read "Vicissitude" and "season" as compound direct objects of the verb "endure," forcing us to find another meaning for the verb.

An unrehearsed in-class performance of the stanza brings to the surface the basic problems of reading the poems. Teacher and students can hear immediately whether the performer understands the syntax. If the reader handles the syntax well, other students have benefited from hearing a decent reading from one of their peers. If the reading works, I ask the rest of the class to imitate or modify the reading, to get the texture deeper into their bones. If the reader bungles it, we stop and analyze the problem; a second, more successful reading usually follows quite soon.

The first in-class performance can do more than patch up misreadings. Some students, with prompting and encouragement, are ready to develop the subtle clues of verse and tone; if so, I use performance to begin a group analysis of the rhetoric and the technique. If I have a reader who can handle the syntax of a whole stanza, I ask the class to listen to the reading with their books shut; then we probe for what they remember of the stanza: What are the most powerful words in the stanza? What does the reading stress or clarify? Introductory students can almost always recognize alliteration, but with eyes alone they may miss the alliteration in line 4: *c* does not look like *s* or *ss*. However, with voice and ears, they can't miss it. A simple beginning, to be sure; but the advantage for a teacher of Donne's complex lyrics is that the students learn to move from familiarity to strangeness, incorporating into their knowledge of the poem more and more of the intricacy of language. So, in a performance and discussion of the above stanza from "Love's Growth," the polysyllable "vicissitude," likely in a preclass reading to be passed over or only glossed (replaced, perhaps, by the footnote equivalent "change") suddenly leaps to attention, highlighted by the line break just before it, the syntactic ambiguity we've discussed earlier, and the surrounding syllabic context—practically monosyllabic for two lines, disyllabically inclined in line 3, peaking at four syllables, and quickly tapering off to the simple monosyllable "grass," the first concrete image in the poem.

In the Royal Shakespeare model, performance workshops deal extensively with meter. With Shakespeare the meter creates an almost constant framework of iambic pentameter with variants (trochaic and spondaic feet, run-on lines, half-lines finished by a second speaker). With Donne, similar metrical variants (with the exception of the half-lines) occur within a framework that itself includes variation: the invented stanza forms of the hymns and *Songs and Sonnets*. Treating metrics not as wearisome prescriptions but as the practical tools of a poet giving clues to the future readers and performers of the poem liberates metrics from its pedantic, hair-splitting reputation. In "Love's Growth," for example, appears the run-on line:

> But if this medicine, love, which cures all sorrow
> With more, not only be no quintessence   (7–8)

The performer who knows the possibility of pausing after "sorrow" to mark the completed line and who also knows the necessity of spilling over to the first foot of the second line ("With more") will understand the underlying paradox of the love that both cures and adds to sorrow.

Scansion of Donne's lyrics is notoriously difficult. It is worthwhile to apply the simplest possible scansion—a strict metrical reading—in performance workshops. Such a reading may have to be abandoned, of course: no one is likely to profit by reading

$$— \; / \quad — \quad /$$
Batter my heart. . . .

But strict metrics often reveal workable and unexpected readings: students need not invert the first foot of

$$/ \quad — \; — / \quad — \quad / \; —$$
Love's not so pure, and abstract (11)

When read iambically, it has a powerful ring of negation:

$$— \; , \quad / \; — \; / \quad — \quad / \; —$$
Love's not so pure, and abstract.

Many students tend to read with prose rhythms, emphasizing, for example, the contrast in line 14 of "Love's Growth":

$$/ \quad / \quad — \quad — \quad / \; — \quad — \; / \quad — \quad /$$
Love sometimes would contemplate, sometimes do.

It's a serviceable but not at all metrical rhythm. To get students to experiment with going beyond such familiar patterns, I insist that they try to fit the actual words to the formal metrical context:

$$— \quad / \quad — \quad / \quad — / \quad — \quad / \quad — \quad /$$
Love sometimes would contemplate, sometimes do.

The verbs are now more subtly contrasted, the longer phrase of more abstract intention, with its stressed auxiliary "would," against the abrupt phrase of action, "do." When a real inversion or substitution occurs, I encourage the students to make the most of it. In the same stanza, they encounter a crucial spondee:

> But if this medicine, love, which cures all sorrow
> With more, not only be no quintessence,
> But mixed of all stuffs paining soul or sense   (7–9)

"Stuffs," with its heavy consonant clusters alliterating with the other /s/ sounds in the context and with its powerful image of materiality, must be elevated to a stress. The best performers deal with that stress, and the students begin to note how often the spondees of the poem refer to the qualities of growth, here ascribed to the mixture of

"all stuffs": "love deeds," "more circles," "new heat," "new taxes"
                                        (9, 19, 21, 25, 27)

and even the title,

"Love's Growth."

Students in performance workshops can learn not just to translate images and figurative language but to use their full potential of expression. One technique is simple and of local application and is especially useful in the introductory workshop: a slight pause, a lift, before a figure gives the impression that the speaker is coining or inventing the figure. The resulting vocal punctuation makes the metaphor stand out from the surrounding texture; and the illusion of invention emphasizes the purposeful and rhetorical aspects of metaphysical imagery, which we later discuss in Rosemond Tuve's terms. In "The Sun Rising," for example, the reader encounters:

> Love, all alike, no season knows, nor clime,
> Nor hours, days, months, which are the rags of time.   (9–10)

A slight pause separates the catalog ("hours, days, months") from the metaphor and brings out the power of the metaphor to encapsulate the values and the attitudes of the speaker.

The coining effect can easily seem mannered if overdone, so, when we start to work on the poem as a whole, I encourage the students to see the image less as a separate invented unit and more as part of a series, with attention to the connections and the flow of the images. The performer studying "Love's Growth" must go beyond the familiar, almost Hallmark-like ease of a single image—"Gentle love deeds, as blossoms on the bough" (19)—to discover the sequence of natural images in the poem—grass, winter, spring, sun, spring again, stars, sun again, blossoms on a bough, root, water, spring, heat, winter, and, finally, spring again. Noting the pattern, the performer sees a large rhythm in the poem. The context of familiarity is broadened; the performer concentrates not just on the easy images but also on the contexts of logic and tone in which they are embedded.

In the performance workshop we stop often to isolate techniques and to try alternative readings. At some point those interruptions become self-defeating; students need to be encouraged to deal with whole poems. At that point I assign memorized, stand-up performances of whole lyrics. I stress that the reader's job is now to deal with local matters of technique—meter, figure, and so forth—as they contribute to a reading of the poem as a whole. An excellent tool for introducing that level of reading is the Royal Shakespeare Company's videotaped sequence in "Speaking Shakespearean Verse" (*Playing Shakespeare* FFH 731F) in which David Suchet is coached to enact a dramatic situation for Shakespeare's sonnet 138 ("When my love swears that she is made of truth"). In the situation that director Trevor Nunn prescribes, a middle-aged philosophy lecturer is trying to explain relativism to his students, and he invents that example of his own not-so-truthful relationship with his lover. The resulting performance takes an already enjoyable poem and makes it unforgettably witty.

With Donne, a reading of the whole poem involves studying and imagining the gaps in the poem. "The Flea" is an obvious example: the student preparing to perform it has to envision the woman's responses in the empty places between stanzas. Similarly, the changes in tone as one moves from stanza to stanza in "The Good-Morrow" or "The Canonization" demand that the student imagine a hidden situation and let it inform the performance. "For God's sake, hold your tongue, and let me love" ("Canonization" 1) is an easy enough beginning, tonally and dramatically, but the challenge in reading the whole poem is to modulate believably from the petulant beginning into the mellow and transcendent ending. The student who has not worked out the implied counterarguments flounders for ways to present each new stanza and is embarrassed by the monotony of the repeated rhyme word *love*.

A performance in my class a few years ago brought "The Relic" to life unforgettably as the student created a specific dramatic situation without props, set, or lights and using only a page of his spiral notebook as the "paper" of the second stanza. The speaker walks through a church, contemplating the tombs; he turns to his imagined lover to explain with playful tenderness his thoughts about his own grave; he shows her the imagined "bracelet of bright hair" (6) about his wrist. The playfulness becomes more serious as the speaker produces the paper itself: "I would have that age by this paper taught / What miracles we harmless lovers wrought" (21–22). The lover, we realize, has thought it out, has prepared the testimony that will prove the relics, has a premeditated purpose. What is it? He reads the paper to his imagined lover in the language of the poem's third stanza with its remarkable distancing—its past-tense description ("we loved"), its vast temporal and ontological perspectives ("nature," "law," "angels," "seals," "miracles"), and its language of negated action ("knew not," "no more we knew," "not between those meals," "ne'er touched"). As he reads, he remains focused on the paper he has written. But at the end, the solemnity of the scenario of desire held in ultimate restraint breaks suddenly as he raises his eyes from the paper to the lover, first summarizing and then abandoning the attempt to bear witness to future ages:

> These miracles we did; but now, alas,
> All measure, and all language, I should pass,
> Should I tell what a miracle she was.   (31–33)

The performer plays the abandonment of language with a half-smile as he reveals that the whole scenario has been an elaborate framework for the most powerful delivery of the simplest of compliments to his lover; in effect, all leads to "you are a miracle."

Of course, that performance excludes alternative readings: perhaps the inarticulateness at the end would be better read as a spontaneous upsurge of desire; perhaps a reading with more satirical elements would be truer to the text. In a discussion or a paper, I expect students to deal with alternatives even while advocating their own theses. After a performance, as students are encouraged to report and discuss what they saw and heard, multiplicity of interpretation is crucial. But in the performance itself we encourage a singleness of intent, a willingness to give up indeterminacy for a moment. To me and to my students, that is the excitement of the technique. We have lived most of our lives with the sense that we can never pin the meaning down. To be sure, we always return to that sense of indeterminacy beyond the limits of the performance. But during a good performance we feel that we are at the single meaning, the momentarily secure core of the poem. As students return to the confusion of new poems and new readings, that confidence remains, enabling them to go on climbing over the blocks to understanding.

Songs and Sonnets Go to Church:
Teaching George Herbert

Richard Strier

A course or unit on metaphysical poetry inevitably approaches George Herbert after studying John Donne. That sequence is proper as well as inevitable. Donne's lyrics are the major and defining examples of metaphysical poetry. To study Herbert's poetry in the context of Donne's provides a number of pedagogical opportunities, although it also presents a number of dangers. One such danger is to try to demonstrate that Herbert is metaphysical in the same way that Donne is. That attempt is not likely to be fruitful. Although one may succeed in finding some bits of scholastic terminology and doctrine here and there in Herbert ("The Quidditie" as a title; sin, in "Sinne" (1), as lacking "the good . . . of being" [5]), they are minor, peripheral, or—as in "The Quidditie," in which the *quidditas* of verse is never conceptually defined—humorously ironic moments. Nowhere in Herbert does a metaphysical assertion like "What ever dyes, was not mixt equally" (Donne, "The Good-Morrow," line 19) have a central or culminating function in the emotional arc of a poem. Herbert is not interested in metaphysics in the way that Donne is. Instead of "affecting" the metaphysics, as Dryden said Donne did, Herbert is fundamentally anti-metaphysical. He is a functionalist, rather than an essentialist. It is no accident that the quiddity of verse for him turns out to be an activity and a personal relationship, rather than a metaphysically defined "thing," just as, for Herbert, the alchemical "elixir" turns out to be an attitude, rather than an essence.

The search for elaborate images or conceits is only slightly more fruitful in approaching Herbert's poetry. Such conceits do exist in significant places in the poems—in the descriptions of the astronomer and the chemist in "Vanitie" (1); in the description of the processes of intellectual and verbal invention in "Sinnes Round" and "Jordan" (2); in the paradoxically strong "rope of sands" in which the speaker of "The Collar" is tempted to see himself imprisoned. Those are all striking moments of verbal and imagistic ingenuity, but they all dramatize or exemplify processes of which Herbert is at least deeply suspicious, if not downright disapproving. The presence of ingenuity in the poetry must not lead us to a false valuation of the status of ingenuity in the poetry. That caution may be true for Donne's poetry as well, but Donne was perhaps more committed than Herbert to the positive functions of ingenuity and ratiocination. However, that ingenuity and ratiocination are present in Herbert's poetry as in Donne's, is beyond dispute.

Thus far, it looks as though Herbert is a metaphysical poet mainly by virtue of the positions and the strategies his poetry shows to be misguided. That is not a bad place to leave the issue, but the relations between Herbert's poetry and Donne's can be more positively exploited. One may expect Donne's religious lyrics to provide a smooth transition to Herbert. In a sense, they do, but the pedagogical opportunity that history apparently provides must be warily and imaginatively exploited. First of all, virtually all students, scholars, and general readers find Donne's religious verse largely inferior in quality and interest to the *Songs and Sonets*. After working with intense and rapturous attention on poems like "The Good-Morrow," "The Anniversarie," and "Loves Growth," students find almost any other poems, especially religious poems, tame and pallid. The teacher's way around that wholly intelligible reaction is to note that religious poetry can be as great as the greatest love poetry; indeed, religious poetry can be great in many of the same ways. That is a daring strategy, but, if it succeeds, it keeps the students from experiencing the course or unit on metaphysical poetry as a steady falling off from an initial plateau that is only partially recovered with Marvell. Moreover, if the strategy succeeds, it establishes a continuity between Herbert and Donne richer than that established by a concern for metaphysics or the presence of conceits.

The strategy requires us to let the students use Donne's greatest love lyrics as touchstones of poetic value for metaphysical poetry. The advantages of doing that are realism—the students do so in any case—and intelligibility. The disadvantage is that most of Donne's religious poems are wanting by that standard. We must be willing to let the chips fall where they will. It is not historically or aesthetically misguided to suggest that Donne's mastery of the holy sonnet was less total than his mastery of the analytical love lyric, for which he had a long and distinguished European tradition behind him and a major English predecessor in Philip Sidney. In the vernacular religious lyric, the general tradition is thinner, and Donne had no equivalent of Sidney. In the love lyric, Donne is building on and playing off a series of masters; in the vernacular religious lyric of the Protestant stripe, he is almost a pioneer. Donne's religious verse is best when it captures or recaptures the gaiety, urbanity, agility, and candor of his greatest love lyrics. That happens, for instance, in "I am a little world made cunningly," in which some of Donne's favorite images and hyperboles reappear; in the humorously detached self-portraits of "Oh might those sighes and teares returne againe" and "Oh, to vex me"; and, most of all, in the wit and gaiety of his greatest religious lyrics, the "Hymne to Christ, at the Authors Last Going into Germany" and the "Hymne to God My God, in My Sicknesse." If we take the probable development of Donne's religious verse seriously, we can say that his project was ultimately to write religious lyrics very much like his greatest love lyrics.

That was Herbert's project as well—to provide in the vernacular, for English Protestants, what Donne, writing of psalm translations, called "formes of joy and art" ("Upon the Translation of the Psalmes by Sir Philip

Sydney, and the Countess of Pembroke His Sister," line 34). That approach to Herbert has the advantage of highlighting some of the most distinctive and distinguished qualities of his poetry, qualities that he shared with and perhaps learned from the *Songs and Sonets*—gaiety, comedy, urbanity, agility, and candor. The relation to Donne provides a number of opportunities. One obvious tactic—obviousness being, I think, a positive rather than a negative feature of pedagogic strategies—is to begin the unit on Herbert with a comparison of Donne's "Death be not proud" and Herbert's "Death." Whatever one says about the Donne sonnet—I myself find it forced in its tone and argumentation and more convincing in its Socratic mode than in its Pauline mode—the Herbert lyric is unequivocal in its gaiety and imaginative freedom. "Death" is a poem that rewards detailed analysis, and it has the useful effect of immediately defusing a crucial preconception that students are likely to have: the idea that religious poetry is a solemn, stiff, and stuffy affair, a business for which one needs one's Sunday-school face. A good reading of the poem shows both its extraordinary gaiety—"an *uncouth* hideous thing" (line 1)—and its awareness of and respect for normal human emotions toward the physical remains of the dead—"Dry dust, which sheds no tears, *but may extort*" (12) (emphasis mine). The poem is a good introduction to a unit on religious poetry (Vaughan and Crashaw after Herbert) because it systematically contrasts a normal perspective, including the Socratic-Platonic one, with the radical and distinctive Pauline stress on the restoration of the body—on resurrection, rather than immortality. The focus on the body is what allows the poem to be both distinctively Christian and tenderly human, both apocalyptic and modulated. Moreover, "Death" is an excellent text with which to demonstrate Herbert's technical mastery. Structurally and syntactically, the turn in the poem comes at its exact center (line 13), and the final "Therefore" (21) changes the grand vision of the penultimate stanza, which had seemed an end in itself, into a means for dealing with the ordinary human condition. Metrical, prosodic, and stylistic analysis reveal similar enhancements and precisions.

In teaching lyric poetry, we must establish connections, relationships, or developments between poems. Each poem analyzed in class should not be simply another one by X but should have some intelligible relation to the previous poem studied, a relation that is explicit or can be made so through class discussion. Herbert's "Death" can coherently lead to a number of other poems in *The Temple*, can enter, in Herbert's image, into various constellations. It may, for instance, lead to other poems recounting bogey-into-beauty transformations, or it may lead into the larger category of retrospective narrative lyrics, one of Herbert's favorite lyrical kinds. In the transformation category, an obvious candidate for treatment is "Justice" (2). Structurally, that poem is closely parallel to "Death," but it is more difficult and less distinguished. It is also a directly theological poem, though that does not account for its lesser distinction. "Justice" (2) dramatizes regeneration as a changed relation to divine justice, a presentation that is based on and duplicates Luther's famous account of his exegetical and religious breakthrough in understanding divine justice. Unlike "Death," which deals with a noncontroversial Christian doctrine, "Justice" (2) is recognizably of a particular Christian coloration, and its interpretation requires some basic knowledge of Reformation theology. The issue of faith versus works can become a focus in class, leading to a discussion of many poems, such as "The Holdfast" (a technically as well as theologically interesting sonnet), "Dialogue," and "Love" (3), poems on the irrelevance of worthiness to salvation.

Building on the category of retrospective narrative can lead in a number of fruitful directions. Herbert is more committed to narrative than Donne is, and at times Herbert creates narratives with fully developed personae. One of the great examples of the technique is the comic and yet quite serious lyric entitled "Artillerie." This poem is particularly useful in studying metaphysical poetry because it contains what may be a direct borrowing from Donne's Songs and Sonets. The penultimate line of "Artillerie," "There is no articling with thee" (32) is close to a line in "Loves Exchange," "I may not article for grace" (27). The likelihood that it was an actual borrowing is intensified by the artillery and parleying context of the entire stanza in which Donne's line appears and by the parallel presentations of each speaker as having rejected the "motions" of a powerful, superhuman interlocutor ("Artillerie," 7; "Loves Exchange," 23). The comparison shows Herbert taking a brilliantly outrageous parody of spiritual experience and bringing it back to the context of actual religious experience while retaining the comic mode. To understand "Artillerie" and many other lyrics, the reader must give full weight to the gentle but firm mockery in Herbert's presentation of his commonsensical and rule-invoking narrator. The explicit rebuke of the narrator's common sense in "Artillerie" should help, for instance, with the rebuke to common sense implied in the mysterious ending of "Redemption," Herbert's most extraordinary sonnet.

First-person comic retrospect is also the mode of one of Herbert's most important poems on poetry, the second of the "Jordan" poems. Any treatment of Herbert should deal with at least one of his poems about poetry. Interesting comments on writing are scattered throughout the Songs and Sonets, but Herbert is extraordinary (for a premodern poet) in the extent of his explicit self-consciousness about writing. In discussing the critique of the grand or elaborate style in "Jordan" (2), students and teachers should see it as a religious critique, not an aesthetic critique. The problem is not with the style itself but with the psychological effects of composing in such a style— the pride, the self-satisfaction, and the self-display that, as Herbert presents it, composing in such a style necessarily entails. The critique of elaborate verbal style in "Jordan" (2) must be connected to the critique of the elaborate architectural style of Solomon's temple in "Sion." What the collocation of these and other poems about God's dislike of "pomp and state" ("Sion," 7) reveals is that Herbert and the God he worshiped and poetically presented valued sincerity above all other things. Herbert's art is never meant to testify to the greatness of art.

Having spoken of the value Herbert placed on sincerity, I urge the inclusion of one other type of Herbertian narrative in an initial survey of Herbert's poetry, the noncomic autobiography. The greatest examples are the first of the "Affliction" poems and the related and probably later poem entitled "The Crosse." They are difficult poems, but they bear comparison with Donne's "A Nocturnall upon S. Lucies Day" and "Twicknam Garden" in the intensity of their presentations of psychological and emotional pain. Herbert's poetry can cure students not only of the idea that religion must be solemn and gloomy but also of the opposed idea that the religious is decorous, serene, and psychologically untroubled. The emotional range of Herbert's lyrics is comparable to that of the *Songs and Sonets*. Resentment, loss, and anguish are as powerfully expressed in "Affliction" (1) and "The Crosse" as in any of Donne's laments and complaints. In teaching the remarkable narrative poem "The Collar," in which we virtually forget the narrative frame, we must present the stunning final resolution as neither a simple condemnation of the recollected opening questions nor a pat and arbitrary intervention of authority.

The *Songs and Sonets* are indeed the perfect context in which to study Herbert's lyrics. I argued at the beginning of this essay that in an important sense Herbert is an antimetaphysical poet. Conceits take us only so far into his work. However, Herbert does belong with Donne among the metaphysical poets. "Their attempts," Dr. Johnson said, "were always analytic" Johnson saw their analytical bent as a liability, as preventing the metaphysical poets from being successful in either "representing or moving the affections" ("Life of Cowley"). T. S. Eliot rightly protested Johnson's separation of the analytical from the affective. Eliot insisted that in Herbert, as in Donne, the analytical and the affective coexist ("Metaphysical Poets"). Like Donne, Herbert is a master of nonundercutting irony. Demonstrating that phenomenon is one of the great challenges of teaching Herbert. The task is to show that in Herbert's most complex poems—"The Temper" (1), "The Forerunners," "The Flower"—powerful emotions are both convincingly represented and located within wider contexts of awareness. Like *Songs and Sonets*, *The Temple* must be shown to be remarkable not only for the variety of tones that different poems in it embody but also for the variety of tones that individual poems embody. We must show that, at his greatest, Herbert, like Donne, simultaneously represented and criticized his deepest emotions.

Representing Vaughan to Undergraduates

Jonathan F. S. Post

Anyone who has taught a survey of English literature of the earlier seventeenth century knows the problem: how to yoke together the vast and seemingly heterogeneous amount of material written during the period without causing too much violence to the students, to the literature, or to yourself. Even for those who find the term useful, metaphysical poetry must compete with the drama and the prose of the period, surely some of the richest and most inventive in literature. Metaphysical poetry must also compete with un-Donne-like poetry, including Jonson's and some by the Caroline poets, like Carew and Herrick, and in some circumstances with Milton and perhaps a representative Spenserian. If one teaches in the quarter system, the yoke can feel like a noose. I have yet to find a fully satisfactory way of presenting and sharing the period in its depth and complexity. A routine question on the final examination, like asking for the approximate date of Charles I's execution, can become an instant lesson in teaching humility as well as a reminder that in California civil wars happen elsewhere.

Henry Vaughan was a civil-war poet. He was also a distant follower of Donne; a poet familiar with pastoralists like William Browne; a court amorist; a Son of Ben, as the followers of Jonson called themselves; a physician and minor virtuoso, perhaps in the Baconian mode; a contemporary of Marvell's; a retirement poet; a Neoplatonist who, like Thomas Traherne, celebrated childhood; a religious mystic or visionary keenly conscious of paradise lost; and George Herbert's best disciple. For someone who spent almost his entire life off the beaten path in Breconshire, Wales, Vaughan's centrality to the seventeenth century is a little unnerving. Even the 1650 date of publication of his best-known collection of poetry, *Silex Scintillans*, strikes at the heart of the century.

Nonetheless, Vaughan is almost always served up to undergraduates as one item among many on the menu, which means that he is probably given two or three meetings at most. In such circumstances, whatever critical theories we cherish are inevitably shaped and modified by our immediate teaching situation. My seventeenth-century classes usually range in size from 35 to 50 students; few have had a previous encounter with Vaughan. Almost all my students are English majors, but their motives for taking the course vary: from the surprised sophomore who thought it was going to be all Donne to the expeditious senior counting the days to graduation to the curious and critically sophisticated student wishing to explore the unknown. I encourage classroom participation, but the presentation is a minilecture. Whatever virtues seminars allow (whenever two or three are gathered . . .), they must be exchanged in part for a potentially different set of rewards: the rights (rites) of introduction.

Vaughan generally follows Herbert in the course and after Vaughan comes Crashaw. By the time we get to Vaughan, we have read many of his most important sources—Donne, Jonson, the Bible (we spend one class on at least one of the Gospels in the King James Version)—and some of his Cavalier contemporaries, who are especially valuable in the curve of Vaughan's career. In conjunction with his poetry, I assign the relevant essays in Mario A. Di Cesare and in William R. Keast; John Hollander's book *Rhyme's Reason* has been on reserve since the first day of the course. (Student access to the secondary literature on Vaughan was improved by Alan Rudrum's 1987 book, *Essential Articles*.) I also ask—and this may be the most important and the most difficult requirement—that the students read Vaughan in a private and quiet place, perhaps even late in the evening. That request may seem overly precious, but Vaughan is an intensely private poet— communing often with the dead, with nature, with another poet, or with Christ and doing so frequently at night. Besides distinguishing him from all other seventeenth-century poets except the Milton of the invocations in *Paradise Lost*, that experience is the one most likely to be sacrificed to the normal hurly-burly of undergraduate life, much of which is spent in the fast lane, going to and from the large, metropolitan-situated university where I teach.

Introducing Vaughan means making sense of anthology selections and editions. Those poems in the *Norton Anthology* (gen. ed. Abrams; 5th ed.) provide a minimal starting place (it excludes familiar poems like "The Retreat," "Vanity of Spirit," and "Peace"). Those in Di Cesare's book give a more substantial overview of the religious verse. Those in Barbara K. Lewalski and Andrew J. Sabol are better yet, since *Silex Scintillans* is printed in full. For teachers who prefer single texts, a handy though no longer inexpensive edition of Vaughan's selected poetry, edited by Robert Shaw, offers an uncluttered approach to most of the important religious lyrics. Alan Rudrum's edition of *Henry Vaughan: The Complete Poems* is lavishly and learnedly annotated. A sensible compromise between the anthology and the individual edition is the combined Herbert and Vaughan in the Oxford series (Martz); it includes from Herbert *The Temple* and *The Priest to the Temple*, both in full, and from Vaughan *Silex Scintillans* in full and selections from his earliest volume of secular verse, *Poems* (1646). Since I like to assign numerous swatches of poetry, I've learned to put an asterisk beside the poems at the center of the day's lecture.

Introducing Vaughan also means having a strategy of presentation, not just an interpretive method. I think the place to begin is not with "Regeneration," the poem given pride of place in *Silex* and often thought to signal the beginning of Vaughan's poetry. "Regeneration" is surely essential to the canon for poetic and theological reasons; but it can be a rough beginning, teasingly obscure in places, and I can imagine losing many students at the outset. I prefer a more direct approach. I give the students a copy of Vaughan's portrait of himself as presented in "Ad Posteros," translations of which are available in Fogle's and Rudrum's complete collections. (Although the cover on the Yale paperback edition depicts a Merlin-like figure with wonderfully wild white hair and a beard, no portraits, drawings, or etchings of the poet are known to exist). "Ad Posteros" requires some decoding, but it has the distinct advantage of locating Vaughan historically as a suffering servant loyal to the king, protesting his innocence, but deeply involved in his country's plight. I also produce the frontispiece of *Eikon Basilike*, subtitled *Portraiture of His Sacred Majesty* [Charles I] *in His Solitude and Suffering*, published in 1649, when it went through sixty-two editions. I discuss the politics of echoing here; I also use the poem to introduce the apocalyptic nature of Vaughan's imagination, and I spend a moment comparing and contrasting Herrick's brand of loyalism, contained within the Cavalier gesture, with Vaughan's more ragged and nervous response.

At that point it is an easy and a necessary move to bring Herbert into the picture. I set Vaughan's "Brittish Church" alongside Herbert's poem of the same title; the juxtaposition emphasizes the radically different moments in church history perceived and represented by each poet. Both poems are concerned with writing, and both identify the church as the authority for a particular aesthetic (beauty in Herbert, woe in Vaughan). In class we discuss how Herbert's voice of the via media becomes disabled and transformed into a sacrificial lament spoken by the church. Vaughan, in fact, recollects the technique of the first-person address in Herbert's "The Sacrifice." The transposition also describes one essential difference between the two poets: if Christ's act of sacrifice is central to Herbert's theology and poetry, the sacrifice of the visible church is essential to Vaughan's.

Introducing Vaughan through history and Herbert ought not diminish his individual poetic attributes—his voice; indeed, comparing the two poets is one of the simplest ways of requiring the students to look closely at both authors. But there are potential dangers. If Herbert was read by an earlier generation as weak Donne, so Vaughan can seem a pale copy of his master. In the past, one way around the problem was to draw attention to Vaughan as a specifically Welsh, proto-Romantic nature poet, one deeply attracted to occult thought. Those features are worth mentioning; I sometimes show some slides of the Usk Valley in Wales and remind the students of Shakespeare's Owen Glendower calling up spirits from the vasty deep (*1 Henry IV* 3.1.51). But Vaughan's Welshness is never easy to recover for American students (oddly enough, only British nonnative speakers of Welsh usually concentrate on that feature), and too much attention to esoteric speculation runs the risk of turning Vaughan's poems into Hermetic commentary. (Those who wish to teach a more Hermetic Vaughan can consult the several publications by Alan Rudrum on that subject.)

Reading "Regeneration" out loud at that point is a dramatically effective way of establishing Vaughan's poetic credentials. With its lush sounds, stunning imagery, restless movement, and climactic prayer, the lyric is a tour de force, like the invocation to *Paradise Lost*, and it often produces in the students a sense of awe and wonder similar to that experienced by the pilgrim. At least, that is how I generously interpret the silence in the class. We then begin our analysis by comparing the poem with Herbert's "Pilgrimage," a comparison that brings to the fore stanzas 5–7 of "Regeneration," in which the invisible church is made suddenly visible (the students always have fun discovering the submerged architectural metaphors), and the underlying biblical text from John 3.5–8 that shapes the narrative and emerges fully at the end of the poem. The students have been prepared for the theological and the potentially controversial significance of the text by reading Calvin's *Commentary on the Gospel According to John* (*Works*) and his remarks on justification in *The Antidote to Canons of Council of Trent* (*Selections*).

"Regeneration" is a demanding poem. The intellectual exhaustion experienced by the pilgrim as a necessary prelude to faith is an experience Vaughan asks the reader to share; the allegory functions deliberately as a dark conceit, never fully accessible to reason in the same way, for instance, that Herbert's conceit is in "The Church-Floore." If the average student's concentration in a lecture begins dwindling after seven minutes, my decision to turn to "Peace" at that point is a belated way of responding to and even capitalizing on potential student fatigue. The poem is luminously simple. We all breathe a little easier, at least until I ask how such simplicity is achieved, a question designed to lead the students not only to discuss rhetorical features—such as diction, meter, and rhyme—but also to see how the peace imaged in heaven is a corrected mirroring of Vaughan's principal concerns on earth: instability, wandering, war, the precarious location of Christ, the loss of childhood (now figured in the nursery rhyme simplicity of the prayer)—all topics either alluded to or considered in the poems already discussed.

"Peace" forms a natural conclusion to a first day's encounter with Vaughan. However much time I have available for further attention to Vaughan, whether one class or two, I structure the presentation so that "The Night" assumes a climactic place in the order of things. If the schedule permits two more days on Vaughan, I range out in the second day to explore the elegiac element of *Silex*, especially powerful in part 1 but still present, though in a subdued mood, in part 2. The discussion centers on "Joy of my life," "Silence and stealth of days," "I walkt the other day," "They are all gone into the world of light," "The Retreate," and "Vanity of Spirit." In a century haunted by elegies and epitaphs, those poems remain unique for their carefully figured isolation; our analysis almost always concentrates on Vaughan's alien presence in the landscape. If I have only one more day, I give an abbreviated account of the elegies, shaping the discussion more in the direction of the nocturnal (by adding "Mid-Night") and the apocalyptic (by adding "The Dawning" and "The Jews"), and I analyze their rich fusion in "The Night." In connection with "The Night," I assign portions of Vaughan's *Man in Darkness* in L. C. Martin's edition (168–90), the account of Nicodemus in John 3.1–22, selections of Saint John of the Cross's *Dark Night of the Soul* (the poem and at least some of the early chapters), and critical interpretations of the poem by R. A. Durr and Rudrum (*Essential Articles*). If time permits, I close with a brief analysis of "The Book" to set the stage for Richard Crashaw, whom we approach by way of his epigram "On Mr. G. Herbert's Book."

It is relatively easy to talk about Vaughan's place on a syllabus. It is even possible to talk about how we may best approach his poetry. But the classroom encounter—the sense of the individual mind and person addressing a complicated text while responding to the particular requirements of a class—is a more problematic transaction to report, and I can only suggest that what I am after in the classroom is to register the inner life of poetry, whether Vaughan's or that of any other author we are studying—and not just that it matters but how it matters and the ways in which, through language, the poet and the reader make it matter. I do not consciously set out to make Vaughan our contemporary; I never feel more irrelevant than when I'm trying to be relevant (I'm always watching the wrong television programs). Nor am I conscious of historicizing Vaughan completely, though his sense of history and our knowledge of histories—literary, personal, religious, and political—are relevant in trying to imagine an approximate context for his poetry. But when a student parenthetically notes that in "The Night" Vaughan "wants to lose himself in God as if he were sailing through a vast black hole," it is impossible not to sense that history and geographical differences have been momentarily relativized; in words appropriated from Vaughan, the veil has been suddenly removed. That cultural exchange, predicated on a knowledge of difference, may not be the only reason why we teach literature, but I cannot imagine teaching without its being one of the reasons. If, in the distant aftermath of Eliot, the seventeenth century no longer seems so critically urgent to the formation of a modern idiom, the response of students can remind us that its literature has yet to lapse into irrelevance. Like other writers from the period, Vaughan never fails to find a kin.

Richard Crashaw: The Neglected Poet

John R. Roberts

The early twentieth-century revival of interest in the metaphysical poets was marked primarily by a renewed appreciation of certain select poems by John Donne, especially those dramatic lyrics that readily lent themselves to New Critical readings. As a result, metaphysical poetry was often defined, whether critics openly acknowledged it or not, as poetry like Donne's, and other seventeenth-century poets were frequently judged on how well or how poorly they demonstrated those particular aspects of Donne's poetry that captured the approval of modern sensibility. The poetry of Richard Crashaw in particular was found wanting when it was compared with that of Donne, for Crashaw was judged devoid of intellectual control and psychological introspection, excessively emotional and embarrassingly sensuous, feminine rather than masculine, and Continental rather than English. In his own time, however, Crashaw was often considered Donne's and Herbert's equal (occasionally their superior); in fact, one critic writing in 1657 ranked Crashaw among the best wits of England, along with Jonson, Shakespeare, Sidney, Bacon, and Donne (B[elasyse] 194). For the most part, much Crashavian criticism of the past was marred by religious prejudice on the one hand and by denominational zeal on the other; and those who disapproved of Crashaw's poetry labeled it unkindly as foreign, grotesque, notoriously baroque, even perverse. A number of more recent literary scholars, however, have examined Crashaw's poetry with greater objectivity and have become increasingly aware of its importance to an adequate understanding of seventeenth-century poetic theory and aesthetics and, on the whole, have tended to agree that Crashaw's poetry occupies a permanent and significant position in the literary, intellectual, and religious history of his time.

As a teacher of Crashaw's poetry, I try to imitate that objectivity and to encourage my students to do likewise; in my lectures and discussion sessions, therefore, I scrupulously avoid using the old labels and clichés about Crashaw's poetry that are found in many literary histories and in the introductions to anthologies. Instead, I find that students arrive at a more just evaluation of Crashaw's poetry if they are introduced as fully as time permits to the tradition from which it comes. Therefore, I comment in some detail on Crashaw's biography, the emblem, discursive meditation and liturgy, and the baroque aesthetic; only after I am satisfied that they have a reasonably sound grasp of those essential background materials do I move on to a discussion of Crashaw's individual style—its imagery, its rhetoric, its form.

Because Crashaw's poetry is generally taught as part of a survey course or a seminar on metaphysical poetry, the students, when they read Crashaw, have probably already begun to define metaphysical poetry for themselves in the light of what they know about Donne's and Herbert's poetry, perhaps even Vaughan's; therefore, it is a good idea to point out that their readings of Crashaw may expand and refine their definitions. And even though by that time in the course the students have been introduced to the major historical events and the religious currents of the period, I find it effective to review that material briefly to show how Crashaw's life, his poetic vision, his choice of models, and his subject matter were specifically shaped and influenced by the world in which he lived.

When commenting on his biography, I stress that Crashaw, like Herbert, greatly loved the English church, its forms of worship, its architecture and art, its hymns and devotional life, but that by the mid-1640s he felt that the radical reformers in England had, for the most part, destroyed the church that had so fully satisfied his own devotional needs and sensibility. Thus, when Crashaw formally became a Catholic, he did not turn his back completely on the tradition of his childhood but, rather, found in Catholicism a continuance, an enhancement, and a fulfillment of that spirit and devotional life that had always been important to him but that seemed lost in the post-Laudian Church of England. I also emphasize that Crashaw, more so than any other English religious poet of the seventeenth century, was familiar with the rich spiritual traditions of the Continent, especially mysticism, and that his self-imposed exile in the Low Countries, France, and Italy made it possible for him to enrich his own spiritual tradition in a way that was not possible for those who had not had his experiences abroad. Further, I point out that early in his life Crashaw was already acknowledged as a highly accomplished student and translator of Latin, Greek, Hebrew, Spanish, and Italian and that he was well read in the literatures of those languages. In other words, he was a learned and even sophisticated master of language; by no means was he simply a dabbler in pious verse.

After that discussion of the historical and religious background and of Crashaw's place in it, I comment on the central importance of emblematic imagery in seventeenth-century poetry, pointing out notable examples that have already been studied earlier in the course, such as Donne's use of the compass in "A Valediction: Forbidding Mourning" or Vaughan's use of the scales in "Regeneration." I stress that, although Crashaw often uses sensuous images, his poetry, like Donne's, is fundamentally intellectual and conceptual, although it clearly lacks the kind of ratiocination that is a hallmark of Donne's poetry. In my discussion I clarify that, although readers must picture those images, they must at the same time recognize the images primarily as vehicles for conveying complex attitudes and intellectual concepts. That is, although readers must see the compass in Donne's poem, they must also immediately find the abstract idea figured forth by what would otherwise be a rather ridiculous picture—Donne leaning on his beloved and being dragged around so that his heels make a circle about his mistress. I direct the students, therefore, to conceptualize Crashaw's emblematic images, not to visualize them, pointing out that in "The Weeper," for example, when the poet states that Mary Magdalen's tears fall *up* when they fall *down* on the feet of the crucified Christ, he is making perfectly good sense. The concept behind the directions of Mary's tears is that, because Christ condescended to become a man, he brought Heaven down to Earth and, at the same time, lifted Earth to Heaven. Thus, the paradoxical movement of the tears upward when they fall downward symbolically represents the theological mystery of the Incarnation, a figurative description that can be traced back as far as the fifth-century *De Conversione Magdalenae* of Peter Chrysologus (Powers 283).

Next I review the nature and the function of discursive meditation and liturgical worship, emphasizing how the aim of such forms of prayer is to re-create with immediacy the major events of Christian history. I explain that liturgical worship, like discursive meditation, does not invite one to go back in time and to imagine oneself present at the Nativity or the Crucifixion or the Resurrection but, rather, attempts to bring those important moments of the past into the present so that one senses the immediacy of divine mysteries. Through the use of memory, as it is understood in Augustinian psychology, the worshiper transcends the limitations of time and space so that the past becomes the present moment.

I have had some success in conveying that difficult concept by use of analogy. I pick out one student in the class, say John, and describe a party we might have to honor him. Knowing that John likes Chianti, lasagna, and Beatles records, we imaginatively design a party that includes all those items. Then I suggest that, some months after that successful party, we learn that John has had a mortal accident on his motorbike during the summer and that naturally we are all deeply disturbed and saddened by the demise of our friend. I point out that, if I were to meet a student from the class on campus in the fall and we commiserated with each other about the tragedy, recalling the party we had all enjoyed, that would be simply memory as we usually think of it. But if in John's honor we held another party at which we re-created as fully as possible the past experience by having Chianti, lasagna, and the music of the Beatles, then we would have an example of the Augustinian concept of memory—bringing the past into the present, not just recalling a past happening. Although all analogies limp, the students seem to understand, sometimes for the first time, how liturgy and discursive prayer function, and they begin to recognize that public celebrations and ceremonies can often be deeply personal experiences for the participants. I point out that something like that operates in Crashaw's poems. He celebrates a past event, such as the Nativity, as though it were happening in the present, and, although he speaks with a public and stylized voice in his poems, he conveys intense feelings and attitudes.

Even though the term *baroque*, when applied to literary texts, creates problems of definition, I find it helpful to bring to class slides of some examples of baroque art as counterparts, in another art form, of Crashaw's poetry. I make it clear, however, that the examples are not meant to suggest borrowings or influences but, rather, that they show that the techniques and the subject matter of a number of baroque paintings and sculptures often reflect attitudes and interests found in Crashaw's poetry. For example, although Crashaw probably never saw Bernini's statue of Saint Teresa in the Cornaro Chapel of Santa Maria della Vittoria in Rome, its subject matter, its blend of eroticism and mysticism, its dramatic and affective qualities, its ability to capture the most sublime yet fleeting experience and to hold it in awe for all time reflect an attitude toward the purpose of art that Crashaw would have found congenial. Also, several paintings by Caravaggio—such as the *Calling of St. Matthew*, the *Conversion of St. Paul*, the *Crucifixion of St. Peter*, and the *Madonna di Loreto*—assist students in understanding both the nature of seventeenth-century Continental devotion and the means used by artists to render it faithfully. Whether or not one calls Crashaw a baroque poet, the devotional spirit and the themes of his poems are by no means unique to him but are almost commonplace in much Continental baroque art; many of the things he attempted to achieve through language, others were attempting to achieve with marble and with paint.

Once those considerations of emblematic imagery, meditation and liturgy, and baroque art have been explored, I begin a discussion of the characteristic features of Crashaw's poetry with some confidence that the students have been reasonably prepared to understand and appreciate them. I stress that the most salient aspects of Crashaw's art are sensuous imagery, such as the presence of colors, odors, and mellifluous music; the extensive use of rhetoric and conceits; and a firm sense of design and structure. I emphasize, in particular, the affective nature of Crashaw's poems; the poet presents his ideas in such a way that the reader is moved by them; he does not simply try to inform or to argue with the reader. Yet I point out that Crashaw's poems, for all their intense feeling, are not self-revelations or analyses of his own spiritual development. His focus is typically on the other—God, the Christ Child, Mary Magdalen, the Magi, the Virgin, Saint Teresa. Because many students are accustomed to admire only introspection, subjectivity, and personal revelation in poetry, I explain in some detail that Crashaw's poems are personal, but only to the extent that they convey the poet's deepest feelings about his subject and his theme, not about himself.

While several of Crashaw's secular poems are particularly remarkable and should be strongly recommended to undergraduate students, especially "Musicks Duell" and "Wishes: To His (Supposed) Mistress," I discuss primarily the religious poems, since it is in them that Crashaw most fully achieves his mark as a poet. Also, rather than comment generally on many poems, I concentrate on only a few, analyzing and discussing them in detail. Depending on the time available in an undergraduate course, I find that the following lend themselves well to class discussion: "Nativity Hymn," "Hymne in the Glorious Epiphanie," "A Hymn to Saint Teresa," "The Flaming Heart," and "The Weeper."

I begin with the "Nativity Hymn," asking the students in advance to read Milton's poem on the same subject and to be prepared to comment on how the two poems are alike and how they differ. Most students recognize that both are highly structured and rather formal but that Milton focuses primarily on the divine mission or salvational role of the God-man, extolling his power to overcome the darkness of sin, ignorance, and superstition; Crashaw, by contrast, focuses primarily on the mystery of God's condescending to become a helpless infant, thereby joining the natural and the supernatural, the human and the divine. Throughout the poem, Crashaw examines the mystery of the Incarnation with rapt awe and with reverent attention to even the smallest details of the Nativity scene. Instead of attempting to explain the incomprehensible to the reader or to analyze in precise theological terms the doctrine of the Incarnation, the poet shows the simple shepherds present at the amazing event, experiencing affectively the inexpressible love that God has for humanity by his willingness to send his Son into the world.

Because the hymn is essentially a dramatic performance—with two soloists, a chorus of shepherds, and a full chorus—and not simply a lyric, I assign the parts to students (or, in the case of the choruses, groups of students) and ask them to recite the poems aloud. At the same time, I urge them to be attentive to the dramatic and musical aspects of the powerful hymn and to notice how the poem is carefully arranged and increases in emotional intensity. I point out that the structure of the poem is clearly that of meditation and liturgy. The movement of meditation is from seeing the event to reflecting on the devotional aspects of the event to making a personal resolution as a result of the exercise. At the end of the poem, the shepherds offer themselves as a sacrifice to the Christ Child, in imitation of his future offering of himself for them. And, like the meditation and the liturgy, the poem unites time and place—bringing together past, present, and future events and places. I illustrate the meditational aspect by the example of Caravaggio's *Adoration of the Shepherds with Sts. Lawrence and Francis*, a typical baroque painting of the Nativity, with saints from a later period present at the birth and with an angel dropping down into the scene, pointing one finger up to Heaven and another down to a sorrowful Mary, who contemplates the future suffering of her child.

Next I ask why the two soloists, Tityrus and Thyrsis, are given Greek, rather than Hebrew, names. At least one student usually points out that

Greek names associate the poem with the pastoral tradition, in which shepherds are singers and poets. That observation opens up the issue of the importance of the art of sacred parody, not only in "Nativity Hymn" but also in seventeenth-century religious poetry in general; the widespread practice of using secular forms, images, and themes and of consciously converting them to the service of divine poetry suggests a triumph of Christianity over paganism and a syncretism between the sacred and the profane. Once alerted to that possibility, the students begin to discover other examples of sacred parody in the poem—for example, the occasional use of Petrarchan diction, such as the phrase "Heavn's fairer ey[e]" in line 7—and thereby become aware that the poem has its roots in several poetic traditions. (All quotations from "Nativity Hymn" are from the second version of the poem in G. W. Williams, *Complete Poetry*.)

A line-by-line explication of the poem follows. I point out, for instance, the imagistic unity of the poem that is established as early as line 2: "Hath mett love's Noon in Nature's night." Throughout the poem, images of heat and light predominate and are vividly juxtaposed with images of cold and darkness. In addition, I note the numerous examples of puns ("sun-son," 4), oxymora ("MIGHTY BABE," 45; "Great little one," 83), paradoxes ("Æternity shutt in a span," 80; "Sommer in winter," 81; "Day in night," 81), synesthesia (the uses of "sweet," 21, 23, 30, 36, 69, 71, 77), and personification ("The North forgot his feirce Intent," 26; "Gloomy night embrac't the Place," 17) and show how those rhetorical figures are effectively used to create a sense of awe, mystery, and rapture. Likewise, I point out the uses of emblematic images, such as the description of the warmth and the purity of the Virgin's breasts in lines 87–90, images that clearly are not intended to be visualized but, rather, are meant to figure forth conceptualized and complex theological ideas. The breasts are called "Two sister-seas of Virgin-Milk" (87), for example, not to offer the reader an erotic picture but, rather, to express the idea that in the Virgin Mary, who is both mother and maid, love and purity have almost no bounds and to present the paradox that she, who is a creature, nourished and sustained the life of the Creator of all life. I also point out that even the central debate within the poem, about finding something or someone worthy to receive into this world the God-man, is primarily a devotional question, not one that could be answered by theological or scriptural proofs; it, like all the rest of the hymn, is only a vehicle to praise God for having settled the debate in advance by creating the Virgin Mary ("The phænix hath built the phænix' nest," 46).

I begin the close reading of Crashaw with the "Nativity Hymn" because its richness illustrates the most important aspects of his art. When I teach "Hymne in the Glorious Epiphanie," I show how it completes the theological significance of the "Nativity Hymn," and I focus on Crashaw's use of intellectual imagery. In teaching the two Teresian poems, "A Hymn to Saint Teresa" and "The Flaming Heart," I illustrate Crashaw's abiding interest in mysticism and sanctity, and I show once more his strong link with the Continent. I reserve "The Weeper" until the end, probably an unusual placement in a survey of Crashaw's poems but a strategic one. Because, of all his poems, it has received the most insulting and adverse criticism, I find that, if it is taught after the students have become familiar with Crashaw's poetic techniques, it is less likely to be condemned out of hand.

Because of the nature of Crashaw's art and subject matter, the poet does not appeal to all modern students. But, if he is given a fair reading and if his poetry is viewed in the light of the tradition from which it comes, the old negative clichés about his art become questionable. In fact, his poetry offers the teacher an excellent opportunity to challenge students' assumptions not only about metaphysical poetry but also about poetry in general. There is no good reason why Crashaw should be the neglected poet in an undergraduate course.

Teaching Marvell

Heather Dubrow

The process of teaching Andrew Marvell's work, like the work itself, is peppered with paradoxes and contradictions. For instance, his chronological position in seventeenth-century literature and hence in most of our courses makes Marvell easy to teach in some ways, singularly difficult in others. We can understand much about Marvell by following T. S. Eliot's recommendation to "squeeze the drops of the essence of two or three poems" ("Andrew Marvell" 251), and yet, as recent studies of the political poetry have reminded us, we can also miss much by doing so.

I have encountered these paradoxes and others when teaching Marvell in a range of courses and to a range of students: I've included his work in a basic lower-level survey of English literature and in the upper-level seventeenth-century survey at the University of Maryland as well as in the counterparts to those courses at Carleton College in Northfield, Minnesota. While the classes have varied in size from about ten students to forty, all have been small enough to permit a combination of discussion and lecture, the format that I enjoy most.

One challenge involved in presenting Marvell to those classes is approaching him after teaching John Donne and George Herbert. Marvell's strengths strike many students as pale in comparison with the pyrotechnics of other metaphysical poets. As John Klause, the author of a book on Marvell, observed in conversation, "What seemed civilized to Eliot seems boring to undergraduates." And, though one is skeptical about the theories of human biorhythms beloved of pop psychologists, I have no doubt that courses themselves have organic rhythms, as anyone attempting to provoke a lively discussion the day a long essay is due has learned. Marvell generally appears at the point in the term when the students are feeling worn down by work and preoccupied with the approach of finals. Changes of pace, such as those generated by the small-group discussions and the slide shows to which I refer below, can be helpful, but the problem of timing is one that we never solve completely.

Yet Marvell's chronological position also carries advantages: because we typically teach him relatively late in our survey courses, by the time we reach him, we have erected solid scaffolding on which to build. For instance, early in the term I generally establish a small group of poetic and pictorial touchstones, works to which we return repeatedly in our discussions; that technique provides a sense of structure and continuity, an antidote to the "ten capitals in ten days" problem that plagues survey classes. Thus in my upper-level seventeenth-century course we read Christopher Marlowe's "Passionate Shepherd to His Love," as well as some other sixteenth-century lyrics, in the first class and refer back to it when studying other persuasion poems like "The Flea"; that framework is useful when we turn to Marvell's "To His Coy Mistress." In preliminary lectures in both that upper-level Renaissance survey and my lower-level survey I use a series of slides to introduce seventeenth-century literature. Though the connection between baroque architecture and metaphysical poetry is problematical, juxtaposed slides of a classical building (I generally use the Parthenon) and a baroque one (my favorite instance is San Carlo alle Quattro Fontane in Rome) effectively engage students in the differences between the metaphysical and the neoclassical strands of seventeenth-century poetry. I relate those styles to analogues on campus and in town, such as the Georgian building in which I teach at Carleton. Some students are initially nonplussed at the thought of comparing buildings to poems, but they quickly become excited. That architectural background, like our early discussions of "The Passionate Shepherd to His Love," proves useful later in the course when we situate Marvell in relation to John Donne and Ben Jonson. Often I include in the same lecture a couple of slides or pictures of emblems, to which we refer when discussing Marvell's complaining nymph. The lecture generally also incorporates a slide of an anamorphic painting and some discussion of that and other forms of illusionist art; that pictorial background illuminates many poetic passages we later encounter but none better than the description of the scythe in "Damon the Mower."

Our discussions of individual Marvell lyrics are funded not only by those earlier classes but also by some contexts and techniques I establish when turning to Marvell himself. Depending on the sophistication of the students, I may refer them to such texts as MacLeish's "You, Andrew Marvell," Peter Beagle's *Fine and Private Place*, and Lynne Sharon Schwartz's novel about a marriage, *Rough Strife*. Above all, whenever the students have the relevant language skills (I find out about language background by asking them to include that information on cards they fill out at the beginning of the term), I draw attention to related readings in foreign languages—notably the Latin counterparts to the country-house tradition, the Latin version of "The Garden," and Marvell's other Latin verse—and encourage the students to consult those works. I facilitate that process by citing specific editions and reminding the students that the Loeb bilingual versions can help when they falter. The declining interest in foreign languages is one of the principal problems in American education, and those of us in English departments should accept the responsibility for encouraging our students to develop their language skills. I am not naive enough to believe that even at Carleton, where students are typically committed and intellectually alert, a crowd of undergraduates rushes joyously from my class to translate "Hortus." I have, however, found that a handful do consult classical and Continental texts if encouraged to do so—texts that one such student charmingly and unselfconsciously referred to as "Marvell's database." Even the students whose software does not include that database are reminded by my references to it that foreign languages and foreign-language requirements can serve substantive purposes.

Each of Marvell's principal lyrics poses distinctive problems in the classroom: in some important respects those lyrics and the process of teaching them differ from each other far more than, say, Donne's "Canonization" and "The Sun Rising" or even "The Canonization" and "Batter my heart." Many of the paradoxes in Marvell stem from the distinctions between his poems.

Most undergraduates in my lower-level course know little about the rest of Marvell's lyrics, but they are often familiar—in a sense, too familiar—with "To His Coy Mistress." One reason is that the poem is frequently taught in high school classes, so we confront the same problem that can complicate classes on "The Canonization": the students are tempted not to read it carefully enough because they have already been given a packaged interpretation. Though "To His Coy Mistress" may be problematical in that way, in most other respects it is a joy to teach. Some reasons are obvious. Students enjoy teasing out the subtleties of the language ("Why think of eternity in terms of deserts?"); most of our discussion of the poem focuses on a close reading. Juxtaposing it with the other persuasion poems already established as touchstones clarifies the paths (and the byways) of literary history, and the reference to that "winged chariot" (line 22) conveniently reminds the members of the group about Marvell's classicism.

Perhaps the main reason I enjoy teaching "To His Coy Mistress" is that it offers a splendid opportunity to engage students in critical challenges that complicate their reading. The phrase "vegetable love" (11) is especially useful pedagogically: I can think of no phrase in the English language that teaches students more about the connotations and the denotations of words and the critical tools with which we elucidate them. I usually start by explaining the concept of the three souls. That explication reminds the group of the importance of scholarly background, and yet it also reminds them of the limitations of that background, for we go on to see that glossing *vegetable* in "vegetable soul" does not resolve the question of whether pejorative connotations cling to the words. Addressing such problems from another angle, we turn to the entry on *vegetable* in the *Oxford English Dictionary*. If I have not used the *OED* earlier in the term, I explain its format and pass it around the room so that everyone has a chance to become fascinated (and often bemused) by its literal and figurative weightiness. I also advise the students, especially advanced ones, that, despite its weightiness, this extraordinary book has its limitations.

In my upper-level class the discussions of "vegetable love" lead to another critical insight. The anthology I generally use, Herschel C. Baker's *Later*

Renaissance in England, glosses the words as "i.e., slowly growing." In discussing the advantages and the disadvantages of that gloss, the students come both to recognize the problems that editors face and to confront their own predilections to accept commentaries uncritically.

Other passages in "To His Coy Mistress" also invite students to think further about critical and scholarly issues. Undergraduates are not and should not be involved in the intricacies of textual editing; nonetheless, I sometimes draw their attention to the frequent emendation of "glew" to "dew" (34). That editorial change can encourage our students to discard an illusion that often beleaguers even the best of them; poems were handed down on stone tablets (probably to the editors of the *Norton Anthology*) in precisely the form in which we read them.

Teaching "To His Coy Mistress," like the poem itself, has its subtle difficulties. The sexual implications of the lyric need to be explicated; not the least of Marvell's achievements is his ability to combine the dignity of the lines with a frankness that occasionally borders on bawdiness, and I think a good reading of the poem should at least consider the possibility that "marble vault" (26) includes a reference to the vagina. Discussing sex in the classroom can, however, be complicated. We sometimes underestimate the range of experience and of attitudes that our students bring to the subject. Other complications stem from our own attitudes; I am fairly comfortable talking about the connotations of the marble vault but far less comfortable when discussing the possible sexual wordplay on "quaint" (29), in part because it involves a word I find offensive. The answer in such cases—and I think in many other awkward situations in the classroom—is to be honest about one's own responses. Students sense them anyway. In this instance I simply mention the reasons for my discomfort when I experience it. Another advantage of honesty is that it establishes one possible model for dealing with one's responses and hence helps students to think through their own responses to sex in literary texts. Unsure how to react, the class will often take their cues from the teacher.

If students consider "To His Coy Mistress" accessible, they face the opposite problem when they read "The Garden." Most find it hard going. To be sure, it offers few of the syntactical complexities that complicate readings of Donne's poems. Yet the problems it does pose are real, and they provide an exemplar of a fundamental challenge that faces us in teaching Renaissance tests: how can we communicate the extensive scholarly background that informs those works without intimidating our students or distancing them from the immediate and accessible pleasures of the poem? As the wealth of scholarship on "The Garden" testifies, readers profit from at least a passing knowledge of Pauline doctrine, Plotinus, and the Cambridge Platonists. I am not wholly satisfied with my responses to that challenge, but I usually break up the scholarly information into segments, rather than inflict a single uninterrupted lecture on the class; that method is more likely to empower, rather than enfeeble, their interpretations of the text. Thus I start with a five- or ten-minute minilecture on the symbolism of gardens (usually the discussion builds on references to the pastoral in earlier classes). We intersperse class discussions of the poem's nuances with further minilectures on subjects like the significance of Plotinus in the middle stanzas of the poem.

Recently I have introduced a feminist perspective into discussions of "The Garden" by eliciting responses to the nostalgic and misogynistic vision of the solitary Adam. I also use feminist discussions to ask: To what extent should our evaluations of writers be affected by their adherence to principles that we do not share or, alternatively, find actively offensive? What do our responses to that issue suggest about the functions of art and the process of valuation? Last year, when preparing my class on "The Garden," I noticed for the first time that the rejection of Eve is part of a broader pattern: the speaker tends to deflect the blame for his own fallings and failings onto others, whether they be apples or women. In sharing such responses in class, I stress that they are recent ideas generated by preparing for the course; that provisional status makes them easier to challenge and also reminds the students that I, too, am discovering the poem as I work on it.

In teaching the Mower poems, I focus on "Damon the Mower": it encapsulates the issues raised by most of the other works in the group, and it is the richest in many ways. A comparison with the double sestina in Philip Sidney's *Arcadia*, "Ye goteherd gods," can clarify Marvell's distinctive pastoral mode. Since "Damon the Mower" is rooted in a less complicated scholarly background than most of the other Marvell lyrics we consider, I often present it through one of my favorite pedagogical strategies: breaking the class into groups of about five students, each of which talks about the work on their own and then reports back to the class. I provide a short list of questions for discussion, though I encourage the students to raise other issues as well, and I move from group to group to answer questions and stimulate debate. One advantage of approaching Marvell or virtually any writer that way is that the students who are intimidated in front of the class often feel comfortable speaking in a small group.

Though the classes I have been describing are generally successful, I am still wrestling with some unresolved problems. In particular, I am not yet happy with my approach to Marvell's political works. Throughout my upper-level course I intersperse lectures on the cultural and the social dimensions of the period. Thus our meeting on Marvell's political poems includes a lecture on the English Civil War (to which I have already referred in the introductory lecture in the course), a discussion of "An Horatian Ode," and selections from "Upon Appleton House." That class meeting provides background and introduces several questions about Marvell's political stance that enliven contemporary critical debates. But in teaching that session I am sometimes conscious that, despite my efforts to the contrary, many undergraduates consider political poetry a contradiction in terms. High school classes embed certain attitudes deeply in our students—witness the difficulties of persuading them that the notion of the tragic flaw is itself flawed—and one of the deepest attitudes is the distrust of political poetry. Another problem I confront is that of teaching "Upon Appleton House" as well as it deserves to be taught; for one thing, covering the whole poem is impractical, but relying on excerpts is frustrating for both the students and me.

I am also working on ways of integrating Marvell into my new strategy for incorporating secondary readings into the course. Such assignments are potentially counterproductive: even the students at Carleton tend to peruse critics uncritically, to approach those sources as a substitute, not a stimulus, for their own responses. In response to those problems, I have introduced a series of readings labeled "critical controversies" into my courses: I assign secondary works that are on the cutting edge of debates in our field, when possible including two texts that sharply contradict each other, and ask the students to hand in notes on three questions: What are the principal arguments of the text? What are its underlying methodological assumptions? What are the advantages and the disadvantages of applying that approach to other authors we have read? Those questions and the fact that the assignments appear under the rubric "critical controversies" encourage my undergraduates to question and evaluate what they are reading, rather than passively accepting it. The unit has been successful—student evaluations regularly cite it as one of the best features of my courses—but I have not yet included an assignment on Marvell. Perhaps a section from Annabel M. Patterson's *Marvell and the Civic Crown* would extend the assignment to Marvell and encourage the students to reconsider his political poetry. In any event, it is appropriate that I am still engaged with some unsolved problems about how to teach Marvell: he himself often delights in crafting answers that raise further questions.

CONTRIBUTORS AND SURVEY PARTICIPANTS

Roy E. Aycock, Old Dominion University; Elizabeth Bieman, University of Western Ontario; Chana Bloch, Mills College; Helen Brooks, Stanford University; Meg Brown, University of Arizona; Thomas O. Calhoun, University of Delaware; Georgia Christopher, Emory University; Ann Baynes Coiro, Rutgers University, New Brunswick; Huston Diehl, University of Iowa; Mary Jane Doherty, Vanderbilt University; Heather Dubrow, Carleton College; Edward E. Ericson, Calvin College; Roy Flannagan, Ohio University; Raymond-Jean Frontain, University of Tennessee, Knoxville; E. R. Gregory, University of Toledo; Marshall Grossman, Fordham University; Janet Halley, Hamilton College; Robert W. Halli, Jr., University of Alabama, University; Burton Hatlen, University of Maine; Judith S. Herz, Concordia University, Loyola Campus; M. Thomas Hester, North Carolina State University; Robert B. Hinman, University of Pittsburgh; John L. Idol, Jr., Clemson University; Nicholas Jones, Oberlin College; R. F. Kennedy, Saint Thomas University; George Klawitter, Viterbo College; Albert C. Labriola, Duquesne University; Anthony Low, New York University; Bridget Gellert Lyons, Rutgers University, New Brunswick; Ronald E. McFarland, University of Idaho; Steven Marx, Stanford University; Nabil Matar, American University of Beirut; Jean Milhaupt, Acquinas College; Edmund Miller, Long Island University, C. W. Post Center; R. L. Montgomery, University of California, Irvine; Janel Mueller, University of Chicago; David Novarr, Cornell University; John Ottenhoff, Wagner College; C. A. Patrides, University of Michigan, Ann Arbor; Annabel Patterson, Duke University; Jonathan F. S. Post, University of California, Los Angeles; Alan Powers, Bristol Community College; Robert H. Ray, Baylor University; Mark Reynolds, Jefferson Davis State College; John R. Roberts, University of Missouri, Columbia; Roger Rollin, Clemson University; Russell Rutter, Illinois State University, Normal; Michael C. Schoenfeldt, University of Michigan, Ann Arbor; William A. Sessions, Georgia State University; William Shaw, LeMoyne College; John T. Shawcross, University of Kentucky; Barry M. Spurr, University of Sydney; P. G. Stanwood, University of British Columbia; Thomas H. Stewart, Blue Mountain, Mississippi; Richard Strier, University of Chicago; William L. Stull, University of Hartford; Joseph H. Summers, University of Rochester; Roger L. Tarr, Illinois State University, Normal; Mark Taylor, Manhattan College; Gene Edward Veith, Jr., Concordia College, Wisconsin; Julia Walker, State University of New York, Geneseo; Faye Pauli Whitaker, Iowa State University; Chauncey Wood, McMaster College; Hilary Yoggerst, Saint John's College, California.

WORKS CITED

Books and Articles

Abrams, M. H., gen. ed. *The Norton Anthology of English Literature*. 5th ed. Vol. 1. New York: Norton, 1986.

Aers, David, Bob Hodge, and Gunther Kress. *Literature, Language and Society in England 1580–1680*. Totowa: Barnes, 1981.

Akrigg, G. P. V. *Jacobean Pageant: Or, The Court of King James I*. Cambridge: Harvard UP, 1962.

Alvarez, A. *The School of Donne*. London: Chatto, 1961.

Andreason, N. J. C. *John Donne: Conservative Revolutionary*. Princeton: Princeton UP, 1967.

Asals, Heather A. R. *Equivocal Predication: George Herbert's Way to God*. Toronto: U of Toronto P, 1981.

Baker, Herschel C. *The Dignity of Man: Studies in the Persistence of an Idea*. Cambridge: Cambridge UP, 1947.

———, ed. *The Later Renaissance in England: Nondramatic Verse and Prose 1600–1660*. Boston: Houghton, 1975.

———. *The Wars of Truth: Studies in the Decay of Christian Humanism in the Earlier Seventeenth Century*. Cambridge: Harvard UP, 1952.

Bald, R. C. *John Donne: A Life*. Ed. Wesley Milgate. New York: Oxford UP, 1970.

Bamborough, J. B. *The Little World of Man*. London: Longman, 1952.

Bantock, Granville, ed. *One Hundred Songs of England*. Boston: Ditson, 1914.

Barker, Arthur E. *The Seventeenth Century: Bacon through Marvell*. Goldentree Bibliographies. Arlington Heights: AHM, 1979.

Barton, John. *Playing Shakespeare*. London: Methuen, 1984.

Beagle, Peter. *A Fine and Private Place*. New York: Viking, 1960.

B[elasyse], Henry. "An English Traveler's First Curiosity: Or, The Knowlege of His Owne Countrey (April 1657)." *Report of Manuscripts in Various Collections*. Historical Manuscripts Commission. Vol. 2. London: Mackei, 1903. 193–204.

Bell, Ilona. " 'Under Ye Rage of a Hott Sonn & Yr Eyes': John Donne's Love Letters to Ann More." Summers and Pebworth, *Eagle* 25–52.

Benet, Diana. *Secretary of Praise: The Poetic Vocation of George Herbert*. Columbia: U of Missouri P, 1984.

Bennett, Joan. *Five Metaphysical Poets*. Cambridge: Cambridge UP, 1964.

———. *Four Metaphysical Poets*. Cambridge: Cambridge UP, 1934.

Bergman, David, and Daniel Mark Epstein, eds. *The Heath Guide to Poetry.* Lexington: Heath, 1983.

Berjeau, Jean Philibert, ed. *Biblia pauperum.* London: Smith, 1859.

———, ed. *Speculum humanae salvationis.* London: Stewart, 1861.

Berry, Lloyd E., ed. *A Bibliography of Studies in Metaphysical Poetry, 1939–1960.* Madison: U of Wisconsin P, 1964.

Berthoff, Ann E. *The Resolved Soul: A Study of Marvell's Major Poems.* Princeton: Princeton UP, 1970.

Bertonasco, Marc F. *Crashaw and the Baroque.* University: U of Alabama P, 1971.

Bethell, S. L. "The Nature of Metaphysical Wit." *Northern Miscellany of Literary Criticism* 1 (1953): 19–40.

Bewley, Marius, ed. *The Selected Poetry of Donne.* New York: NAL, 1966.

Bloch, Chana. *Spelling the Word: George Herbert and the Bible.* Berkeley: U of California P, 1985.

Bloom, Harold, ed. *John Donne and the Seventeenth-Century Metaphysical Poets.* New York: Chelsea, 1986.

Bottrall, Margaret. *George Herbert.* 1954. London: Folcroft, 1971.

Bourdette, Robert E., Jr. "Recent Studies in Henry Vaughan." *English Literary Renaissance* 4 (1974): 229–310.

Bradbrook, M. C., and M. G. Lloyd-Thomas, *Andrew Marvell.* Cambridge: Cambridge UP, 1940.

Bradbury, Malcolm, and David Palmer, eds. *Metaphysical Poetry.* London: Arnold, 1970.

Bredvold, Louis I. *The Intellectual Milieu of John Dryden: Studies in Some Aspects of Seventeenth-Century Thought.* Ann Arbor: U of Michigan P, 1934.

Brett, R. L., ed. *Andrew Marvell: Essays on the Tercentenary of His Death.* Oxford: Oxford UP, 1979.

Briggs, Julia. *This Stage-Play World: English Literature and Its Background, 1580–1625.* Oxford: Oxford UP, 1983.

Brinsley, John. *Ludus Literarius: Or, The Grammar School.* Ed. E. T. Campagnac. Liverpool: Liverpool UP, 1917.

Brooks, Cleanth. *The Well-Wrought Urn: Studies in the Structure of Poetry.* New York: Harcourt, 1947.

Brown, John Russell. *Discovering Shakespeare: A New Guide to the Plays.* New York: Columbia UP, 1981.

Bush, Douglas. *English Literature in the Earlier Seventeenth Century, 1600–1660.* Oxford History of English Literature 5. Ed. F. P. Wilson and Bonamy Dobrée. Oxford: Clarendon, 1962.

Calhoun, Thomas O. *Henry Vaughan: The Achievement of Silex Scintillans.* Newark: U of Delaware P, 1981.

Calvin, John. *John Calvin: Selections from His Writings.* Ed. John Dillenberger. New York: Doubleday, 1971.

——. *Works*. Vols. 34, 35. Edinburgh: Calvin Translation Soc., 1847. 52 vols. 1844–56.

Carey, John, ed. *Andrew Marvell*. Penguin Critical Anthologies. Harmondsworth: Penguin, 1961.

——. *John Donne: Life, Mind, and Art*. New York: Oxford UP, 1981.

Cathcart, Dwight. *Doubting Conscience: Donne and the Poetry of Moral Argument*. Ann Arbor: U of Michigan P, 1975.

Charles, Amy M. *A Life of George Herbert*. Ithaca: Cornell UP, 1977.

——, ed. *The Williams Manuscript of George Herbert's Poems*. Delmar: Scholars', 1977.

Charles, Amy M., and Mario A. Di Cesare, eds. *The Bodleian Manuscript of George Herbert's Poems: A Facsimile of Tanner 307*. Delmar: Scholars', 1984.

Chernaik, Warren L. *The Poet's Time: Politics and Religion in the Work of Andrew Marvell*. Cambridge: Cambridge UP, 1983.

Chute, Marchette. *Two Gentle Men: The Lives of George Herbert and Robert Herrick*. New York: Dutton, 1959.

Cirillo, Albert R. "Recent Studies in Crashaw." *English Literary Renaissance* 9 (1979): 183–93.

Clark, George N. *The Later Stuarts, 1660–1714*. 1934. Oxford History of England 10. Oxford: Clarendon, 1955.

Clark, Ira. *Christ Revealed: The History of the Neotypological Lyric in the English Renaissance*. Gainesville: U of Florida P, 1982.

Clements, A. L., ed. *John Donne's Poetry*. Norton Critical Editions. New York: Norton, 1966.

Coffin, Charles M. *John Donne and the New Philosophy*. New York: Columbia UP, 1937.

Colie, Rosalie. *"My Ecchoing Song": Andrew Marvell's Poetry of Criticism*. Princeton: Princeton UP, 1970.

——. *Paradoxia Epidemica: The Renaissance Tradition of Paradox*. Princeton: Princeton UP, 1966.

——. *The Resources of Kind: Genre Theory in the Renaissance*. Ed. Barbara K. Lewalski. Berkeley: U of California P, 1973.

Collins, Dan S. *Andrew Marvell: A Reference Guide*. Boston: Hall, 1981.

Collinson, Patrick. *The Religion of Protestants: The Church in English Society 1559–1625*. Oxford: Clarendon, 1982.

Combs, Homer C., and Zay R. Sullens, eds. *A Concordance to the English Poems of John Donne*. Chicago: Packard, 1940.

Cooper, Robert M., ed. *A Concordance to the English Poetry of Richard Crashaw*. Troy: Whitson, 1981.

——, ed. *Essays on Richard Crashaw*. Salzburg: Institut für Anglistik und Amerikanistik, Universität Salzburg, 1979.

Cox, Hyde, and Edward Connery Lathem, eds. *Selected Prose of Robert Frost*. New York: Collier, 1968.

Craik, T. W., and R. J. Craik, eds. *John Donne: Selected Poetry and Prose*. London: Methuen, 1986.

Craze, Michael. *The Life and Lyrics of Andrew Marvell*. London: Macmillan, 1979.

Cullen, Patrick. *Spenser, Marvell, and Renaissance Pastoral*. Cambridge: Harvard UP, 1970.

Daniélou, Jean C. *From Shadows to Reality: Studies in the Typology of the Fathers*. Trans. Wulston Hibberd. London: Burns, 1960.

Davies, Godfrey. *The Early Stuarts, 1603–1660*. Oxford History of England 9. Oxford: Oxford UP, 1959.

Davies, Horton. *Worship and Theology in England*. Vol. 1: *From Cranmer to Hooker, 1534–1603*. Vol. 2: *From Andrewes to Baxter and Fox, 1603–1690*. Princeton: Princeton UP, 1970, 1975.

Dees, Jerome S. "Recent Studies in the English Emblems." *English Literary Renaissance* 16 (1986): 391–420.

Di Cesare, Mario A., ed. *George Herbert and the Seventeenth-Century Religious Poets*. Norton Critical Editions. New York: Norton, 1978.

Di Cesare, Mario A., and Rigo Mignani, eds. *A Concordance to the Complete Writings of George Herbert*. Ithaca: Cornell UP, 1977.

Dickson, Donald R. *The Fountain of Living Waters: The Typology of the Waters of Life in Herbert, Vaughan, and Traherne*. Columbia: U of Missouri P, 1987.

Didron, Adolphe Napoléon. *Christian Iconography*. Trans. E. J. Millington. 2 vols. New York: Ungar, 1965.

Diehl, Huston. "Graven Images: Protestant Emblem Books in England." *Renaissance Quarterly* 39 (1986): 49–66.

Docherty, Thomas. *John Donne, Undone*. New York: Methuen, 1987.

Dollimore, Jonathan. *Radical Tragedy: Religion, Ideology and Power in the Drama of Shakespeare and His Contemporaries*. Chicago: U of Chicago P, 1984.

Donno, Elizabeth Story, ed. *Andrew Marvell: The Complete English Poems*. New York: St. Martin's, 1972.

———, ed. *Andrew Marvell: The Critical Heritage*. Boston: Routledge, 1978.

Dryden, John. "A Discourse concerning the Original and Progress of Satire" (1693). Clements 106.

Dubrow, Heather. "Shakespeare's Undramatic Monologues: Toward a Reading of the Sonnets." *Shakespeare Quarterly* 32 (1981): 55–68.

Dubrow, Heather, and Richard Strier, eds. *The Historical Renaissance: New Essays on Tudor and Stuart Literature and Culture*. Chicago: U of Chicago P, 1988.

Duncan, Joseph E. *The Revival of Metaphysical Poetry: The History of a Style, 1800 to the Present*. Minneapolis: U of Minnesota P, 1959.

Durr, R. A. *On the Mystical Poetry of Henry Vaughan*. Cambridge: Cambridge UP, 1962.

Dyson, A. E., ed. *English Poetry: Select Bibliographical Guides*. London: Oxford UP, 1971.

Eisenstein, Elizabeth L. *The Printing Press as an Agent of Change*. Cambridge: Cambridge UP, 1979.

Eliot, T. S. "Andrew Marvell." 1921. *Selected Essays*. 251–63.

―――. *Complete Poems and Plays 1909–1950*. New York: Harcourt, 1952.

―――. *George Herbert*. Writers and Their Work. London: Longmans, 1962.

―――. "Lancelot Andrewes." *Selected Essays* 299–310.

―――. "The Metaphysical Poets." 1921. *Selected Essays* 241–50.

―――. *Selected Essays, 1917–1932*. London: Faber, 1932.

―――. "Tradition and the Individual Talent." 1919. *Selected Essays* 3–11.

Ellrodt, Robert. *L'inspiration personelle et l'esprit du temps chez les poètes métaphysiques anglais*. Paris: Corti, 1960.

Empson, William. *Seven Types of Ambiguity*. 3rd ed. New York: Meridian, 1955.

―――. *Using Biography*. Cambridge: Harvard UP, 1984.

Fiore, Peter Amadeus, ed. *Just So Much Honor: Essays Commemorating the Four Hundredth Anniversary of the Birth of John Donne*. University Park: Pennsylvania State UP, 1972.

Fish, Stanley E. *The Living Temple: George Herbert and Catechizing*. Berkeley: U of California P, 1978.

―――. *Self-Consuming Artifacts: The Experience of Seventeenth-Century Literature*. Berkeley: U of California P, 1972.

Fletcher, Angus. *Allegory: The Theory of a Symbolic Mode*. Ithaca: Cornell UP, 1964.

Fogle, French, ed. *The Complete Poetry of Henry Vaughan*. Garden City: Doubleday, 1964.

Ford, Boris, ed. *From Donne to Marvell*. Rev. ed. New Pelican Guide to English Literature 3. New York: Penguin, 1982.

Foucault, Michel. *The Order of Things: An Archaeology of the Human Sciences*. New York: Pantheon, 1970.

Fraistat, Neil, ed. *Poems in Their Place: The Intertextuality and Order of Poetic Collections*. Chapel Hill: U of North Carolina P, 1986.

Freeman, Rosemary. *English Emblem Books*. London: Chatto, 1948.

―――. "Parody as a Literary Form: George Herbert and Wilfred Owen." *Essays in Criticism* 13 (1963): 307–22.

Freer, Coburn. *Music for a King: George Herbert's Style and the Metrical Psalms*. Baltimore: Johns Hopkins UP, 1972.

Friedenreich, Kenneth. *Henry Vaughan*. Boston: Twayne, 1978.

―――, ed. *Tercentenary Essays in Honor of Andrew Marvell*. Hamden: Archon, 1977.

Friedman, Donald M. *Marvell's Pastoral Art*. Berkeley: U of California P, 1970.

Friedrich, Carl. *The Age of the Baroque*. New York: Harper, 1962.

Gardiner, Samuel R. *History of England from the Accession of James ı to the Outbreak of the Civil War*. 10 vols. London: Longmans, 1883–85.

Gardner, Helen, ed. *John Donne: A Collection of Critical Essays*. Twentieth Century Views. Englewood Cliffs: Prentice, 1962.

——, ed. *John Donne: The Divine Poems*. Oxford: Clarendon, 1952.

——, ed. *John Donne: The Elegies and the* Songs and Sonnets. Oxford: Clarendon, 1965.

——, ed. *The Metaphysical Poets*. Rev. ed. Baltimore: Penguin, 1966.

Garner, Ross. *Henry Vaughan: Experience and the Tradition*. Chicago: U of Chicago P, 1959.

——. *The Unprofitable Servant in Henry Vaughan*. Lincoln: U of Nebraska P, 1963.

Gaston, Paul L. "Britten's Donne and the Promise of Twentieth Century Settings." Summers and Pebworth, *Eagle* 201–13.

George, Charles H., and Katherine G. George. *The Protestant Mind of the English Reformation, 1570–1640*. Princeton: Princeton UP, 1961.

Gilman, Ernest B. *The Curious Perspective: Literary and Pictorial Wit in the Seventeenth Century*. New Haven: Yale UP, 1978.

——. "Word and Image in Quarles' *Emblemes*." *Critical Inquiry* 6 (1980): 385–410. Rpt. in *The Language of Images*. Ed. W. J. T. Mitchell. Chicago: U of Chicago P, 1980. 59–89.

Ginsberg, Allen. *Allen Verbatim*. Ed. Gordon Ball. New York: McGraw, 1974.

Goldberg, Jonathan. *James ı and the Politics of Literature*. Baltimore: Johns Hopkins UP, 1983.

——. *Voice Terminal Echo: Postmodernism and English Renaissance Texts*. New York: Methuen, 1986.

Gottlieb, Sidney. "The Social and Political Backgrounds of George Herbert's Poetry." Summers and Pebworth, *"Muses Common-Weale"* 107–18.

Grabar, André. *Christian Iconography: A Study of Its Origins*. Trans. Terry Grabar. Princeton: Princeton UP, 1968.

Grant, Patrick. *Images and Ideas in Literature of the English Renaissance*. Amherst: U of Massachusetts P, 1979.

——. *The Transformation of Sin: Studies in Donne, Herbert, Vaughan, and Traherne*. Amherst: U of Massachusetts P, 1974.

Greaves, Richard L. "The Puritan-Nonconformist Tradition in England, 1560–1700: Historiographical Reflections." *Albion* 17 (1985): 449–86.

——. *Society and Religion in Elizabethan England*. Minneapolis: U of Minnesota P, 1981.

Greenblatt, Stephen. *Renaissance Self-Fashioning: From More to Shakespeare*. Chicago: U of Chicago P, 1980.

Grierson, Herbert J. C., ed. *Donne: Poetical Works*. New York: Oxford UP, 1971.

———. *Metaphysical Lyrics and Poems of the Seventeenth Century*. Oxford: Clarendon, 1921.

Guffey, George R., ed. *A Concordance to the English Poetry of Andrew Marvell*. Chapel Hill: U of North Carolina P, 1974.

Guss, Donald L. *John Donne, Petrarchist: Italianate Conceits and Love Theory in the* Songs and Sonets. Detroit: Wayne State UP, 1966.

H. A. [Henry Hawkins]. *Parthenia Sacra: Or, The Mysterious and Delicious Garden of the Sacred Parthenes*. [Paris], 1633. In facsim. Ed. John Horden. Menston: Scolar, 1971.

Halewood, William. *The Poetry of Grace: Reformation Themes and Structures in English Seventeenth-Century Poetry*. New Haven: Yale UP, 1970.

Haller, William. *The Rise of Puritanism*. New York: Columbia UP, 1938.

Harman, Barbara Leah. *Costly Monuments: Representations of the Self in George Herbert's Poetry*. Cambridge: Harvard UP, 1982.

Harris, Victor. *All Coherence Gone: A Study of the Seventeenth-Century Controversy over Disorder and Decay in the Universe*. Chicago: U of Chicago P, 1949.

Hauser, Arnold. *Mannerism: The Crisis of the Renaissance and the Origin of Modern Art*. London: Routledge, 1965.

Hester, M. Thomas. *Kinde Pitty and Brave Scorn: John Donne's* Satyres. Durham: Duke UP, 1982.

Hill, Christopher. *The Century of Revolution, 1603–1714*. 1961. New York: Norton, 1966.

———. *Collected Essays of Christopher Hill*. 3 vols. to date. Amherst: U of Massachusetts P, 1985–.

———. *Intellectual Origins of the English Revolution*. Oxford: Oxford UP, 1965.

———. *Puritanism and Revolution: Studies in Interpretation of the English Revolution in the Seventeenth Century*. London: Secker, 1958.

———. *Society and Puritanism in Pre-Revolutionary England*. London: Secker, 1964.

Hirsch, E. D. *Cultural Literacy: What Every American Needs to Know*. Boston: Houghton, 1987.

Hodge, R. I. V. *Foreshortened Time: Andrew Marvell and Seventeenth Century Revolutions*. Cambridge: Brewer, 1978.

Hollander, John. *Rhyme's Reason: A Guide to English Verse*. New Haven: Yale UP, 1981.

———. *The Untuning of the Sky: Ideas of Music in English Poetry, 1500–1700*. Princeton: Princeton UP, 1961.

Holmes, Elizabeth. *Henry Vaughan and the Hermetic Philosophy*. Oxford: Blackwell, 1932.

Hoover, L. Elaine. *John Donne and Francisco de Quevedo: Poets of Love and Death*. Chapel Hill: U of North Carolina P, 1978.

Hughes, Richard E. *The Progress of the Soul: The Interior Career of John Donne.* New York: Morrow, 1968.

Hughes, Robert. *Heaven and Hell in Western Art.* New York: Stein, 1968.

Hulse, Clark. "Recent Studies of Literature and Painting in the English Renaissance." *English Literary Renaissance* 15 (1985): 122–40.

Hunt, Clay. *Donne's Poetry: Essays in Literary Analysis.* New Haven: Yale UP, 1954.

Hunt, John Dixon. *Andrew Marvell: His Life and Writings.* Ithaca: Cornell UP, 1978.

Husain, Itrat. *The Mystical Element in the Metaphysical Poets of the Seventeenth Century.* Edinburgh: Oliver, 1948.

Hutchinson, F. E. *Henry Vaughan: A Life and Interpretation.* Oxford: Clarendon, 1947.

———, ed. *The Works of George Herbert.* 1941. Rev. ed. Oxford: Clarendon, 1945.

Hyman, Lawrence W. *Andrew Marvell.* Boston: Twayne, 1964.

Jenner, Thomas. *The Soules Solace.* London, 1626. In facsim. in *The Emblem Books of Thomas Jenner.* Ed. Sidney Gottlieb. Delmar: Scholars', 1983.

Jensen, H. James. *The Muses' Concord: Literature, Music, and the Visual Arts in the Baroque Age.* Bloomington: Indiana UP, 1976.

John of the Cross, Saint. *The Dark Night of the Soul.* Trans. and ed. Kurt F. Reinhardt. New York: Ungar, 1957.

Johnson, Samuel. "Life of Cowley." *Samuel Johnson: Rasselas, Poems, and Selected Prose.* Ed. Bertrand H. Bronson. New York: Holt, 1958.

Jones, R. F. *Ancients and Moderns: A Study of the Rise of the Scientific Movement in Seventeenth-Century England.* Rev. ed. New York: Dover, 1982.

Jonson, Ben. *Ben Jonson.* Ed. Ian Donaldson. Oxford: Oxford UP, 1985.

Keast, William R., ed. *Seventeenth-Century English Poetry: Modern Essays in Criticism.* Oxford: Oxford UP, 1971.

Kenner, Hugh, ed. *Seventeenth-Century Poetry: The Schools of Donne and Jonson.* New York: Holt, 1964.

Kermode, Frank, ed. *Discussions of John Donne.* Boston: Heath, 1962.

———, ed. *The Metaphysical Poets.* Greenwich: Fawcett, 1969.

———. "The Private Imagery of Henry Vaughan." *Review of English Studies* 1 (1953): 206–25.

Kermode, Frank, and John Hollander, gen. eds. *The Oxford Anthology of English Literature.* Vol. 1. New York: Oxford UP, 1973.

Kilpatrick, William Kirk. *Psychological Seduction: The Failure of Modern Psychology.* Nashville: Nelson, 1983.

King, Bruce. *Marvell's Allegorical Poetry.* Cambridge: Oleander, 1977.

Kinney, Arthur F., and Dan S. Collins, eds. *Renaissance Historicism: Selections from* English Literary Renaissance. Amherst: U of Massachusetts P, 1988.

Klause, John. *Theodicy and the Moral Imagination of Andrew Marvell*. Hamden: Archon, 1983.

Korshin, Paul J. *Typologies in England 1650–1820*. Princeton: Princeton UP, 1982.

Koyré, Alexander. *From the Closed World to the Infinite Cosmos*. Baltimore: Johns Hopkins UP, 1957.

Kuhn, Thomas S. *The Copernican Revolution: Planetary Astronomy in the Development of Western Thought*. Cambridge: Harvard UP, 1957.

Le Comte, Edward S. *Grace to a Witty Sinner: A Life of Donne*. New York: Walker, 1965.

Legouis, Pierre. *Andrew Marvell: Poet, Puritan, Patriot*. 1928. Rev. and abr. Oxford: Clarendon, 1965.

———. *Donne the Craftsman: An Essay upon the Structure of the* Songs and Sonets. 1928. New York: Russell, 1962.

Leishman, J. B. *The Art of Marvell's Poetry*. London: Hutchinson, 1966.

———. *The Metaphysical Poets: Donne, Herbert, Vaughan, Traherne*. Oxford: Clarendon, 1934.

———. *The Monarch of Wit: An Analytical and Comparative Study of the Poetry of John Donne*. London: Hutchinson, 1951.

Letts, Rosa Marie. *The Renaissance*. Cambridge Introduction to the History of Art 3. Cambridge: Cambridge UP, 1981.

Lewalski, Barbara Kiefer. *Donne's "Anniversaries" and the Poetry of Praise: The Creation of a Symbolic Mode*. Princeton: Princeton UP, 1973.

———. *Protestant Poetics and the Seventeenth-Century Religious Lyric*. Princeton: Princeton UP, 1979.

Lewalski, Barbara Kiefer, and Andrew J. Sabol, eds. *Major Poets of the Earlier Seventeenth Century*. New York: Odyssey, 1973.

Lewis, C. S. *The Discarded Image: An Introduction to Medieval and Renaissance Literature*. Cambridge: Cambridge UP, 1964.

Long, Michael. *Marvell, Nabokov: Childhood and Arcadia*. Oxford: Clarendon, 1984.

Longnon, Jean, and Raymond Cazelles, eds. *The* Très Riches Heures *of Jean, Duke of Berry*. New York: Braziller, 1969.

Lord, George deF., ed. *Andrew Marvell: A Collection of Critical Essays*. Twentieth-Century Views. Englewood Cliffs: Prentice, 1968.

———, ed. *Andrew Marvell: Complete Poetry*. 1968. London: Dent, 1984.

———, ed. *Poems on Affairs of State: Augustan Satirical Verse, 1660–1714*. Vol. 1. New Haven: Yale UP, 1963.

Lovejoy, A. O. *The Great Chain of Being: A Study in the History of an Idea*. Cambridge: Harvard UP, 1936.

Low, Anthony. *Love's Architecture: Devotional Modes in Seventeenth-Century English Poetry*. New York: New York UP, 1978.

Lowrie, Walter. *Art in the Early Church*. Rev. ed. New York: Harper, 1965.

Lytle, Guy Fitch, and Stephen Orgel, eds. *Patronage in the Renaissance*. Princeton: Princeton UP, 1981.

McCanles, Michael. *Dialectical Criticism and Renaissance Literature*. Berkeley: U of California P, 1975.

McCloskey, Mark, and Paul R. Murphy, eds. and trans. *The Latin Poetry of George Herbert: A Bilingual Edition*. Athens: Ohio UP, 1965.

McGee, J. Sears. *The Godly Man in Stuart England: Anglicans, Puritans, and the Two Tables, 1620–1670*. New Haven: Yale UP, 1976.

McQueen, William A., and Kiffin A. Rockwell, eds. and trans. *The Latin Poetry of Andrew Marvell*. Chapel Hill: U of North Carolina P, 1964.

Madsen, William G. *From Shadowy Types to Truth: Studies in Milton's Symbolism*. New Haven: Yale UP, 1968.

Mahood, M. M. *Poetry and Humanism*. New Haven: Yale UP, 1950.

Mainstone, Madeleine, and Rowland Mainstone. *The Seventeenth Century*. Cambridge Introduction to the History of Art 4. Cambridge: Cambridge UP, 1981.

Malcolmson, Cristina. "George Herbert's *Country Parson* and the Character of Social Identity." *Studies in Philology* 85 (1988): 245–66

Mâle, Emile. *The Gothic Image: Religious Art in France of the Thirteenth Century*. Trans. Dora Nussey. New York: Harper, 1958.

Maleski, Mary, ed. *A Fine Tuning: Studies of the Religious Poetry of Herbert and Milton*. Binghamton: Medieval and Renaissance Texts and Studies, 1989.

Manley, Frank, ed. *John Donne: The Anniversaries*. Baltimore: Johns Hopkins UP, 1963.

Marcus, Leah Sinanoglou. *Childhood and Cultural Despair: A Theme and Variations in Seventeenth-Century Literature*. Pittsburgh: U of Pittsburgh P, 1978.

———. *The Politics of Mirth: Jonson, Herrick, Milton, Marvell, and the Defense of Old Holiday Pastimes*. Chicago: U of Chicago P, 1986

Margoliouth, H. M., ed. *The Poems and Letters of Andrew Marvell*. 1927. Rev. Pierre Legouis with E. E. Duncan-Jones. Oxford: Clarendon, 1971.

Marilla, E. L. *A Comprehensive Bibliography of Henry Vaughan*. Tuscaloosa: U of Alabama P, 1948.

———, ed. *The Secular Poetry of Henry Vaughan*. Cambridge: Harvard UP, 1958.

Marilla, E. L., and James D. Simmonds. *Henry Vaughan: A Bibliographical Supplement, 1946–1960*. Tuscaloosa: U of Alabama P, 1963.

Marotti, Arthur F. *John Donne, Coterie Poet*. Madison: U of Wisconsin P, 1986.

Martin, L. C., ed. *The Poems, English, Latin, and Greek, of Richard Crashaw*. 2nd ed. Oxford: Clarendon, 1957.

———, ed. *The Works of Henry Vaughan*. 2nd ed. Oxford: Clarendon, 1957.

Martindale, Adam. *Life of Adam Martindale, Written by Himself*. Ed. Richard Parkinson. Chetham Society Publications 4. Manchester: Simms, 1845.

Martz, Louis L. "English Religious Poetry, from Renaissance to Baroque" *Explorations in Renaissance Culture* 11 (1985): 1–28.

———, ed. *English Seventeenth-Century Verse*. Vol. 1. Garden City: Doubleday, 1969.

———, ed. *George Herbert and Henry Vaughan*. Oxford: Oxford UP, 1986.

———. *The Paradise Within: Studies in Vaughan, Traherne, and Milton*. New Haven: Yale UP, 1964.

———. *The Poetry of Meditation: A Study in English Religious Literature of the Seventeenth Century*. Rev. ed. New Haven: Yale UP, 1962.

———. *The Wit of Love: Donne, Carew, Crashaw, Marvell*. Notre Dame: U of Notre Dame P, 1969.

Mazzeo, Joseph A. "A Critique of Some Modern Theories of Metaphysical Poetry." *Modern Philology* 50 (1952): 88–96.

———. *Renaissance and Revolution: Backgrounds to Seventeenth-Century Literature*. New York: Random, 1965.

Meiss, Millard, and Edith W. Kirsch, eds. *The Visconti Hours*. New York: Braziller, 1972.

Milgate, Wesley, ed. *John Donne: The Epithalamions, Anniversaries and Epicedes*. Oxford: Clarendon, 1978.

———, ed. *John Donne: The Satires, Epigrams and Verse Letters*. Oxford: Clarendon, 1967.

Miller, Edmund, and Robert DiYanni, eds. *Like Season'd Timber: New Essays on George Herbert*. New York: Lang, 1987.

Miller, Perry. *The New England Mind: The Seventeenth Century*. Cambridge: Harvard UP, 1954.

Mills, Jerry Leath. "Recent Studies in Herbert." *English Literary Renaissance* 6 (1976): 105–18.

Miner, Earl, ed. *Literary Uses of Typology from the Late Middle Ages to the Present*. Princeton: Princeton UP, 1977.

———. *The Metaphysical Mode from Donne to Cowley*. Princeton: Princeton UP, 1969.

———, ed. *Seventeenth-Century Imagery: Essays on Uses of Figurative Language from Donne to Farquhar*. Berkeley: U of California P, 1971.

Minor, Robert N., and Robert D. Baird. "Teaching about Religion at the State University: Taking the Issue Seriously and Strictly." *The Council on the Study of Religion Bulletin* 14 (1983): 69–72.

"More Collegians Turn to Religion." *Christianity Today* 17 June 1983: 43–44.

Mulder, John R. *The Temple of the Mind: Education and Literary Taste in Seventeenth-Century England*. New York: Pegasus, 1969.

Nicolson, Marjorie Hope. *The Breaking of the Circle: Studies in the Effect of the "New Science" upon Seventeenth-Century Poetry*. Rev. ed. New York: Columbia UP, 1960.

Norbrook, David. *Poetry and Politics in the English Renaissance.* London: Routledge, 1984.

Novarr, David. *The Disinterred Muse: Donne's Texts and Contexts.* Ithaca: Cornell UP, 1980.

Nuttall, A. D. *Overheard by God: Fiction and Prayer in Herbert, Milton, Dante and St. John.* London: Methuen, 1980.

Ogg, David. *England in the Reign of Charles II.* 2nd ed. Oxford: Oxford UP, 1984.

———. *England in the Reign of James II and William III.* 1955. Oxford: Oxford UP, 1984.

Ong, Walter J. "From Allegory to Diagram in the Renaissance Mind: A Study in the Significance of the Allegorical Tableau." *Journal of Aesthetics and Art Criticism* 17 (1959): 423–40.

———. *Interfaces of the Word: Studies in the Evolution of Consciousness and Culture.* Ithaca: Cornell UP, 1977.

———. *The Presence of the Word: Some Prologomena for Cultural and Religious History.* 1967. Minneapolis: U of Minnesota P, 1981.

Oxford English Dictionary. 1933.

Parfitt, George. *English Poetry of the Seventeenth Century.* London: Longman, 1985.

Parrish, Paul A. *Richard Crashaw.* Boston: Twayne, 1980.

Parry, Graham. *Seventeenth-Century Poetry: The Social Context.* London: Hutchinson, 1985.

Patrides, C. A., ed. *Approaches to Marvell: The York Tercentenary Lectures.* London: Routledge, 1978.

———, ed. *The Complete English Poems of John Donne.* London: Dent, 1985.

———, ed. *The English Poems of George Herbert.* London: Dent, 1974.

———, ed. *George Herbert: The Critical Heritage.* London: Routledge, 1983.

———. *The Grand Design of God: The Literary Form of the Christian View of History.* London: Routledge, 1972.

———. *Premises and Motifs in Renaissance Thought and Literature.* Princeton: Princeton UP, 1982.

Patrides, C. A., and Raymond B. Waddington, eds. *The Age of Milton: Backgrounds to Seventeenth-Century Literature.* Manchester: Manchester UP, 1980.

Patterson, Annabel M. *Censorship and Interpretation: The Conditions of Writing and Reading in Early Modern England.* Madison: U of Wisconsin P, 1984.

———. *Marvell and the Civic Crown.* Princeton: Princeton UP, 1978.

Peacham, Henry. *Minerva Britanna.* London, 1613. In facsim. Ed. John Horden. Menston: Scolar, 1973.

Petersson, Robert T. *The Art of Ecstasy: Teresa, Bernini, and Crashaw.* London: Routledge, 1970.

Pettet, E. C. *Of Paradise and Light: A Study of* Silex Scintillans. Cambridge: Cambridge UP, 1960.

Pickering, F. P. *Literature and Art in the Middle Ages.* Coral Gables: U of Miami P, 1970.

Pinka, Patricia Garland. *This Dialogue of One: The* Songs and Sonnets *of John Donne.* University: U of Alabama P, 1982.

Plummer, John, ed. *The Hours of Catherine of Cleves.* New York: Braziller, 1966.

Post, Jonathan F. S. *Henry Vaughan: The Unfolding Vision.* Princeton: Princeton UP, 1982.

———, ed. Special Issue on Henry Vaughan. *George Herbert Journal* 7 (1983–84): 1–119.

Powers, Perry J. "Lope de Vega and *Las lágrimas de la Madalena.*" *Comparative Literature* 8 (1956): 273–90.

Praz, Mario. 1958. *The Flaming Heart: Essays on Crashaw, Machiavelli, and Other Studies in the Relations between Italian and English Literature from Chaucer to T. S. Eliot.* New York: Norton, 1973.

———. *Studies in Seventeenth-Century Imagery.* 2nd ed. Rome: Edizioni di Storia e letteratura, 1964.

Press, John. *Andrew Marvell.* Writers and Their Work. London: Longmans, 1958.

Quarles, Francis. *Emblemes.* London, 1635.

Raspa, Anthony. *The Emotive Image: Jesuit Poetics in the English Renaissance.* Fort Worth: Texas Christian UP, 1983.

Ray, Robert H., ed. *The Herbert Allusion Book: Allusions to George Herbert in the Seventeenth Century.* Texts and Studies. *Studies in Philology* 83 (1986): 1–182.

———. "Recent Studies in Herbert, 1974–1986." *English Literary Renaissance* 18 (1988): 460–75.

Réau, Louis. *Iconographie de l'art chrétien.* 3 vols. Paris: Presses Universitaires de France, 1955–59.

Redpath, Theodore, ed. *The* Songs and Sonets *of John Donne.* London: Methuen, 1956.

Reeves, Gareth, ed. *Selected Poems of George Herbert.* New York: Barnes, 1971.

Rickey, Mary Ellen. *Rhyme and Meaning in Richard Crashaw.* Lexington: U of Kentucky, 1961.

———. *Utmost Art: Complexity in the Verse of George Herbert.* Lexington: U of Kentucky P, 1966.

———. "Vaughan, *The Temple,* and Poetic Form." *Studies in Philology* 59 (1962): 162–70.

Rivers, Isabel. *Classical and Christian Ideas in English Renaissance Poetry.* London: Allen, 1979.

Roberts, John R., ed. *Essential Articles for the Study of George Herbert's Poetry.* Hamden: Archon, 1979.

———, ed. *Essential Articles for the Study of John Donne's Poetry.* Hamden: Archon, 1975.

———. *George Herbert: An Annotated Bibliography of Modern Criticism, 1905–1984.* Rev. ed. Columbia: U of Missouri P, 1988.

————. *John Donne: An Annotated Bibliography of Modern Criticism, 1912–1967*. Columbia: U of Missouri P, 1973.

————. *John Donne: An Annotated Bibliography of Modern Criticism, 1968–1978*. Columbia: U of Missouri P, 1982.

————. *Richard Crashaw: An Annotated Bibliography of Criticism, 1632–1980*. Columbia: U of Missouri P, 1985.

Rollins, Hyder Edward, ed. *Tottel's Miscellany*. 2 vols. Cambridge: Harvard UP, 1965.

Rorimer, James J., ed. *The Belles Heures of Jean, Duke of Berry*. New York: Metropolitan Museum of Art, 1958.

Ross, Malcolm M. *Poetry and Dogma: The Transfiguration of Eucharistic Symbols in Seventeenth Century English Poetry*. 1954. New York: Octagon, 1969.

Roston, Murray. *The Soul of Wit: A Study of John Donne*. Oxford: Clarendon, 1974.

Rothe, Edith. *Medieval Book Illumination in Europe*. Trans. Mary Whittall. New York: Norton, 1968.

Rudrum, Alan. "An Aspect of Vaughan's Hermeticism: The Doctrine of Cosmic Sympathy." *Studies in English Literature* 14 (1974): 129–38.

————, ed. *Essential Articles for the Study of Henry Vaughan*. Hamden: Archon, 1987.

————, ed. *Henry Vaughan: The Complete Poems*. Harmondsworth: Penguin, 1976.

————. "The Influence of Alchemy in the Poems of Henry Vaughan." *Philological Quarterly* 49 (1970): 469–80.

————. "Vaughan's 'The Night': Some Hermetic Notes." *Modern Language Review* 64 (1969): 11–19. Rpt. in Rudrum, *Essential Articles* 141–53.

Ruffo-Fiore, Silvia. *Donne's Petrarchism: A Comparative View*. Florence: Grafica Toscana, 1976.

Russell, Conrad. *The Crisis of Parliaments: English History 1509–1660*. London: Oxford UP, 1971.

Sanders, Wilber. *John Donne's Poetry*. Cambridge: Cambridge UP, 1971.

Schaar, Claes. *Marino and Crashaw: Sospetto d'Herode: A Commentary*. Lund: Gleerup, 1971.

Schiller, Gertrud. *Iconography of Christian Art*. Trans. Janet Seligman. 2 vols. Greenwich: New York Graphic Soc., 1971–72.

Schleiner, Louise. "Recent Studies in Poetry and Music of the English Renaissance." *English Literary Renaissance* 16 (1986): 253–68.

Schoenfeldt, Michael C. " 'Subject to Ev'ry Mounters Bended Knee': Herbert and Authority." Dubrow and Strier 242–69.

Schwartz, Lynne Sharon. *Rough Strife*. New York: Harper, 1980.

Sessions, William A. *Henry Howard, Poet-Earl of Surrey*. Boston: Twayne, 1986.

Seznec, Jean. *The Survival of the Pagan Gods: The Mythological Tradition and Its Place in Renaissance Humanism and Art*. Trans. B. Sessions. New York: Pantheon, 1953.

Sharpe, Kevin, and Steven N. Zwicker, eds. *Politics of Discourse: The Literature and History of Seventeenth-Century England.* Berkeley: U of California P, 1987.

Shaw, Robert B. *The Call of God: The Theme of Vocation in the Poetry of Donne and Herbert.* Cambridge: Cowley, 1981.

———, ed. *Henry Vaughan: Selected Poems.* Manchester: Carcanet, 1983.

Shawcross, John T., ed. *The Complete Poetry of John Donne.* Garden City: Doubleday, 1967.

———. "Research and the State of Studies in Seventeenth-Century British Literature (1600–1660)." *Literary Research Newsletter* 9 (1984): 3–19.

Sherwood, Terry G. *Fulfilling the Circle: A Study of John Donne's Thought.* Toronto: U of Toronto P, 1984.

Simmonds, James D. *Masques of God: Form and Theme in the Poetry of Henry Vaughan.* Pittsburgh: U of Pittsburgh P, 1972.

Sinfield, Alan. *Literature in Protestant England 1560–1660.* Totowa: Barnes, 1983.

Singleton, Marion White. *God's Courtier: Configuring a Different Grace in George Herbert's Temple.* Cambridge: Cambridge UP, 1987.

Slights, Camille Wells. *The Casuistical Tradition in Shakespeare, Donne, Herbert, and Milton.* Princeton: Princeton UP, 1981.

Smith, A. J., ed. *John Donne: The Complete English Poems.* Baltimore: Penguin, 1975.

———, ed. *John Donne: The Critical Heritage.* London: Routledge, 1975.

———, ed. *John Donne: Essays in Celebration.* London: Methuen, 1972.

Spencer, Theodore, ed. *A Garland for John Donne.* Cambridge: Harvard UP, 1931.

———. *Shakespeare and the Nature of Man.* 1942. New York: Macmillan, 1961.

Spencer, Theodore, and Mark Van Doren, eds. *Studies in Metaphysical Poetry: Two Essays and a Bibliography.* New York: Columbia UP, 1939.

Stampfer, Judith. *John Donne and the Metaphysical Gesture.* New York: Funk, 1970.

Stein, Arnold. *George Herbert's Lyrics.* Baltimore: Johns Hopkins UP, 1968.

———. *John Donne's Lyrics: The Eloquence of Action.* Minneapolis: U of Minnesota P, 1962.

Stewart, Stanley. *The Enclosed Garden: Tradition and Image in Seventeenth-Century Poetry.* Madison: U of Wisconsin P, 1966.

———. *George Herbert.* Boston: Twayne, 1986.

Stocker, Margarita. *Apocalyptic Marvell: The Second Coming in Seventeenth-Century Poetry.* Athens: Ohio UP, 1986.

Stone, Lawrence. *The Crisis of the Aristocracy, 1558–1641.* New York: Oxford UP, 1965.

———. *The Family, Sex and Marriage in England 1500–1800.* New York: Harper, 1977.

Strachan, James. *Early Bible Illustrations.* Cambridge: Cambridge UP, 1957.

Strier, Richard. *Love Known: Theology and Experience in George Herbert's Poetry.* Chicago: U of Chicago P, 1983.

Styan, J. L. *The Shakespeare Revolution: Criticism and Performance in the Twentieth Century.* Cambridge: Cambridge UP, 1977.

Summers, Claude J., and Ted-Larry Pebworth, eds. *"Bright Shootes of Everlastingnesse": The Seventeenth-Century Religious Lyric.* Columbia: U of Missouri P, 1987.

———, eds. *The Eagle and the Dove: Reassessing John Donne.* Columbia: U of Missouri P, 1986.

———, eds. *"The Muses Common-Weale": Poetry and Politics in the Seventeenth Century.* Columbia: U of Missouri P, 1989.

———, eds. *"Too Rich to Clothe the Sunne": Essays on George Herbert.* Pittsburgh: U of Pittsburgh P, 1980.

Summers, Joseph H. *George Herbert: His Religion and Art.* Cambridge: Harvard UP, 1954.

———. *The Heirs of Donne and Jonson.* New York: Oxford UP, 1970.

———, ed. *The Selected Poetry of George Herbert.* New York: NAL, 1971.

Sypher, Wylie. *Four Stages of Renaissance Style: Transformations in Art and Literature 1400–1700.* Garden City: Doubleday, 1955.

Szanto, Gillian. "Recent Studies in Marvell." *English Literary Renaissance* 5 (1975): 273–86.

Taylor, Mark. *The Soul in Paraphrase: George Herbert's Poetics.* The Hague: Mouton, 1974.

Thomas, Keith. *Religion and the Decline of Magic.* New York: Scribner's, 1971.

Thomson, Patricia. *Sir Thomas Wyatt and His Background.* Stanford: Stanford UP, 1964.

Tillyard, E. M. W. *The Elizabethan World Picture: A Study of the Idea of Order in the Age of Shakespeare, Donne and Milton.* London: Chatto, 1943.

Todd, Richard. *The Opacity of Signs: Acts of Interpretation in George Herbert's The Temple.* Columbia: U of Missouri P, 1987.

Toliver, Harold. *Lyric Provinces in the English Renaissance.* Columbus: Ohio State UP, 1985.

———. *Marvell's Ironic Vision.* New Haven: Yale UP, 1965.

Trevelyan, G. M. *England under the Stuarts.* 1904. 19th rev. ed. London: Methuen, 1947.

Tuttle, Imilda, ed. *Concordance to* Silex Scintillans. University Park: Pennsylvania State UP, 1969.

Tuve, Rosemond. *Allegorical Imagery: Some Medieval Books and Their Posterity.* Princeton: Princeton UP, 1966.

———. *Elizabethan and Metaphysical Imagery: Renaissance Poetic and Twentieth-Century Critics.* Chicago: U of Chicago P, 1947.

———. *A Reading of George Herbert.* Chicago: U of Chicago P, 1952.

————. "Sacred 'Parody' of Love Poetry, and Herbert." Roberts, *Essential Articles for the Study of Herbert's Poetry* 129–59.

Tyacke, Nicholas. *Anti-Calvinists: The Rise of English Arminianism, 1590–1640.* Oxford: Clarendon, 1987.

————. "Puritanism, Arminianism, and Counter-Revolution." *Origins of the Civil War.* Ed. Conrad Russell. New York: Harper, 1971. 119–43.

Unger, Leonard. *Donne's Poetry and Modern Criticism.* Chicago: Regnery, 1950.

Van Veen, Otto. *Amorum Emblemata.* Antwerp, 1608. In facsim. Ed. Stephen Orgel. New York: Garland, 1979.

Veith, Gene Edward, Jr. *Reformation Spirituality: The Religion of George Herbert.* Lewisburg: Bucknell UP, 1985.

————. "Whiskey and Religion." *Christianity and Literature* 29 (1980): 50–61.

Vendler, Helen. *The Poetry of George Herbert.* Cambridge: Harvard UP, 1975.

Wall, John N., Jr., ed. *George Herbert:* The Country Parson, The Temple. 2nd ed. New York: Paulist, 1984.

————. *Transformations of the Word: Spenser, Herbert, Vaughn.* Athens: U of Georgia P, 1988.

Wallace, John M. *Destiny His Choice: The Loyalism of Andrew Marvell.* Cambridge: Cambridge UP, 1968.

Wallerstein, Ruth. *Richard Crashaw: A Study in Style and Poetic Development.* Madison: U of Wisconsin P, 1935.

————. *Studies in Seventeenth-Century Poetic.* Madison: U of Wisconsin P, 1950.

Walton, Izaak. *The Lives of John Donne, Sir Henry Wotton, Richard Hooker, George Herbert, and Robert Sanderson.* London: Oxford UP, 1927.

Warner, Marina. *Alone of All Her Sex: The Myth and Cult of the Virgin Mary.* New York: Knopf, 1976.

Warnke, Frank J., ed. *European Metaphysical Poetry.* 2nd ed. New Haven: Yale UP, 1974.

————. *John Donne.* Boston: Hall, 1987.

————, ed. *John Donne: Poetry and Prose.* New York: Modern Library–Random, 1967.

Warren, Austin. *Richard Crashaw: A Study in Baroque Sensibility.* Baton Rouge: Louisiana State UP, 1939.

————. "True and False Shepherds." *Teacher and Critic: Essays by and about Austin Warren.* Ed. Myron Simon and Harvey Gross. Los Angeles: Plantin, 1976.

Webster, Charles. *The Great Instauration: Science, Medicine, and Reform, 1626–1660.* New York: Holmes, 1975.

Wedgwood, Cecily Veronica. *Poetry and Politics under the Stuarts.* Cambridge: Cambridge UP, 1960.

Westerweel, Bart. *Patterns and Patterning: A Study of Four Poems by George Herbert.* Amsterdam: Rodopi, 1984.

White, Helen C. *English Devotional Literature, 1600–1640.* Madison: U of Wisconsin P, 1931.

———. *The Metaphysical Poets: A Study in Religious Experience.* New York: Macmillan, 1936.

White, Helen C., Ruth C., Wallerstein, Ricardo Quintana, and A. B. Chambers, eds. *Seventeenth-Century Verse and Prose. Volume 1: 1600–1660.* Rev. ed. New York: Macmillian, 1971.

Whitney, Geoffrey. *A Choice of Emblemes.* Leyden, 1586. In facsim. Ed. John Horden. Menston: Scolar, 1973.

Wiersma, Stanley M. "Jonson's 'To Johne Donne.' " *Explicator* 25 (1966): item 4.

Wilcher, Robert, *Andrew Marvell.* Cambridge: Cambridge UP, 1985.

———, ed. *Andrew Marvell: Selected Poetry and Prose.* London: Methuen, 1986.

Wilding, Michael, ed. *Andrew Marvell.* Modern Judgments. London: Macmillan, 1969.

Willey, Basil. *The Seventeenth-Century Background: Studies in the Thought of the Age in Relation to Poetry and Religion.* 1934. New York: Columbia UP, 1952.

Williams, George Walton, ed. *The Complete Poetry of Richard Crashaw.* New York: Norton, 1974.

———. *Image and Symbol in the Sacred Poetry of Richard Crashaw.* Columbia: U of South Carolina P, 1963.

Williams, Raymond. *The Country and the City.* New York: Oxford UP, 1973.

Williamson, George. *The Donne Tradition: A Study of English Poetry from Donne to the Death of Cowley.* Cambridge: Harvard UP, 1930.

———. *Six Metaphysical Poets: A Reader's Guide.* New York: Farrar, 1967.

Winn, James Anderson. *Unsuspected Eloquence: A History of the Relation between Poetry and Music.* New Haven: Yale UP, 1981.

Winny, James. *A Preface to Donne.* Rev. ed. London: Longman, 1981.

Wintle, Justin, and Richard Kenin, eds. *Dictionary of Biographical Quotation of British and American Subjects.* London: Routledge, 1980.

Wither, George. *A Collection of Emblemes.* London, 1935. In facsim. Ed. Rosemary Freeman. Columbia: U of South Carolina P, 1975.

Witherspoon, Alexander M., and Frank J. Warnke, eds. *Seventeenth-Century Prose and Poetry.* 2nd ed., enl. New York: Harcourt, 1982.

Wolf, A. A. *A History of Science, Technology, and Philosophy in the Sixteenth and Seventeenth Centuries.* New York: Macmillan, 1939.

Wright, Louis B. *Middle-Class Culture in Elizabethan England.* Ithaca: Cornell UP, 1958.

Young, R. V. *Richard Crashaw and the Spanish Golden Age.* New Haven: Yale UP, 1982.

Zunder, William. *The Poetry of John Donne: Literature and Culture in the Elizabethan and Jacobean Period.* Sussex: Harvester, 1982.

Films and Recordings

Bronowski, Jacob, writer and narr. *The Ascent of Man*. ViIdeocassette. Prod. Richard Gilling. Series ed. Adrian Malone. 12 programs. BBC, 1973.

Burton, Richard. *Love Poems of John Donne*. Caedmon Records, TC-1141, 1962.

Clark, Kenneth, writer and narr. *Civilisation*. Videocasette. Dir. Michael Gill and Peter Montagnon. 12 programs. BBC, 1969.

Damon the Mower. Film. Animation by George Dunning. American Federation of Arts Film.

Hardwicke, Cedric, and Robert Newton. *Metaphysical Poetry*. Audiocassette. Caedmon, SWC 1049.

Hardy, Barbara, and A. J. Smith. *Donne's Poetry*. Audio Learning Cassette, ELA042.

Kermode, Frank, and A. J. Smith. *Seventeenth-Century Literature*. Audio Learning Cassette, A2.

Marshall, Herbert. *Sermons and Meditations of John Donne*. Caedmon, SWC 1051.

Milton and Seventeenth-Century Poetry. Videocassette. Princeton: Films for the Humanities.

Palmer, Paulina, and Paul Merchant. *Herbert and Marvell*. Audio Learning Cassette, ELS093.

Palmer, Paulina, and Paul Merchant. *Metaphysical Poetry*. Audio Learning Cassette, ELS092.

Royal Shakespeare Company. *Playing Shakespeare*. 11 videocassettes. Princeton: Films for the Humanities, 1984.

Index of Works

The following index includes all works by Donne, Herbert, Vaughan, Crashaw, and Marvell mentioned in the text. Poems from Donne's *Holy Sonnets* and *Songs and Sonnets*, Herbert's *The Temple*, and Vaughan's *Silex Scintillans* are listed alphabetically under the titles of those collections.

Index of Names

WITHDRAWN

JUN 2 7 2024

DAVID O. McKAY LIBRARY
BYU-IDAHO